DØ769350

Migration, Minorities and Citizenship

General Editors: Zig Layton-Henry, Professor of I
and **Danièle Joly**, Director, Centre for Research in Ethnic Relations, University
of Warwick

Titles include:

Muhammad Anwar, Patrick Roach and Ranjit Sondhi (*editors*)
FROM LEGISLATION TO INTEGRATION?
Race Relations in Britain
Naomi Carmon (*editor*)
IMMIGRATION AND INTEGRATION IN POST-INDUSTRIAL SOCIETIES
Theoretical Analysis and Policy-Related Research

Malcolm Cross and Robert Moore (*editors*)
GLOBALIZATION AND THE NEW CITY
Migrants, Minorities and Urban Transformations in Comparative Perspective

Adrian Favell
PHILOSOPHIES OF INTEGRATION
Immigration and the Idea of Citizenship in France and Britain

Sophie Body-Gendrot and Marco Martiniello (*editors*)
MINORITIES IN EUROPEAN CITIES
The Dynamics of Social Integration and Social Exclusion at the
Neighbourhood Level

Simon Holdaway and Anne-Marie Barron
RESIGNERS? THE EXPERIENCE OF BLACK AND ASIAN POLICE OFFICERS

Atsushi Kondo (*editor*)
CITIZENSHIP IN A GLOBAL WORLD
Comparing Citizenship Rights for Aliens

Danièle Joly
HAVEN OR HELL?
Asylum Policies and Refugees in Europe

SCAPEGOATS AND SOCIAL ACTORS
The Exclusion and Integration of Minorities in Western and Eastern Europe

Jørgen S. Nielsen
TOWARDS A EUROPEAN ISLAM

Jan Rath (*editor*)
IMMIGRANT BUSINESSES
The Economic, Political and Social Environment

Peter Ratcliffe (*editor*)
THE POLITICS OF SOCIAL SCIENCE RESEARCH
'Race', Ethnicity and Social Change

John Rex
ETHNIC MINORITIES IN THE MODERN NATION STATE
Working Papers in the Theory of Multiculturalism and Political Integration

Carl-Ulrik Schierup (editor)
SCRAMBLE FOR THE BALKANS
Nationalism, Globalism and the Political Economy of Reconstruction

Steven Vertovec and Ceri Peach (editors)
ISLAM IN EUROPE
The Politics of Religion and Community

Östen Wahlbeck
KURDISH DIASPORAS
A Comparative Study of Kurdish Refugee Communities

John Wrench, Andrea Rea and Nouria Ouali (editors)
MIGRANTS, ETHNIC MINORITIES AND THE LABOUR MARKET
Integration and Exclusion in Europe

Migration, Minorities and Citizenship
Series Standing Order ISBN 0-333-71047-9
(outside North America only)

You can receive future titles in this series as they are published by placing a standing order.
Please contact your bookseller or, in case of difficulty, write to us at the address below with
your name and address, the title of the series and the ISBN quoted above.

Customer Services Department, Macmillan Distribution Ltd, Houndmills, Basingstoke,
Hampshire RG21 6XS, England

Globalization and the New City

Migrants, Minorities and Urban Transformations in Comparative Perspective

Edited by

Malcolm Cross
Director of the Centre for European Migration and Ethnic Studies

and

Robert Moore
Eleanor Rathbone Professor of Sociology
The University of Liverpool

palgrave

First published 2002 by
PALGRAVE
Houndmills, Basingstoke, Hampshire RG21 6XS and
175 Fifth Avenue, New York, N. Y. 10010
Companies and representatives throughout the world

PALGRAVE is the new global academic imprint of
St. Martin's Press LLC Scholarly and Reference Division and
Palgrave Publishers Ltd (formerly Macmillan Press Ltd).

ISBN 0–333–80260–8 hardback

This book is printed on paper suitable for recycling and made from the British
Library

A catalogue record for this book is available from the British Library.

Library of Congress Cataloging-in-Publication Data

Globalization and the new city: migrants, minorities and urban transformations in comparative perspective/edited by Malcolm Cross and Robert Moore.
       p. cm. — (Migration, minorities, and citizenship)
       Includes bibliographical references and index.
       ISBN 0–333–80260-8 (cloth)
       1. Urban economics—Cross-cultural studies.   2. Immigrants—Social
conditions—Cross-cultural studies. 3. Sociology, Urban—Cross-cultural studies. I. Cross, Malcolm. II. Moore, Robert, 1936-III. Series.
    HT321 .G555 2001   2001045126
    307.76—dc21

10   9   8   7   6   5   4   3   2   1
11   10 09 08 07 06 05 04 03 02

Printed and bound in Great Britain by
Antony Rowe Ltd, Chippenham, Wiltshire

Contents

List of Tables

List of Figures

Preface and Acknowledgements

This book arises from the work of the 'Migrants in European Cities', a thematic network funded by the European Commission (Fourth Framework Programme). The network brought together research teams from Belgium, France, Germany, Italy, Portugal, Spain and the United Kingdom.

We are very grateful to the European Commission for the funding that made the network possible. A meeting to discuss early drafts of the papers contained in this book was held at the University of Warwick. We are also grateful to the then director of the ESRC Centre for Research on Ethnic Relations, Professor Zig Layton-Henry, for his kindness in making this possible.

MC and RM

Notes on the Contributors

William A.V. Clark is Professor of Geography at the University of Los Angeles (e-mail: wclark@geog.ucla.edu). He is the author of *California Cauldron: Immigration and the Fortunes of Local Communities (1998)*.

Malcolm Cross is Director of the Centre for European Migration and Ethnic Studies (e-mail: director@cemes.org).

Jürgen Friedrichs is Professor of Sociology and Director of the Institute of Sociological Research at the University of Cologne (e-mail: friedrichs@wiso-r610.wiso.uni-koeln.de).

Chris Hamnett is Professor of Geography at Kings' College, University of London (e-mail: chris.hamnett@kcl.ac.uk).

David R. Howell is Professor of Economics at the Robert J. Milano Graduate School, New School for Social Research, New York (e-mail: howell@newschool.edu).

Connie Hum is an undergraduate student at the University of California at Los Angeles.

Rebecca Kim is a graduate student in sociology at the University of California at Los Angeles.

Ivan Light is Professor of Sociology at the University of California, Los Angeles. He is author most recently of *Ethnic Economies: Pursuing the American Dream* (San Diego: Academic, 1999) with Steven Gold. Correspondence on Chapter 8 should be directed to Ivan Light (e-mail: light@soc.ucla.edu).

Suzanne Model is Professor in the Social and Demographic Research Institute and Department of Sociology, University of Massachusetts (e-mail: Model@SADRI.UMass.Edu).

Robert Moore is Eleanor Rathbone Professor of Sociology at the University of Liverpool (e-mail: rsmoore@liverpool.ac.uk).

Elizabeth J. Mueller is Associate Professor of Economics at the Robert J. Milano Graduate School, New School for Social Research, New York (e-mail: lizmueller@juno.com).

Jeffrey G. Reitz is Robert F. Harney Professor of Ethnic, Immigration and Pluralism Studies at the University of Toronto, and also professor in the University's Department of Sociology and Centre for Industrial Relations (e-mail: reitz@chass.utoronto.ca). Among his most recent publications is *Warmth of the Welcome: the Social Causes of Economic Success for Immigrants in Different Nations and Cities* (1998).

Alisdair Rogers is at the School of Geography at Oxford University (e-mail: ali.rogers@geog.ox.ac.uk).

Loïc Wacquant is Professor of Sociology at the University of California (Berkeley) and Researcher at the *Centre de Sociologie Européenne du Collegè de France* (e-mail: loic@uclink4.berkeley.edu).

Roger Waldinger is Professor and Chair of the Department of Sociology at the University of California, Los Angeles (e-mail: waldinge@soc.ucla.edu).

1
Globalization and the New City

Malcolm Cross and Robert Moore

On both sides of the Atlantic, there is a growing realization that the advent of the global economy is having profound effects on the structure and functions of cities. While cities have never conformed to a simple typology but have reflected economic, political, geographical and cultural differences, so called 'global cities' have come to be seen as critical nodes in the restructured economies of today's advanced economies. It has been suggested, for example, that both the increasing cultural complexity in major cities and increased inequalities of income and wealth are related to the advent of the global economy (Sassen 1991, 1994). Whether this is true or not is one major question to which this book is addressed. Another purpose is to explain what is occurring on both sides of the Atlantic in relation to apparent increases in migration and the effects this may have on established ethnic minorities. A third objective is to re-examine old divisions in the light of these new changes, particularly those relating to the isolation of some social groups in spatial zones, or what in North America are usually referred to as 'ghettos'.

These three themes will be considered separately in this introduction. Before that, however, some clarification is necessary on our use of the over-used term 'globalization'. Moreover, the title of this book makes the bold claim that that there is a link between whatever this term connotes and the city, such that the latter may be described as possessing 'new' features. It behoves us to set out this proposition in more detail. An additional claim we shall make is that there are more *similarities* between Europe and North America in relation to this theme than is commonly supposed. In providing a context for this claim, we have to say something about the obvious differences. These are many but we shall focus on one alone, namely the nature and extent of welfare provision.

Globalization and globalism

The globalization thesis in its strong form as a new and potentially uncontrollable domination by transnational corporations, with associated curtailment of the power of states, is not without its critics (Hirst and Thompson 1996). Certainly we would agree that writing off the state as an agent of control or assuming that global trade is necessarily greater as a proportion of total trade than it was a century ago, or that large corporations are more powerful now than then, would be misplaced. From the vantage point of urban communities, however, changes since the oil price recession of the early 1970s have been significant. From the industrial revolution onwards, there has been an assumption that the city was the motor of employment. Migrants only had to make it to the city to maximize their employment possibilities. Those that arrived in many European cities from former colonies, for example, or those recruited under *gastarbeiter* systems in the 1960s and early 1970s, originally revealed very low rates of unemployment. After 1980, this pattern changed rather dramatically and migrants and ethnic minorities became strongly over-represented in the ranks of the long-term unemployed (cf. Cross 1994; Dangschat 1994; Hollifield 1992; Kloosterman 1994, 1996a).

Today's global order differs from the 19th century. It is less overtly based upon direct military domination and plunder, although puppet regimes of the great powers may practise both and the United States' military force is the ultimate guarantor of global stability. There are, however, features of today's world order that, when taken together, constitute a new form. First we have seen the rise of transnational and supranational military, political and economic organisations that transcend the nation-states that were formed in the 19th century. These include NATO, SEATO, the European Union, NAFTA, the World Bank, the IMF and the United Nations. More important still we see transnational corporations of such wealth and power that many of the world's governments are only minor pieces on the global chessboard. Second we see features of *globalism*, the culture of McDonalds and Coca-Cola, pop singers, film stars, sports people and filmmakers who are known throughout the world and whose appeal transcends language and nationality. To some extent globalism may be equated with the

Americanization of the world but not the homogenization of world culture. Regional, ethnic, religious and local cultures flourish in the face of globalism and aspects of cultures transport themselves to new societies so that, in addition to developing a taste for Coca-Cola the British, for example, have developed a taste for curry. Nonetheless the persistence of localism, and to some extent its renaissance, have become more visible and more salient precisely because of burgeoning commonalities, and it is these that deserve the label, 'globalism'. Third, the speed and density of information transfers is unique in human history. It is all very well to refer to the telegraph as evidence that nothing is new but the volume of data transfers now justifies a paradigm shift in our ways of understanding cultural communications. National media, for example, have become internationalized, not least through the existence of strong transnational networks of migrants.

If the first global cities were based upon empires what is the economic base of contemporary globalization and globalism? Light *et al.* (1994) remind us that 'Global restructuring theory proclaims the supremacy of big capital.' With the end of the cold war we may say that globalization is based not just upon big, but *triumphant* capitalism. It is also a *triumphalist* capitalism and many features of globalism are a celebration of capitalism and its triumphal advance. The extent of the triumph of capitalism can be seen in the response to the economic crisis in Russia in 1998. The condition under which the western powers (and the USA in particular) promised to continue to support the regime was that the state did not intervene in the market. Goods and capital were to flow freely – at whatever cost to the Russian people. Thus the interests of the global capitalists and the new small class of wealthy Russians were secured while ordinary Russians, and even those with some savings, faced poverty and hunger. These events not only illustrate the extent of what we have called 'the triumph of capitalism', they draw our attention to the globalization of economies. The economic crisis in Russia was not self-contained, its effect was felt in western markets and in Latin America, and raised questions about whether it would amplify the crisis in Japan and eventually cause a meltdown of economies worldwide. By late 1998 the global economic order looked distinctly precarious. In the days of the electric telegraph, the steamship and handwritten market transactions such precipitate international reactions to an economic crisis in one country would not have been possible. But one nation's crisis nearly became everyone's crisis in a world linked by rapid communications and automated financial transactions.

Globalization theory often has a deeply pessimistic ring, every painful economic situation is blamed on the forces of globalization and national politicians seek to either evade or displace responsibility by citing global forces. But who, in 1989, would have foreseen the end of the Soviet empire or the fall of the apartheid regime? Apparently impregnable bastions of power and domination collapsed with bewildering speed. After these events who can say with certainty that any economic or political arrangements will last forever, or even until next year?

The crisis in Russia and eastern Europe not only highlights the power of capitalism and the globalization of human relations, it is a motor driving migration as evidenced by the presence of Russian street traders in the major towns and cities of Poland. The extent to which globalization alone can account for migration is also challenged by Light and his colleagues who warn us to avoid 'one dimensional explanations' of immigration. On the other hand, we detect in the debates on globalization, and in particular on globalism, a difference of perspective between North America and Europe. For one it is the logical outcome of winning the cold war, the making over of the world in an American image; for the other it is a more troublesome process with great perils as well as gains. It is perceived as giving an 'unfair' advantage to US corporations; it propagates a vapid culture through immensely powerful channels, such as the Internet, and it throws into doubt the feasibility of continuing to support institutions, like the welfare state, upon which civic duties are seen in Europe to rest.

Global cities?

The global city is not new. Rome and Constantinople were global cities and people from the entire known world were to be found on their streets. More recently Liverpool, for example, stood at a prime node in the transport and commercial networks of a global empire, and in its dockside streets emigrants from throughout Europe *en route* to the New World mixed with citizens of the empire. Today only Rome remains, in part, a global city with pilgrims and tourists thronging its streets. Liverpool by contrast has lost its global position, it is one of the poorest cities in Europe and many of its streets are empty. All variants of globalization theory suggest a growing polarization in which the life experiences of those within the pale of knowledge diverge widely from those without, but they are less consistent on what will become of the mass of people who cannot enjoy the benefits which accrue from being at the nodal points of information flows, or indeed, who those people are. In some variants of a globalization approach, the result is mass unemployment, as demand shifts from products with low information content provided locally to those high in knowledge content that sustain an increasingly self-servicing lifestyle (Gershuny 1983). Computer-based products, which are themselves manufactured overseas, undermine jobs by removing the need for the services on which service-based professionals once depended.

Paradoxically, the 'loss of jobs' perspective was specifically applied to cities that were left behind by the onward march of global forces. William Julius Wilson, for example, in a series of widely acclaimed studies (1979; 1987; 1996) argued that de-industrialization had devastating effects in some cities as what disappeared were the jobs on which the low-skilled previously depended. He suggested that a consequence of this process was the generation of social exclusion within clear spatial boundaries, or a process of *ghettoization*. Social isolation, the growth of single parent households and declines in the quality of local leaders were all claimed to flow from these dynamics of urban change. This was a powerful set of ideas for it went some way in showing why the battle in the United States against racism through civil rights legislation and other measures was only partially successful. If you managed to break out of the city into the black middle class then you would not be caught in this ebb tide of prosperity. If you did not, then any amount of anti-racist policy would not create opportunities for advancement. Many black Americans were, therefore, seen as trapped in zones of relegation from which there were few legitimate paths of escape.

Wilson's thesis produced a fierce controversy in the United States. From the left he was lambasted for overlooking the continued significance of race, particularly as discrimination closes off options for escape from the ghetto (Massey and Denton 1993). Spatial segregation in this critique is founded on a form of apartheid as cities become urban reservations or perhaps the equivalent to 'homelands'. On the right, the debate was highjacked by the moral majority who proclaimed the virtues of orthodoxy in family relationships, of traditional gender roles and in parental authority. In this thesis the 'underclass' was a self-perpetuating sink of immorality whose festering state could only be countered by a return to Christian values and the ethic of individual self reliance (Murray 1990).

The echoes of this debate can undoubtedly be heard in the pages of this book. All three arguments successfully made the passage across the

Atlantic. New minorities in Europe were indeed recruited into manufacturing in the postwar years and Wilson's argument helps us understand why cities whose fortunes were firmly wedded to metal bashing
or mining are still suffering the consequences of their decline. In the
UK, for example, minorities of Pakistani and Bangladeshi origin have
found great difficulty in repeating the success stories of other 'Asians'
in Britain or elsewhere. This is partially because they in particular were
incorporated into the secondary sector as a way of trying to reduce
costs as the fierce winds of global competition first blew through the
factory gates. Some would also wish to reassert the role of cultural racism
in this example by pointing to the added burden of Islamaphobia
(Modood 1998).

These approaches, however, still leave the question of the 'global
cities' untouched. The decline of manufacturing and the need to sustain the knowledge-based elite are said to lead to a growth in low-level
service jobs, usually accompanied by short-term labour contracts, pri-
vatized services, part-time work and a growing dependence on female
labour. Saskia Sassen (1991, 1994, 1996) suggests that this produces a
polarized class structure in which migrants and minorities are crowded
towards the bottom end. In contrast to the Wilson approach this is a
theory of social exclusion *in* employment, rather than through a rise in
the level of the long-term unemployed. It is especially helpful in
explaining how an apparent decline in the jobs for which migrants
were once recruited has not been followed by a fall in inward migration. An 'hourglass' shape to the occupational structure is said to have
replaced the traditional cone. In other words there has been a significant expansion in low-level service jobs which migrants (particularly
migrant women) were ideally placed to fill.

The possibility of a new form of emergent polarization and inequality within work has aroused considerable interest and controversy
(Cross 1993; Dieleman and Hamnett 1994; Hamnett 1994b; Thrift
1994). Chris Hamnett in this volume, for example, challenges the evidence for the hour-glass shape arguing that what the recent past has
shown is simply a growth in income inequality consequent upon
'Thatcherite' social and economic policies (Chapter 9). Perhaps, therefore, Europe is not like the United States. Saskia Sassen continues,
however, to argue in recent work that the similarities outweigh the
differences. In an interpretation of the European debate on immigration she suggests that migrants are the new settlers, and that within
the large cities of both continents we can see the emergence of new
frontiers (Sassen 1999: 156). Thus, on both sides of the Atlantic the

dynamics of urban change are perceived as remarkably similar. Modern urban systems are more, not less, likely to depend on new labour sources whose role and existence changes both the appearance and the contours of the city.

Welfare regimes

Capitalism is an abstract concept standing for concrete realities. It summarizes complex sets of institutions and processes that ultimately serve the material interests of the owners of productive wealth and property. These interests override all others and have historically been expressed most obviously through the demand for free trade, or the free movement of goods and capital (and sometimes the free movement of labour). In the late 19th and early 20th century organized labour however was able to modify the relations between workers and employers in Europe and North America. Governments too recognized the importance of both meeting some of the social costs of producing and maintaining labour and maintaining political stability, through the provision of education, health and welfare services. This required the regulation of unrestrained market forces and, therefore, became a cost to capitalists. The pattern of modification of raw capitalism was not uniform. The European 'social' model of the welfare state grew out of the twin traditions of Catholic social thought and the solidarities of working class movements. The welfare state entailed deeper modification to the rights of employers. The European model is expressed today through the idea of partnership between employers, workers and the state. It embodies an essentially Durkheimian view of industrial society.

The Anglo-American model of the welfare state never incorporated ideas of social solidarity but was a minimalist approach based on the need to achieve social cohesion in times of economic crisis or war. It uneasily coexisted with views of humanity that were essentially individualistic and market-based. Indeed the very idea of society may itself be questioned, as when Margaret Thatcher famously observed that 'there is no such thing as society'. The Europeans saw humankind as essentially social; the Anglo-American view embodies a more purely economic view of human nature.

In the UK, and especially in its relations with the EU, one finds tensions between the two models of the welfare state. The deregulation of the labour market and the reduction of the welfare state reduce the social costs of labour to employers, but the government remains concerned to ensure minimum wages and social cohesion. When in power, both main political parties have wanted to be 'good Europeans' but rather than expanding the welfare state they have urged their European partners to curtail theirs. Cutting the welfare state can increase unemployment as well as increasing poverty. Friedrichs notes how curtailing the welfare state's provisions leads to loss of disposable incomes which in turn impact upon the very companies and employers' federations that have urged the cuts. Occupational diversity, he argues, protects cities to some extent from these effects.

There have been recent attempts to modify the technological determinism that lies at the core of post-industrial thinking by stressing the role of institutions and of the choices made by individuals (Dieleman and Clark 1996). Acting either in an intermediary or determinative role, institutions such as the welfare state, education and training systems or labour organizations are seen as shaping the contours of the post-industrial labour market, and thereby accounting for the divergence that some commentators note in modern western economies (Esping-Andersen 1990, 1993). Gosta Esping-Andersen has argued that institutional arrangements have a significant impact on post-industrial employment trajectories, both qualitatively (in terms of the social stratification) and quantitatively (in terms of the level of employment). This argument gives rise to a number of important questions. To what extent can national employment protection policies and minimum wage legislation reduce social exclusion, as some major contributors to the central debates believe (Wilson 1987, 1991a)? What is the role of social housing in ameliorating social exclusion or maintaining insulation from employment prospects, and is it sustainable (Dieleman 1994)? Does the level of welfare benefit appear to make a difference to the fortunes of migrants and minorities? Do national training policies provide a solution to the problem of a 'mismatch' between skill needs and those available in the workforce, particularly that drawn from migrant or minority origins? Do different types of national institutional frameworks generate divergent patterns of selection and exclusion for migrants?

Esping-Andersen and his associates posit the existence of three ideal types. The first is the gendered, welfare state economies of Scandinavia in which the public or social services are instrumental in achieving high rates of labour participation. The second is typified by the low-level consumer-services and free market structures of North America. The near absence of state intervention enables a huge expansion of low wage jobs in the (private) personal services, and thus creates a relatively high rate of labour participation. The third type is the so-called 'corporatist' welfare state. Here, in marked contrast to both other types, the labour market policy is directed to reducing the supply of labour by, on the one hand, creating comfortable exit routes for the unemployed, the disabled and older workers, and, on the other, throwing up barriers for women wanting to enter the labour market (for example, fiscal barriers and avoiding child-care provision). This last type of welfare state is exemplified by Germany or the Netherlands. The suggestion is that '... these differences can be traced to the impact of their respective welfare state and industrial relations institutions ...' (Esping Andersen 1993: 4). A central theme is that different welfare states may generate different patterns of social stratification and thus different forms of social exclusion.

Despite these important differences there are three processes that emerge from the studies in this book where the comparison between both sides of the Atlantic, and within Europe also, point to similarities. These are the kinds of social divisions emerging in cities, the increase in what has been called the 'new migration' and in forms of social exclusion.

Urban social divisions

While racial and ethnic discrimination may be widespread and severe, it cannot be a *complete* explanation when city-related problems appear to have got so much worse in recent years and when some migrant communities appear to be much more affected than others (Cross 1994). The great merit of globalization theory is that it depends on analyzing the new division of labour and on understanding new processes of class closure (Parkin 1979). Not all migrants necessarily gravitate, as if by some unseen hand, towards the bottom of the new class system. They may become *integrated*, in the sense that the differentials within the existing labour market largely come to be mirrored in the structure of the new group itself. Second, they may be *concentrated* in one part of the employment structure, either at a higher or lower level. The third possibility is that the labour *market* proves to be impenetrable; that is the chances of employment, which may have been the reason for migrating in the first place, prove illusory and the most probable destination becomes long-term unemployment. The most common outcome is some form of what has been termed 'segmented assimilation' where individual groups end up in identifiable niches

(Portes and Zhou 1993). An important debate arises, however, between adherents of alternative explanations for the rather complex mosaic that occurs as a result. Many niches are clearly associated with entrepreneurial effort, which might suggest that 'social capital' was a powerful determinant of success or failure. It is certainly true that the overseas Chinese, for example, have consistently shown a capacity to build entrepreneurial independence on the basis of community networks and occupational specialization. On the other hand, they have also been associated, on both sides of the Atlantic, with a rapid growth in 'human capital', particularly in terms of educational success. Jürgen Friedrichs in earlier work on the assimilation of Yugoslavs and Turks showed that the neighbourhood had only a very small effect on assimilation of these ethnic groups. Friedrichs and his co-authors showed that the percentage of the minority in the neighbourhood had less impact than individual characteristics (Esser and Friedrichs 1990; Friedrichs and Alpheis 1991). On the other hand, recent studies of particular urban quarters show just how important neighbourhoods can be and how they are moulded by official interventions (Simon 1997).

The original creator of the term 'segmented assimilation', Alejandro Portes, has argued that both of these arguments account for less of the variance in outcome than how a particular group of migrants and their offspring are viewed and treated by majorities (Portes and MacCleod 1999). Thus the 'mode of incorporation' cannot be separated from data on outcomes. In this context, it is plausible to argue that countries will differ according to how they evaluate the qualities and potential of each group. This approach is also useful in helping to understand why some communities with many benefits in terms of human capital experience a downward spiral as they face hostile media reports, indifferent teachers and targeted policing. In Britain and the Netherlands, for example, communities of Caribbean origin have experienced a particular difficulty in utilizing the resources of language and education that an earlier generation of migrants bequeathed them (Berthoud 2000).

The challenges of handling issues like these in a comparative context are very considerable. Yet real advances have been made, not least in the work of Suzanne Model and her co-authors (Chapter 5; and Model *et al.* 1999). A further major difficulty has come, however, in integrating this research at the national level with the study of cities. What happens to migrant and minority groups when compared with the indigenous population in those cities that are at the cutting edge of technology and economic progress? Do they benefit from new opportunities and thereby experience upward social mobility? Do they take the new, low-level jobs, or do they join the ranks of those excluded from secure employment and become an increasingly ghettoized underclass? Does it make any difference which ethnic groups are involved and in which country? To what extent do processes that influence the position of others affect migrants and minorities? Are the same processes found in more traditional cities whose fortunes lie more with the processing of goods rather than with information transfers? Which groups are worst affected and why? What are the processes that lead to employment success? Is this the result of anti-discrimination measures or urban redevelopment strategies, or does it depend upon the entrepreneurial endeavours of migrants and minorities themselves? It is clear that a rich and rewarding research agenda lies at the interstices of 'ethnic studies' on the one hand and urban studies on the other.

Moreover, it is also important to remember that relevant populations are not homogeneous in other respects. For example, are the children of migrants, particularly those of minority ethnic origin, destined to join the mainstream, or will they stay identifiable and apart? If the latter applies then is it more likely than for others that these young people will be socially excluded? For some ethnic groups the portents do not look very encouraging. Notwithstanding the prosperity of cities overall, levels of unemployment have remained high in some cases, being approximately double that for indigenous young people. Given population concentrations of migrant and minority populations in major urban centres, and the proportion of these populations that are less than 25 years old, this may mean that in some locales, *a majority* of young people in the labour market may be without work. It is among young people that policy challenges are particularly acute. Young people are overrepresented in police statistics for those apprehended on suspicion of having committed an offence. They are also overrepresented among the homeless. While much is made of improving educational provision in many countries of the European Union this may be insufficient. As William Clark argues in the case of Mexican migrants to California, where migrants have very low educational backgrounds there are grounds for pessimism in terms of intergenerational social mobility.

The new migration

In a labour market that becomes more global it is possible either for the worker or the job to migrate. This book is about the migration of workers to the global cities of the USA and Europe. Studies have tended to concentrate on 'push' and 'pull' factors in migration, suggesting that migration may be explained by external forces acting upon migrants. But there may be migration based on 'pure' choice; for example, a diasporic community may see a niche for entrepreneurial activity in a booming city. Globalization cannot explain everything and in Chapter 8 in the volume Light *et al.* highlight the importance of migration networks in sustaining migration. Of course the existence of such networks is part of what we recognize as globalization but they have an autonomous impact on migration behaviour.

The first migrants might be highly qualified with an identified niche in the labour market but their kin, friends and co-villagers who follow them might have fewer qualifications or none. If the labour market becomes saturated they might enter informal employment to service either the ethnic 'colony' itself or the needs of the newly affluent indigenous population. The informal economy generates further demands for immigrant labour. In the informal economy migrants might join downwardly mobile indigenous workers who have either been replaced by migrants or been displaced by economic restructuring. There is now a substantial body of work on the informal economy including studies reported in a parallel publication to this volume.[1]

A central proposal contained in many studies of the 'new migration' is that today's migrant networks are more fluid and denser than those before. The degree of autonomy and closure that these networks can attain has led some to propose that 'transnationalism' represents a new form of economic relationship (Portes 1995). The thesis exists in a weak and a strong form. In the weak form, the proposal is that transnational communities have created a nexus of economic relations, based usually on trade but mediated by ethnic and kinship ties, which constitute a *new variant* of capitalism. In this form, global economic ties are seen as not only benefiting the growth of transnational corporations (TNCs) but also the emergence of a form of smaller scale ethnic capitalism in which the bonds of culture, language and religion serve as a resource or lubricant for world trade. In its stronger form, the proposition is that these bonds are of such importance that they could be called 'post-capitalist', not in the sense of eschewing the profit motive entirely, but in terms of priorities and ultimate goals. In this thesis, the strengthening of cultural bonds and the sustenance of ethnic loyalties displaces the quest for maximization, which becomes subordinate to affective ties.

If the globalization literature has been slow to explore the implications of this thinking, so too has the study of 'ethnic business'

(Waldinger *et al.* 1990). Debates within this literature have moved slowly from the assumption that the ethnic entrepreneur was only in the business of shielding himself and his family from rapacious racism, to the gradual recognition that he or she might also be making enough money to live quite well (Lyon and West 1995; Srinivasan 1992). Even in a more sophisticated form the debate has focused on whether globalization or ethnic networks were more significant in shaping economic activity (Light 1996). While it would be a mistake to suggest that ethnic networks could not exist in a pre-globalized world, nonetheless they have been energized by the communications revolution, itself perhaps the most important strand in globalization. In other words, ethnic networks are able to become so significant precisely because they operate in a globalized economy. Neither of these approaches has explored what could be called the 'generational transition'; in other words raising the question of whether entrepreneurship is an alternative for the first generation to educational achievement that confers on the following generation enhanced mobility choices for the professions or for management. If that was so the growth of transnationalism might be a transitional phenomenon.

Forms of social exclusion

Even without a 'global city perspective', it is plausible to argue that shifts in the labour market can be intricately linked to neighbourhood and spatial structures. Migrants in neighbourhoods with strong concentrations of co-ethnics may fare very differently from their counterparts in more mixed neighbourhoods in the same city (cf. Massey and Denton 1993; Schmitter-Heisler 1994). A neighbourhood with a strong concentration of migrants, for instance, may contribute to stigmatization and discrimination against migrant job applicants, but it may also stimulate ethnic entrepreneurship by offering a captive market. An analysis of social exclusion from a labour market point of view has to incorporate, therefore, the context of the neighbourhood. This context is strongly dependent on national housing policies, but we also have to take account of local policies in this respect (Dieleman and Clark 1996; Priemus and Dieleman 1997).

Globalization cannot explain all of the pattern of change in migration and labour markets in even the most 'global' of cities. One-dimensional explanations simply do not work. Similarly explanations that deal in terms of migrants and ethnic minorities to the neglect of race fail to explain the changes we see in global cities. Wacquant (Chapter 3) reminds us forcefully of the failure of the significance of race to decline, but he too warns about simplistic notions of the ghetto. Certainly in Europe we find little evidence of the institutional parallelism accompanying spatial segregation that characterizes a 'real' ghetto. Furthermore Rogers (Chapter 11) shows that there is little spatial mismatch between ethnic minorities and occupational opportunities in London. So in London the 'blackest' areas are actually remarkably 'white', and black workers commute to their occupations much as white workers do, sometimes travelling longer distances than whites. Perhaps this is a real difference between North America and Europe. Spatial concentrations in conditions of social and economic exclusion may occur on both continents but in the former case, the walls are higher and less easy to breach.

Race is important in the global cities of the USA although according to Howell and Mueller (Chapter 10) its impact is mediated by gender. Migrants *are* replacing African-Americans and especially African-American males (and out-migrating whites) and they find tentative evidence for a negative effect on black wages. Further research will elaborate the impact of migration on wages, but if Light *et al.* are correct we might expect labour market saturation by migrants to depress wages for African-American men. Race seems to lose none of its significance. African-Americans as a *racial* minority have been continuously superseded by new arrivals from outside the USA. Thus, they are caught between the decline of the occupations that they acquired during the Second World War and the accession of new migrants in areas of economic expansion. Model's chapter describes the pattern of supercession in New York and explores the gender differences in more detail. She suggests that migrant women take dead-end jobs to underwrite their husband's training. Migrant men thus become more upwardly mobile than women and the gap between the incomes of native and migrant women is wider than the gap for men. By contrast Clark argues that the strategies currently adopted by new Hispanic migrants could, if they become trapped and isolated in inner city neighbourhoods, eventually lead to a 'long downward spiral into poverty and hopelessness'.

The strategies described by Model are not adopted by African-Americans, where poorer women may seek advancement to support their family in circumstances that make marriage an economic handicap. Model reports that the oppositional subculture of African-American men may in part block their occupation opportunities. It would be impossible to offer an explanation of any of this without referring to race.

Conclusion

The spectre of concentrated pockets of poverty affecting identifiable minorities in certain zones of Europe's greatest cities haunts the minds of many of us who are concerned with formulating economic and social strategies over the next decade. Too little is known about the causes of social exclusion to be certain as to why this is. We know that discrimination plays a part and also that the changing patterns of work are important. We know that some of the worst affected groups lack the skills necessary to participate to the full in the opportunities that are emerging. We know that young people are particularly likely to be affected. What we do *not* know, or know insufficiently well, is the balance of these factors, or whether they are made worse or better by state intervention, city type and the cultures of specific neighbourhoods.

On the other side of the Atlantic, the historical separation between two great research traditions has closed off some important areas of inquiry. On the one hand, the literature on the entrapment of black Americans in urban centres abandoned by whites is now enormous and, although there is little consensus on why this continues, its existence is indisputable. On the other hand, the new migration continues apace and has stimulated an equally rich research tradition. European debates have much to learn from each of these bodies of work. In return, European debates can offer three valuable lessons. First, on the advantages of not making a hard and fast distinction between these two sets of issues; second, on the gains and losses associated with various forms of welfare state (and social market perspectives in general) in coping with the economic and social repercussions of these changes and, third, on the implications of quite different historical and legal traditions. In one way or another, all the studies in this book address issues directly or indirectly related to these themes.

Note

1. Special issue of the *Journal of Ethnic and Minority Studies* Vol. 24, No. 2 (April 1998).

2
Migrants and the Urban Labour Market in Europe and North America

Malcolm Cross and Roger Waldinger

The question of the relationship between new ethnic populations and the urban economic base is central to both research and policy agendas. That question is also troubling because the relationship between urban economic and demographic bases that held during the initial, postwar age of migration has changed drastically. At the earlier period, cities had a thriving manufacturing economy, which allowed them to serve as staging grounds for unskilled newcomer groups. The US experience was one in which the old factory-based economy allowed for a multi-generational move up the totem pole. Immigrant children could do better if they just hung on through the high school years, after which time well-paid manufacturing jobs would await them. The third generation would continue on through university and beyond, completing the move from peddler to plumber to professor. Although the story of immigration is more recent in Europe, the early years of incorporation were very similar with high levels of employment in manufacturing and transport services.

The past 25 years, however, have seen a transformation of urban economies and social structures in ways that make a repeat of the past unlikely. There are various interpretations of the new urban reality and each has different implications for migrants and established minorities.

Skills mismatch and the underclass

This argument emphasizes the decline of manufacturing and its replacement by services. For the most part, the concern here is with *employment* and the shifting distribution of jobs by skill. At the earlier

16

period, manufacturing jobs were plenty and offered opportunities to workers with low or modest levels of schooling. But those jobs have now declined, due to suburbanization; relocation to lower-cost, domestic areas; internationalization; and the advent of the post-industrial metropolis. These changes have robbed urban areas of their absorptive capacity so that the urban economy no longer constitutes the first rung in the ladder of social mobility.

A second version of the skills mismatch argument emphasizes the *spatial* mismatch. In the USA version of this argument, the problem has to do with the suburbanization of employment, on the one hand, and the continued confinement of ethnic minorities – black Americans, in particular – to inner cities. Within the inner cities, the job structure has been transformed as described in the paragraph above. But the suburbs have been growing much faster than inner cities. Not only do the suburbs offer more jobs, but they provide a much richer supply of low-skilled jobs, in part due to the relocation of manufacturing, but more importantly, because the expanding suburban population base has given rise to a large, diversified service and retailing sector where educational requirements are relatively low.

Both versions of the spatial mismatch hypothesis may apply to European cities, though possibly in very different ways given the different relationship between inner city and suburban ring (Friedrichs 1993). Clearly, the key issue has to do with the relationship between the spatial distribution of the ethnic population, on the one hand, and the spatial distribution of the jobs to which they are best matched, on the other. In some European cities, the ethnic population may be in the suburbs, and the jobs in the central cities; in other cases, the situation may more closely resemble that in the USA. The intensity of the problem is also related to the constraints on spatial redistribution: few groups are likely to experience levels of housing discrimination as extreme as those encountered by USA blacks. State interventions have also been more effective in changing spatial distributions, as noted in a study of Amsterdam, where '...the welfare state has made it possible for the immigrants to improve their housing situation in a time of rising unemployment' (van Amersfoort and Cortie 1996: 685).

Both types of mismatch formulations are related to the *underclass* hypothesis developed in the United States by William J. Wilson, and applied, with important modifications to a number of other countries. This hypothesis contends that urban job erosion has been paralleled by an outflow of the more skilled, better educated members of the USA black population; these two shifts have undermined the institutional infrastructure of urban black communities. The end result is a pattern of concentrated poverty, in which poor, low-skilled blacks are concentrated in urban communities with few jobs, few institutions that can provide help, and few residents with connections to either employers or helping institutions. As Wilson has written:

> Neighborhoods that offer few legitimate employment opportunities, inadequate job information networks, and poor schools lead to the disappearance of work. That is, where jobs are scarce, and where people rarely, if ever have the opportunity to help their friends and neighbors find jobs, and where there is a disruptive or degraded school life... many people eventually lose their feeling of connectedness to work in the formal economy, they no longer expect work to be a regular, and regulating force in their lives.
>
> (Wilson 1996: 52)

The underclass hypothesis flows logically from the various mismatch formulations. However, it is not clear, even in the USA, how well it applies to other ethnic minorities (for example, Mexican Americans), or to various immigrant groups, though as noted below, it may provide a better fit with the situation of various second generation groups. Moreover, Wilson essentially offers a theory of *black* poverty; yet, the majority of the poor in the USA are not black and none of Wilson's research concerns that phenomenon. While some of the same processes affecting African-Americans similarly displace less skilled whites in rustbelt cities, they do not lead to concentration and segregation in spatially isolated zones of enduring poverty. In Europe, moreover, the socially excluded are highly heterogeneous in ethnic terms, to that extent the concept of *the* underclass is also of very limited value since it appears to suggest that a common labour market position will be accompanied by a common identity.

Globalization and city type

An alternative view, most closely associated with Saskia Sassen (1988, 1991, 1996), emphasizes the new sources of urban growth and dynamism. Sassen and others contend that the urban economy has been reorganized around a complex of service industries linked to the global economy; urban areas remain crucial for their role in assembling a highly skilled labour force engaged in transactions where agglomeration and face-to-face contacts remain important. But the growth of services also involves a process of economic restructuring, in which service growth at the top simultaneously generates jobs for chambermaids and waiters, investment bankers and lawyers, while positions in between these extremes are slowly, but steadily, reduced.

The global city thus provides the perfect setting for *new forms* of migration. The ban on formal entry is highly functional for this new labour supply because it means that workers, many of them women, are available at wage levels below the legal minimum, constrained to docility, flexibility and compliance by their non-legal status. Consequently, the growth of migration from poorer countries in general, and undocumented migration in particular, cannot be assumed to derive from those countries themselves but, rather, from demands created in the richest cities.

The arrival of new immigrant streams helps explain why the past two decades have seen a new 'urban renaissance'. The influx of foreign-born workers has given the comatose manufacturing sector a new lease on life. Immigrants have been a more pliable labour force, and so factory employers have not been obliged to keep wages at parity with national norms. In contrast to that of nationals, immigrant labour can also be deployed in more flexible ways, thereby giving urban manufacturers the scope to customise production and place greater reliance on subcontracting. As yet another plus, urban manufacturers can also draw on a large, vulnerable population of illegal immigrants. Their presence has given new meaning to the word exploitation, making 'the new immigrant sweatshop... [a] major USA central city employment growth sector in the past decade' (Smith 1988: 200).

To some extent, the globalization hypothesis represents an abstraction from urban trends of the late 1970s and early to mid 1980s, when cities like New York, London, or Tokyo were in a state of vigorous expansion. But that earlier boom collapsed, and all three cities have since undergone a difficult period of adjustment. It is also not clear whether specialization or diversification is the key to urban growth. New York and London are far more specialized in services and finance than Tokyo, which retains a stronger manufacturing base, and for that reason may encounter greater difficulties in generating future growth on a sustainable basis. The globalization hypothesis also emphasizes the centrality of the very largest cities, but, on the global scale, the cities mentioned above are far from the largest. Even if the global scale is reduced to the ranks of advanced societies, it is not clear that the largest cities are the most competitive. Globalization does also imply increased competition among metropolitan areas, and it may be that the salient feature of the

current situation is the *instability* of the urban hierarchy, not the place-
ment of cities on the hierarchy at any one time. In that case, it would
be important to know how cities that vary in their immigrant density,
or in the relative size of their immigrant population, rate in terms of
global competitiveness.

The urban agglomeration

The two hypotheses outlined above imply that manufacturing is a
declining activity in metropolitan areas. This is almost certainly true in
relative employment terms, but there are various reasons to think that
manufacturing may prove to be a more persistent urban phenomenon,
as suggested by the writings associated with 'flexible specialization' and
'new industrial districts'. Here the argument is that manufacturing is
shifting from mass to flexible production, in which advantage goes to
small producers, capable of responding quickly to shifts in demand
and linked, through networks, to sources of labour, supply, information and capital. Because these network systems flourish 'in regional
agglomerations where repeated interaction builds shared identities and
mutual trust while at the same time intensifying competitive rivalries'
(Saxenian 1994: 4), the regional factor in economic growth is increasing in importance. Competitive differences among regions are linked
to regional differences in the cultures and social structures supportive
of new, more co-operative, more flexible work arrangements.

This body of research is more concerned with manufacturing than with
services, though given trends in technology, the boundary between
manufacturing and services is less clear than ever before. In general,
the research emphasizes historical factors that produce regional advantage; this raises questions as to whether the 'flexible specialization' or
the 'industrial district' model can be imported or adopted by regions with
varying historical experiences.

Though the classic industrial district was once a big city phenomenon,
it is not clear that it still is; many of the industrial districts described in
the literature are found in areas of smaller or medium-sized cities. The
very large, primate cities with large immigrant concentrations appear
not to harbour thriving industrial districts. The immigrant-employing
industries of the labour-importing period were concentrated in the
mass production sector; some of the persistent immigrant-employing
manufacturing industries have characteristics that are reminiscent of
flexible specialization, for example, the clothing industry, but these
also hark back to the days of the sweatshop. In other cases, as in

Los Angeles or Silicon Valley, high technology firms that appear to belong to local 'industrial districts' have nonetheless recruited immigrants, deploying their foreign-born workers in low-skilled, repetitive, poorly paid jobs, differing little from the immigrant role in the mass production industries during the postwar economic heyday (Scott 1993).

Ethnicity and immigrant adaptation

Apart from the classical approach to ethnic assimilation, consideration of the economic fortunes of migrants and minorities in cities have tended to focus on the opportunity structure they face, or the barriers to opportunity that have to be overcome. Migrants and their descendants are, however, far from being *passive* – they adapt to changing conditions, creating new opportunities and openings and using well-trodden paths for social mobility. One of the main reasons why the story of migrant incorporation is so varied is because of the different forms of adaptation that are possible. Running through the literature on these issues is an unresolved puzzle; whether closeness in cultural terms to majority communities is beneficial for positive adaptive responses, or whether strength may be gained from difference. There are examples both ways round. East African Asians in the UK, for example, have achieved remarkable economic successes utilizing the strength of their experience as traders and entrepreneurs and their facility in the English language. Koreans in the USA have mobilized ethnic distinctiveness as one method of providing community strength. African-Americans are not immigrants and have no major cultural traditions that would explain their circumstances, which appear to be largely shaped by discrimination.

Attempts to measure the specific effects of *ethnic* as distinct from *class* resources are not entirely clear. Partly this turns on problems of specific ethnic groups (as distinct from nominal categories) but it also entails separating out interaction effects between the two (Light and Rosenstein 1995). There are some indications that even when controlling for human capital, age and other factors, specifically *ethnic* resources do make a difference – either positive or negative – in affecting, for example, the chances of ethnic entrepreneurship.

Ethnic networks

While immigrants might be stigmatized, with a cost to be attached to those stigmas, they might also be distinctive in other ways that promote more fruitful adaptations to restructuring. Migrant network theory, which depends upon the proposition that the social and economic ties which matter are ultimately *ethnic*, has been used to account both for established migration processes themselves and new forms of movement. Thus Douglas Massey argues, in the Mexican case, that networks are a prime determinant of continued flows while Alejandro Portes contends that 'transnational migration', in which the fluidity of movement is perhaps the key characteristic, offer a new form of capitalist accumulation (Massey 1988; Portes 1995).

We also know that immigrant communities develop through the mobilization of informal recruiting chains and networks, and these may assist immigrants in responding to the new *circumstances*. Because getting a job remains very much a matter of whom one knows, immigrants and members of ethnic minorities get hired through networks; the repeated action of network recruitment leads to ethnic employment concentrations, or 'ethnic niches' as these have been termed. The process of niche formation can often be a story of ethnic disadvantage turned to good account, enabling social outsiders to compensate for the background deficits of their groups and the discrimination they encounter. The networks that span ethnic communities comprise a source of 'social capital', providing social structures that facilitate action, in this case, the search for jobs and the acquisition of skills and other resources needed to move up the economic ladder (Portes and Sensenbrenner 1993). Networks between ethnic incumbents and job-seekers allow for rapid transmission of information about openings *from* workplaces to the communities. And the networks provide better information *within* workplaces, reducing the risks associated with initial hiring. Once in place, ethnic hiring networks are self-reproducing, since each new employee recruits others from his or her own group.

Urban entrepreneurship

While the development of an ethnic niche provides a group with privileged access to jobs, one classic example – that of small business – suggests that it can do far more. Ethnic businesses emerge as a consequence of the formation of ethnic communities, with their sheltered markets and networks of mutual support. Though individual firms often die off at an appalling rate, business activity offers a route to expansion into higher profit, more dynamic lines. Retailers evolve into wholesalers; construction firms learn how to develop real estate; garment contractors gain the capital, expertise, and contacts to design and merchandise their own clothing. As the ethnic niche expands and diversifies, the opportunities for related ethnic suppliers and customers also grow.

With an expanding business sector comes both a mechanism for the effective transmission of skill and a catalyst of the entrepreneurial drive. From the standpoint of ethnic workers, the opportunity to acquire managerial skills through a stint of employment in immigrant firms both compensates for low pay and provides a motivation to learn a variety of different jobs. Employers who hire co-ethnics gain a reliable workforce with an interest in skill acquisition – attributes that diminish the total labour bill and make for greater flexibility. Thus, a growing ethnic economy creates a virtuous circle: business success gives rise to a distinctive motivational structure, breeding a community-wide orientation towards small business and encouraging the acquisition of skills within a stable, commonly accepted framework.

In early approaches to the growth of ethnic enterprise, there was a tendency to be dismissive about its positive effects. The argument was that small businesses were a route of necessity to avoid the exclusionary effects of discrimination. They tended to operate only within the 'enclave economy' relying almost solely on co-ethnics as customers and clients. Limited by the poverty of those they served, and the dilapidated urban areas in which they operated, such businesses were forced either to exploit family labour to sustain marginal profitability in the niche market of ever-open retailing, or to exploit co-ethnics in manufacturing 'sweat-shops' which – often in defiance of basic safety standards – brought Third World wages and work conditions into decaying corners of large cities. This depiction is not wholly false, and it is certainly true that illegal status can be as readily exploited *within* ethnic communities as elsewhere, but it leads to a pessimism that is not entirely warranted. Later research has shown that ethnic business can penetrate well beyond the enclave economy; that opportunities for capital accumulation are real and that typical forms of business expansion, such as horizontal and vertical integration, are by no means unknown in the evolution of what were once marginal activities (Aldrich and Auster 1984).

Network ties are, therefore, the most formidable community resource. Migrants will typically work in areas below their level of education and in this sense, entrepreneurship must be seen in part as a strategy to overcome the effects of discrimination. Levels of entrepreneurship will often be remarkably high, even for relatively newly arrived migrants. Networks, particularly those based on blood ties, will also provide business finance and thus lessen dependence upon mainstream institutions. Perhaps the central point, however, is that globalization itself increases the likelihood that these networks will be mobilized for entrepreneurship. Entrepreneurship by migrants is both a creature of economic globalization and a response to it. On the one hand, it is able to utilize the communications technologies developed by and for large corporations; on the other it is a way of escaping the levelling down effects of wage competition between rich and poor countries (Portes 1995).

Network theory is also important not just as an account of migration dynamics or as a wellspring for entrepreneurship, but also as a source of informalization in advanced economies. If migrants generate certain kinds of businesses, sweatshops in the garment industry for example, then they are adding support to sectors of the informal economy which cannot then be said to depend solely upon the demands for labour emanating from the globalized economy. Most probably the effect is interactive in the sense that *both* new kinds of demand and social processes of network construction that arise in response may generate freestanding systems which sustain continued population movement. Ivan Light terms this 'spill-over immigration' which is a condition where '...demand conditions trigger a migration, but immigrant social networks thereafter expand it beyond what the initiating demand would support' (Light 1996: 9).

Informalization and cities

In countries with highly controlled corporatist approaches to labour market regulation, the relative advantage of the informal economy is increased. Where the relative advantage is higher, the size of the informal economy may increase. Partly because of exclusion from the formal labour market and partly because of physical concentration, migrants are well placed to apply entrepreneurial skills in this segment of employment. These opportunities increase again as large retail outlets and manufacturing operations leave certain zones of central cities for more profitable terrain elsewhere. Indeed, until very recently, population outflows from many cities have tended to exceed job decline in both manufacturing sectors and in some branches of consumer services again resulting in new opportunities for migrants and minorities (Cross and Waldinger 1992). Many of these will be in the formal sector but there are clear structural reasons why a link should exist between migrants and informal economic activity.

In fact by focusing on a comparison of cities, it is possible to see that what is part of the informal (that is, uncontrolled) sector in one will not be in another; that rules will vary over time, both in theory and in their application; and that links with various forms of criminal activity will also be fluid and flexible. This still 'Unknown City' provides a range of opportunities for undocumented migrants, only some of which relate to the informal economy (Burgers and Engbersen 1996).

The highly skilled

The circulation of high-level labour has increased world-wide. This type of movement does not necessarily fall under the rubric of 'immigration', with its implication of settlement and eventual membership in the host society itself. Many of the high-level migrants are purely transitory, heading back to the home country after a brief sojourn, or on to another stop on the international circuit. Numerically, however, they are of growing importance, and it is useful to understand how and why global economic integration changes the international circulation of labour.

Skilled labour migration comes in two main forms. First there are those in that large and increasing army of multinational company employees who are in long-term employment with one firm, but are relocated around the world in response to instructions from headquarters, often on the other side of the globe. Well paid, well protected and well cushioned against the risks of working outside their own country, these workers have no real interest in learning languages, or becoming otherwise embedded in their country of temporary sojourn. Similar in some respects are the other group of skilled migrants but these are employed as individuals under contract. Lacking the cushioned life of the multinational mover, such experts are paid even higher levels of remuneration to compensate for the short-term bursts of expertise that they have been contracted to supply. They are likely to be younger, and more technically specialist, than the company-movers, often taking off lengthy periods of time between spurts of work.

Though some high-level migrants are sojourners, many also belong to the classical 'immigrant' category, either by design, as with the countries actively engaged in recruiting high-level immigrants, or by default, when a sojourn ends up lasting a lifetime. More than 160 000 foreign engineers and scientists, for example, immigrated to the USA as permanent residents between 1966 and 1984, and annual rates of immigration among engineers and scientists appear to have grown in recent years. With numbers like these, immigrant professionals have become an important presence in certain branches of American industry. For example, tabulations from the 1990 Census of Population show that Asians, a largely foreign-born population, comprise seven per cent of all engineers, but 14 per cent of those with Masters degrees and 22 per cent of those with doctorates.

The advent of high-level immigration raises a different, though not utterly distinctive, set of issues from those concerning migrants of the labour type. For the most part, employment as such is not in danger, as high-level migrants find themselves favourably situated relative to the changing labour market trends. The more important issue, rather, has to do with the full use of the human capital of these high-level migrants. It may be the case, that for all their education, the training is somehow inappropriate to the demands of host society employers. Or perhaps other attributes – language, culture, what have you – limit progress. To the extent that higher-level immigrants are also distinctive ethnically, discrimination is always a possibility; the claim that highly-skilled immigrants encounter a 'glass ceiling' that curbs their career development is heard with increasing frequency.

The new second generation

The advent of the hourglass economy appears to confront the immigrant children with a cruel choice: either acquire the college, and other advanced degrees needed to move into the professional/managerial elite, or else accept the same menial jobs to which the first generation was consigned. However, the latter possibility is unlikely, precisely because acculturation has successfully socialized the children of immigrants for the types of jobs that the native-born population also wants. Theories of 'second generation decline' (Gans 1992) or 'segmented assimilation' (Portes and Zhou 1993) suggest that the children of immigrants will run into trouble, trapped by a mismatch between their aspirations, on the one hand, and the requirements of the jobs which they seek, returning us back to the 'skills mismatch' argument.

While plausible, this scenario is too crude, ignoring both inter-ethnic differences within countries and inter-country variations. Second generation options are likely to be shaped by the circumstances of their parents, and these will vary greatly. The greatest problems are likely to be encountered by the children of low-level, manual workers, especially those dislocated by industrial restructuring. While this is a sizeable group, especially in the USA, a large portion of today's second generation comes from more advantaged circumstances.

Moreover, the declining demand for less educated labour may threaten the prospects for second generation advance; but it need not be determining. Like their peers, immigrant offspring realize that more education will yield dividends, and act accordingly. Seventy-four per cent of all college-age immigrants are enrolled in some form of post-secondary schooling as opposed to 65 per cent among the native-born; likewise, in-school rates for immigrant 18–21 year old are above native-born levels (Vernez and Abrahamse 1996). Movement into higher education is a realistic prospect for many, precisely because a large fraction of the immigrants do not start at the bottom and a similarly substantial portion of immigrant offspring do not seek positions that only represent 'incremental improvements' over low-skill jobs.

As in other areas, migrants will adapt to these changing circumstances. While education may have always been prized, its objective value may now be enhanced. Migrant communities have, therefore, to consider the strategy which will improve school performance, often in city zones where general levels of achievement are poor. The evidence from Germany suggests that cultural assimilation can play a positive role in educational success. Although foreign children tend to do poorly in the basic qualification, *Hauptschule*, the longer they have lived in Germany, the more young people achieve (Alba *et al.* 1994). On the other hand, cultural separation and solidarity can sometimes serve as a useful insulation against the corrosive effects wrought by poverty on native populations. One serious consequence, however, of community isolation, whether or not by choice, is that it may lead to a low level of knowledge concerning local occupational possibilities and routes into work. Penn and Scattergood's study of South Asian young people in the north of England, for example, concluded that the best characterization of their results was '... the interaction of high ambitions and lack of a comprehensive knowledge of occupational possibilities outside higher education ....' (1992: 94).

Directions for research and policy

Contemporary research on immigrants in urban economies points to new sources of difficulty: the engine that previously propelled the lower-skilled members of society up the social ladder no longer works, or no longer works with similar force. However, this formulation emphasizes the problems encountered by all the less skilled members of society, not those of distinctive, or distinctively perceived, ethnic backgrounds. Thus, the question needs refinement in order to specify the factors impinging on foreign-born populations and their descendants. Even this specification requires further modification and attention to internal differences among both the immigrants and their descendants. Leaving aside the second generation, for the moment, it is clear that the foreign-born population is highly diverse; the axes of variation are several, not one, having to do with country of origin, timing of migration, circumstances of migration (whether economic migrant or refugee), skill level and so on. Moreover, the degree of concern associated with the foreign-born, as opposed to their descendants, will vary from country to country, depending on whether the foreign-born population is long established, in which case the focus primarily switches to the second generation, or whether immigration is ongoing at reasonably high levels, in which case matters of immigrant adjustment gain priority.

For labour migrants of the traditional type, any one of the scenarios of urban economic change outlined earlier in the chapter spells bad news. The worst may be the skills mismatch, since it suggests that the immigrants no longer have a function in urban economies; for many of the labour migrants of the 1960s and 1970s, who now find themselves redundant, the skills mismatch hypothesis may ring a depressingly true note. But the skills mismatch view seems likely to overstate its case: skill requirements have indeed gone up in the USA, but only to a modest degree, with the tendency toward skill deepening having slowed substantially since 1960 (Howell and Wolff 1991). Consequently, people with modest levels of schooling have continued to fill a surprising number of jobs. As the USA is not the only post-industrial economy to attract immigrants of a traditional type, there seems to be a sustained demand for low-skilled labour, notwithstanding the tenets of the mismatch hypothesis.

It is also unclear whether the decline in large cities relative to smaller industrial districts and small towns is a long-term phenomenon or whether it is part of a cyclical pattern. For example, it was a tenet of faith amongst planners that inner areas of major cities would continue to decline in population terms as telecommunications and the relocation of companies made central business districts undesirable places to live and to work. Yet in the UK, the Office for National Statistics predicts that six inner-London boroughs will be among the 11 fastest growing local authority areas in the country in the next ten years. It is *suburbanization* which appears now to be in decline as transport delays and high costs are leading to a renaissance of urban living.

The globalization hypothesis would help explain the persisting scope for low-skilled immigration, but it too has disturbing implications, since it suggests that the immigrants move into an ethnic mobility trap, in which there are few, if any opportunities to move ahead. As with the skills mismatch hypothesis, the globalization hypothesis offers, at best, an incomplete account, entirely neglecting the role of highly skilled immigrants. And as we have noted, the migration process itself generates resources, which allow at least some immigrants to surmount the obstacles they confront.

Urban regeneration

If the past is any guide, then newcomers will continue to converge on urban areas, and in particular, on a handful of large cities that have absorbed a disproportionate share of the immigrant flows. As emphasized in this chapter, the economies of urban areas have been changing in ways that will impede the mobility of immigrants with lower than average skills. Can governments shape urban economies in ways that might facilitate immigrant adaptation?

One answer might involve stimulating entrepreneurial development, but governments do not appear to have the resources or the foresight to pick winners and losers from among competing small businesses. This is not to say that governments should do nothing. Effective policies might be developed along two lines: first, building an infrastructure that fosters small business development in general and, second, enacting and enforcing systemic policies of equal economic opportunity for ethnic and racial minorities. It is not the purpose of this study to take sides in the debate over the welfare state, but we do note a likely tension between labour market regulation and entrepreneurship in the *formal* economy, with the former constricting the latter. If the informal economy is the only one available then migrants will congregate within it. The problem then is that governments may have unwittingly created the conditions for low levels of social mobility, increased urban concentrations and the stimulation of xenophobia.

Education and training

Notwithstanding discrimination, and the possibility that some cities will go on offering opportunities at the lower end of the skill range, there is widespread agreement that the possession of a good education is more important now than ever before if aspirations for advancement are ever to be realized. What happens in schools is, therefore, of major importance in shaping mobility options.

In the USA, there is evidence that a substantial portion of the second generation is progressing beyond their parents, but their ability to do so on a sustained basis depends both on their ability to obtain and complete a decent secondary schooling and on proceeding to at least some post-secondary education. To a large extent, the problems confronted by the children of immigrants are not all that different from the problems faced by the much larger population of children with US-born, working-class parents: the supply/demand equation for less skilled workers has become highly unfavourable, making extended schooling an imperative. Improving the quality of secondary schooling and improving access to higher education will do much for all of the USA's working-class families, including those with foreign-born children or parents.

In Europe the pattern is very mixed. Some groups of the second or third generation are achieving above the level of their peers nationally and much above when considered locally. The story is, however, very variable and the children of some other communities are much less likely than average to complete a secondary education. Some of those in the latter group are full citizens with language skills equal to the majority. In other cases, they are foreigners without fluency in dominant languages. While language acquisition is a necessary condition for successful incorporation, it is not itself sufficient to guarantee relative success.

Anti-discrimination policy

If the children of immigrants do succeed in obtaining extended education of adequate quality, then the key issue will be guaranteeing that they enjoy equal rewards for the skills they possess. This, of course, is the problem raised by the 'glass ceiling' controversy. Those analysts and advocates who detect a 'glass ceiling' concede that higher-skilled immigrants are doing well, but then argue that these better educated immigrants are not doing as well as they *should*. It is not clear what normative expectations inform that 'should': is it reasonable to anticipate that the foreign-born – as distinct from their children – will ever catch-up with comparably schooled natives? Perhaps not, but it would probably be better if the gap would get smaller rather than larger. Given immigration's contribution to greater diversity, it is not clear that policies of an affirmative action type would be beneficial – especially since affirmative action now gives foreign-born persons an entitlement that USA-born citizens with a class, but no ethnic, disadvantage do not currently enjoy. A better objective, rather, would be to ensure that majority groups are not able to use ethnicity as a weapon against ethnic minorities. Legal and political strictures against discrimination are needed: at the very least, immigrants and their descendants should be able to play the game on an equal footing.

While there is some reason for thinking that positive action policies may have a positive effect, the processes involved are not well understood. It may be that minority applicants are drawn to apply to organizations emphasizing their open entries. In any case, while the level of discrimination in employment may be worse in some groups of countries than others, there is no overwhelming evidence that countries, which have pursued anti-discrimination rules, have lowered discrimination, or that countries without such rules demonstrate more. On the other hand, the law has a salutary and educational effect. It is probable that 'race-specific' policy has helped foster the black middle class in the USA even though it may have done little for the black poor. On balance, therefore, anti-discrimination legislation is important as long as it is *not* assumed that alone it can resolve the socio-economic issues addressed in this chapter.

3

Gutting the Ghetto: Political Censorship and Conceptual Retrenchment in the American Debate on Urban Destitution

Loïc Wacquant

There is an unnoticed irony in the moral panic about 'ghettoization' that has swept through Europe over the past decade. It is that Old and New World analysts of the urban scene have been unknowingly moving in opposite directions while using increasingly similar terminology and jointly pondering the likelihood, modalities, or reality of transatlantic convergence. For just as European scholars and state experts were importing the concept of 'ghetto' from the USA to spotlight with anguish the putative *racialization* of social and physical space in their metropolis, American social scientists have been busy *deracializating* that same concept, ostentibly eliminating from it any reference to ethno-racial division and domination. Yet, even as their conceptual language shunned overt reference to the country's colour line, USA urban researchers have maintained their empirical and policy focus on the predicament of African-Americans. The result is a great deal of confusion and misunderstanding, on both sides of the Atlantic, as to what makes a ghetto and how such an entity might be unmade, ameliorated, or prevented from emerging in the first place.[1]

This chapter offers a critical examination of the strange drift towards an income-based notion of ghetto in the recent American debate on urban destitution. Retracing the semantic trajectory of the 'ghetto' in the USA over the past century reveals how this drift marks in fact a sharp break with the established meaning of the term: from the 1860s to the 1970s, the ghetto always conjugated ethno-racial separation with socio-spatial closure. Only in the 1980s does race suddenly drop out of the picture, when a number of influential analysts propose to equate ghetto with any perimeter of 'extreme poverty', no matter its ethnic composition and institutional make up.

This 'gutting' of the ghetto – the *expurgation of race from a concept expressly forged to denote a mechanism of racial domination* – is not reflective of a brusque transformation of the structure and dynamics of urban relegation in the USA. Rather, it is expressive of the growing heteronomy of research on poverty and of the intensifying suppression of race in policy-oriented scholarship in this country (which itself is the academic retranslation of the taboo that weighs on segregation in the political field). It also reveals the obdurate incapacity of USA social science to conceptualize ghettoization as a distinct form of ethno-racial domination that has been imposed uniquely upon blacks (Wacquant 1998).

The three faces of the ghetto in American society and history

The meaning of the 'ghetto' in American society and social science has shifted over time as a function of the ways in which the country's political and intellectual elites have conceived of the intertwined problems of ethnicity and poverty in the metropolis. With only minor simplification, one may distinguish three broad stages in the semantic trajectory of the term leading up to the contemporary debate.[2]

A European import of medieval origins, the word *ghetto* was initially applied strictly to residential concentrations of Eastern European Jews who settled in seaports along the Atlantic at the close of the 19th century. During this period, neighbourhoods of physical and social degradation thought to thwart efforts at individual uplift and group improvement were labelled *slums* (Bender 1975). In these notorious territories, moral isolation and environmental disability were said to combine with genetic inferiority to produce depravity, destitution, popular disruption and pauperism. The 'discovery' of the slum in the period between 1840 and 1875 was the major impetus behind the growth of philanthropy, moral reform and urban inquiry, as manifest by the creation of the American Social Science Association in 1865 and by the onset of the settlement house movement a few decades later.

During the progressive era, the referent of 'ghetto' expanded 'to describe the segregation of exotic minorities in the crowded sections of the inner city' (Ward 1989: 95). This new usage expressed widespread scepticism as to whether the new immigrant streams – of southern and

East-Central European provenance as well as of lower class composition – could be or should be assimiliated within the predominant Anglo-Saxon pattern of the nationalizing USA. It also signalled intensifying hostility towards African-Americans whose numbers were growing as they fled the oppressive regime of the southern states to rally the 'promised land' of the northern city after the outbreak of the First World War (Grossman 1989). In this second phase, the ghetto was thus redefined as the '*intersection between the ethnic neighborhood and the slum*', where segregation combined with housing dilapidation to exacerbate urban ills and exclude residents from full participation in societal life (Lubove 1962).

The terms (German, Swedish, Russian, Greek and so on) 'colony' and (black) 'belt' were also employed to differentiate European immigrant quarters and African-American enclaves in the city.[3] 'Colony' refered to the propensity of some migrant groups, particularly the Irish, Sicilians and Polish, to settle together by originating kinship cluster, village or region. 'Belt', by contrast, signalled the compressed and contiguous character of the bounded districts reluctantly conceded to African-American; the term 'Black Belt' originally designated those regions of the South where the plantation economy was dominant owing to the dark and fertile soil fit for the cultivation of cotton.

Yet 'ghetto' came increasingly to subsume lower-class white, black, as well as Hispanic and Asian neighbourhoods where deprivation overlapped with ethno-national, racial, or religious segmentation. This reflected the (mistaken) view of the newly professionalized urban experts that African-Americans were but the latest immigrant stream to come into the city's ambit and that, as their predecessors, they would eventually assimilate into American society. Thus the founders of the Chicago school of sociology:

> believed and taught their students to believe that all ethnic neigh-borhoods were – or once had been – ghettos, like the Black Belt. They viewed Negroes as just another ethnic group, whose segrega-tion was largely voluntary and would prove to be only temporary.
>
> (Philpott 1978: 136)[4]

Only after the Second World War did the semantic range of the 'ghetto' contract again to refer nearly exclusively to the '*forcible relega-tion of African-Americans*' to compact and oft dilapidating central-city districts (Hannerz 1969: 11; Weaver 1948). The institutional and cogni-tive disruptions wrought by the war; the escalating influx of southern blacks into northern cities and the resulting tensions over housing and access to the other prerogatives of citizenship; the glaring contrast between the smooth residential dispersal of 'ethnic whites' and the persistent spatial seclusion of African-Americans; the growing contestation of caste rule by blacks mobilizing against exclusionary violence and state policies: all helped dramatize the structural as well as experiential differences between ethnic cluster and black ghetto.

To be sure, there were still references to 'white ghettos' in the 1960s and after (for example, Darden 1981; Forman 1971; Goldfield and Lane 1973; Warner and Burke 1969) and influential voices persisted in denying any institutional or cultural specificity to the location of African-Americans in the metropolitan system – most famously Glazer and Moynihan in *Beyond the Melting Pot* (1963) and Edward Banfield (1970) in *The Unheavenly City*.[5] But the upsurge of black militancy and the historiographic revolution that accompanied it solidified identification of the term with the uniformly segregated Black Belts of the industrial city. The Chicago school thesis, reiterated by Oscar Handlin (1959) in *The Newcomers: Negroes and Puerto-Ricans in the Metropolis* and modernized by Milton Gordon (1964) in *Assimilation in American Life*, that it was only a matter of time until African-Americans would fully benefit from the 'urban elevator' and find their rightful place in a multi-ethnic metropolitan order, was thoroughly and repeatedly refuted by a wave of rigorous monographs on the historical formation of the ghettos of New York City, Chicago, Detroit and Cleveland. The 'immigrant analogy' was finally exposed for what it had been all along: a historical fallacy as well as 'the greatest miscalculation' (Wade 1990: 6) of all those who had hoped that urbanization would eventually attenuate if not erase America's colour line.

By the time Kenneth Clark published his acclaimed account of the *Dark Ghetto*, the expression was well-nigh reserved to denote, and denounce, the uniquely virulent form of territorial, economic and socio-cultural exclusion imposed by whites upon urban blacks (Clark 1965: 11):

> America has contributed to the concept of the ghetto the restriction of persons to a special area and the limiting of their freedom of choice on the basis of skin color. The dark ghetto's invisible walls have been erected by the white society, by those who have power.

The conjugation of racial schism and urban marginality as the signal feature of the black urban predicament was reiterated with vigour by the Kerner Commission in its painstaking analysis of 'civil disorders' in the nation's cities: 'The term "ghetto" as used in this report refers to an area within a city characterized by poverty and acute social disorganization, *and inhabited by members of a racial or ethnic group under conditions of involuntary segregation*' (Kerner Commission 1989: 12, my emphasis). And in an oft quoted passage, the Commission left no doubt as to the origins of the ghetto in group domination:

> What white Americans have never fully understood – but what the Negro can never forget – is that white society is deeply implicated in the ghetto. White institutions created it, white institutions maintain it, and white society condoned it.
>
> (Kerner Commission 1989: 2)

In all three of its past American incarnations, then, the notion of ghetto encompassed and tied together the ideas of *ethno-racial* division (and homogeneity) with those of *spatial concentration* and *social closure*.[6] New York's Harlem, Chicago's South Side and Detroit's Paradise Valley were never simply desolate territories of ecological disrepair and social destitution: they were, and are, manifestations of a power relation between the dominant white society and its subordinate black caste, as materialized by the twin conditions of rigid segregation and inordinate poverty thrust upon their residents.

The expurgation of race in 'underclass' research

Recent studies of race and urban marginality in the USA carried out within the ambit of the 'underclass' deviate sharply from this semantic lineage in that they tend to equate the ghetto with any perimeter of high poverty irrespective of population and organizational make up.[7] It is as if, suddenly, in nary a decade, a century-old institution of ethno-racial control had mutated into a mere agglomeration of very poor households whose position in America's caste hierarchy is somehow irrelevant to the process of urban relegation visited upon them.

At first sight, it might appear that such redefinition involves merely a technical adjustment needed, perhaps, to capture emergent structures of urban exclusion that blur or cut across the colour line. On closer examination, it turns out that this seemingly anodine lexical shift is a veritable conceptual *coup de force* driven by tactical 'policy' considerations: it effectively 'expurgates race' from the causal equation and 'collapses the ghetto into the slum' even though everything indicates that the black/white schism continues to be a primary determinant of dispossession in the urban core. In so doing, it transforms a 'relational' notion, designating a 'deeply entrenched dominant–subordinate racial arrangement', to borrow the language of Herbert Blumer (1958), into a falsely neutral, 'gradational construct' ostensibly pegged on income level.[8] All of this because income is a variable that policy analysts and designers find more 'friendly': it is at once uncontroversial, ideologically innocuous and, seemingly, easy to measure and manipulable, everything that race is not. The result is that, for the first time in its long life in America, the concept of 'ghetto' has been *stripped of its ethno-racial referent and denuded of any mention of group power and oppression*. A multi-sided institutional capsule is thus reformulated into a flat, one-dimensional, demographic descriptor that obfuscates the history and enduring reality of racial division in the USA.

The elimination of race is immediately detectible in the works of the leading scholars of the 'underclass' and its derivatives. Thus, in the sequel to his much-acclaimed book, *The Truly Disadvantaged: The Underclass, the Inner City, and Public Policy*, William Julius Wilson (1996: 12, original emphasis) reports approvingly that 'in attempts to examine the problem of ghetto poverty across the nation empirically, social scientists have tended to define ghetto neighborhoods as those located in the *ghetto poverty* census tracts', that is, tracts 'in which at least 40 per cent of the residents are poor'. The country's foremost authority on the question endorses this conceptual alteration, which he justifies by citing the investigations of two public policy scholars from Harvard's Kennedy School, Paul Jargowsky and Mary-Jo Bane. And, indeed, Jargowsky and Bane offer an exemplar of this increasingly common elision of the racial and institutional dimension of the ghetto when they write:

> We have defined a ghetto as an area in which the overall poverty rate in a census tract is greater than 40 per cent. The ghetto poor are then those poor, *of any race or ethnic group*, who live in such high-poverty census tracts. ... Visits to various cities confirmed that the 40 per cent criterion came very close to identifying areas that *looked like ghettos* in terms of their *housing* conditions. Moreover, the areas selected by the 40 per cent criterion corresponded closely with the neighborhoods *that city officials and local Census Bureau officials considered ghettos*. ... It is important to distinguish our definition of ghetto tracts based on a poverty criterion from a definition based on

racial composition. Not all majority black tracts are ghettos under our definition nor are all ghettos black.

(1991: 239, 241, emphasis added)

This (re)definition of the term deserves to be quoted at length, first, because it cumulates nearly all of the flaws that have marred recent such usages of 'ghetto' and, second, because it is widely cited by other scholars of urban poverty. Its careful dissection offers a unique opportunity to pinpoint the manifold empirical anomalies and severe theoretical truncation of the object it entails in the name of operational efficiency and political palatability.

First, this specification of the ghetto is impeccably *arbitrary* (as Jargowsky and Bane readily concede on page 239): why use census tracts rather than city blocks as catchment area, the official 'poverty line' as measuring rod and a rate of 40 per cent poor persons as cut-off point? Systematic field observation in various inner-city areas reveals that census tracts are poor proxies of what residents construe and construct as neighbourhoods in their daily round (Sánchez-Jankowski 1996). The federal 'poverty line' does not quantify destitution, need, or the capacity for self-sufficiency. 'A bureaucratic category designed to facilitate the routine collection of statistics and the determination of eligibility for public assistance' (Katz 1989: 117), it is geared to the managerial concerns of the state and is egregiously unfit for capturing urban social structures and strategies.[9] In addition, there is not a shred of sociological theory or observation to document that 40 per cent (or any other poverty ratio) constitutes a 'threshold' beyond which special social dynamics and patterns take over. By contrast, there is strong empirical evidence as well as solid theorizing to indicate that high levels of racial segregation (defined by an index of dissimilarity above 60) do produce distinct socio-economic constellations and processes (Massey 1990). Why then substitute an ill-suited and highly inexact instrument of measurement for a more pertinent and accurate one?

Second, why leave out rural counties and suburban tracts wherein we encounter extreme income deprivation? What is so special about *central-city* dispossession that we should grant it exclusivity in the analysis of concentrated poverty – if that is what we are really after? Neither Jargowsky and Bane nor Wilson provide a rationale for such discounting, which is typically accepted as a given by students of the 'underclass', even though overall poverty is at once more concentrated and more persistent for all ethno-racial groups in nonmetropolitan areas. In 1985, the poverty rate for African-Americans was 32 per cent in central cities and 42.6 per cent in nonmetropolitan areas (making such areas immense 'ghettos' according to the Jargowsky–Bane definition); the corresponding figures were 30.7 per cent and 38.7 per cent for Mexican-Americans (Sandefur 1988: 54–7). Only eight per cent of urban blacks who were 'persistently poor' (that is, poor at least eight years in the period 1974–83) lived in zip codes with poverty rates of 40 per cent and more. This means that by focusing on residents of areas of extreme poverty, we miss the overwhelming majority (perhaps as many as nine in ten) of the persistently poor black urbanites (Adams *et al.* 1988: 88).

The protracted sociomental journey of urban dread in America from the Jacksonian to the Clintonian era intimates the likely reason why the stagnant counties of the backwoods of Mississipi and the desolate Indian reservations of the north central states do not qualify as 'ghettos', even when their poverty rates far exceed the 40-per cent mark: rural poverty has never been viewed as morally corrosive and socially threatening in the way that its metropolitan counterpart has. This is why there has been no talk of a 'rural underclass', only an urban one.

Third, Jargowsky and Bane's conception of the ghetto is fundamentally *asociological* insofar as it is pegged on household income – a notoriously unreliable item in standardized surveys, especially among irregularly employed populations – and on the visual state of the built environment, irrespective of the system of social and economic relations that determine these. Now, a dilapidated housing stock is a serious urban problem in its own right but it does not a ghetto make. 'Broken glass, litter, stripped and abandoned automobiles and many young men hanging out on street corners' (Jargowsky and Bane 1991: 240) may be outward 'signs of urban decay', but such signs do not reveal what produced this decay. And unthinking use of the 'poverty line' as the key conceptual device ensures the elimination of social structure and institutions (Schram 1995: 79–84) – precisely that which sociological analysis is concerned with.

Fourth, and this accounts for its sociological vacuity, the income-based concept of the ghetto is quintessentially *bureaucratic*, derivative of administrative categories and practices: its content and viability are entirely premissed on the existence and availability of government data and measurements such as the Census Bureau designation of 'poverty area'.[10] By importing this administrative construct into the realm of scholarly research, Jargowsky and Bane unabashedly conflate a historical–analytical concept with the *lay notions held by municipal and state elites* ('what city officials and local Census officials considered ghettos'). And they do so without explicating what these folk perceptions are, whether they are stable and uniform across locations, and more importantly why they should serve as warrant for the delineation of the object under study. Note also that we are not told what municipal authorities have in mind when 'they show on a map the neighbor-hoods they consider ghettos' (Jargowsky and Bane 1991: 238); is their criterion poverty, segregation, dilapidated housing, commercial blight, crime, disrepute, historical ghetto status, or some combination of these? We are informed that Jargowsky and Bane's definition agrees with that of census bureaucrats but are left in the dark as to the basis for this agreement.

Last but not least, the income-based notion of ghetto is 'ostensibly deracialized' when in fact it denotes urban enclaves of coloured poverty to the near-total exclusion of poor white areas. Wilson (1996) invokes the work of Jargowsky and Bane as justification for eliminating racial entrapment from his characterization of the ghetto. But what rationale do the latter adduce for this excision? The two Harvard scholars first call on the common sense meaning of the term, as codified by the *Random House Dictionary*: 'a slum area inhabited predominantly by members of a minority group, often as the result of social and eco-nomic restrictions'. But then, in splendid ignorance of three decades of historical research on the black American ghetto, they summarily assert that 'current usage, however, almost always implies impover-ished residents and run-down housing' (Jargowsky and Bane 1991: 237) and, inexplicably, pretext such 'current usage' for purging ethno-racial restriction and homogeneity from the definition they cite!

Absent any theoretical or empirical argument, one must conclude that the sole reason for dropping segregation from the picture is the consensus of a circle of like-minded policy-oriented scholars for whom mention of race is deemed superfluous, disagreeable, or ill-advised.[11] Silently recapitulating the immigrant fallacy, Jargowsky and Bane have redefined the ghetto as 'nothing more than a slum', if a particularly bad one: an area characterized by intense poverty, a concentration of vulnerable households, and substandard housing and living condi-tions, independently of ethno-racial domination.

Conceptual camouflaging as self-imposed political censorship

But social reality is stubborn and racial division is not so easily made to vanish. Indeed, no sooner has it been pushed out the front door than it slips in through the back door. After reiterating that theirs is a race-blind definition of the 'ghetto', Jargowsky and Bane proceed to confine their analysis to blacks and Hispanics on grounds that the 'the percentage of white poor living in ghettos was extremely low and varied little among regions and cities'.[12]

For 'ghetto poverty' is a condition that *de facto* impacts nearly exclusively subordinate ethno-racial groups. And, try as they might, Jargowsky and Bane cannot hide that race figures among its primary determinants. For not only does 'the proportion of the poor who live in the ghetto (vary) dramatically by race', with only two per cent of poor whites residing in one, as against 16 per cent of poor Latinos and 21 per cent of poor blacks. The pattern of growth in 'ghetto poverty' (that is, poor persons living in very poor areas) also suggests a racial dynamic at work: eight of the ten cities with the largest increases (New York, Chicago, Philadelphia, Newark, Detroit, Columbus, Baltimore and Paterson, New Jersey) are northeastern and midwestern industrial centres with large, entrenched and long-established 'Black Belts' (Teaford 1993). Furthermore, such increases occurred 'largely among blacks' (and secondarily among Latinos in southern cities). Finally, the fact that 'ghetto' poverty areas expanded from an established segregated core outward by engulfing 'adjacent mixed-income tracts' is further indication of a process of turnover consistent with the racial ghetto and not a socio-spatially random variation in tract income levels.

In short, the very data that Jargowsky and Bane marshall in defence of their allegedly non-racial conception of the ghetto cry out for bringing race back into its definition. If 'ghetto tracts are a subset of a city's majority black or Hispanic tracts' and if the 'pattern of dispersion' (or concentration) of the poor results from interactions between 'changes in the poverty rate and *continuing high levels of racial segregation*' (Jargowsky and Bane 1991: 241, 268, emphasis added), then 'segregation must be a constitutive, not a derivative, feature of the ghetto'.[13] To maintain otherwise is to engage in conceptual legerdemain. It is, in effect, to disfigure the ghetto and to render it inscrutable.

The various labels and indicators deployed to capture the putatively new types of destitution and populations said to have coalesced in and around the metropolitan core in the past two decades, 'underclass' and 'underclass neighbourhood', 'concentrated deviance' and 'antisocial behaviour', 'the severely distressed' and 'the nonworking poor', 'social isolation' and 'new urban poverty', are so many euphemistic devices for *not talking about racial exclusion* while actually fastening social analysis, and the disciplinary arm of the state, on black and Latino families trapped in the territories of socio-ethnic relegation made into emblems of danger by the latest cycle of moral panic over the city. And just as the fixation of urban anxiety onto the 'inner city' following the racial upheavals of the 1960s partakes of a century-long tradition of disquiet over the intersection of class and ethnicity in the metropolis, the reluctance to recognize and thematize the role of racial segregation in recent 'underclass' scholarship manifests the congenital indisposition of American social scientists to confront the abiding pervasiveness, forcible nature and destructive consequences of spatial seclusion as a preeminent *form of ethnoracial domination* distinct from (albeit intimately linked to) prejudice and discrimination.[14]

In the 1930s, Louis Wirth preferred to talk of 'isolation' rather than segregation, for the latter term swore with the inveterate liberal belief that the modernization of America – propelled by the twin forces of urbanization and industrialization – would inexorably erode all ethnoracial boundaries and ultimately lead to the residential integration of blacks (Miller 1992). In the 1980s, William Julius Wilson reintroduces this same term, 'social isolation', purportedly to ward off the discredited notion of 'culture of poverty' (Wilson 1987: 61–2, 137–8) but also, whether consciously or not, as a conceptual shield to obviate coming to terms with the continuing, and not simply 'historic', reality of segregation. Subsequently, in *When Work Disappears*, Wilson (1996) explicitly acknowledges racial segregation but only as an inert 'background' condition or an unbendable if not immutable constraint, not as an *active force*, a nexus of institutionalized devices and practices that ongoingly co-determines social fates and strategies in the 'inner city' and, therefore, ought to be kept at the centre of the analytic stage.[15] And this timid acknowledgement itself is undercut by his endorsement and use of the income-based notion of 'ghetto'.

Thus, much as Louis Wirth mistook a relation of ethno-racial power, upheld by inflexible caste hostility and state violence, for a mere 'specialization of interests and cultural types' fuelled by ecological dynamics (Wirth 1928: 285), the redefinition of the 'ghetto' as a central-city area of extreme poverty contributes to the obfuscation of racial domination in contemporary American society and social science. The early Chicago school legitimated segregation by presenting it as the natural outcome of a biotic 'process of competition' over urban space 'akin to the competition that underlies the plant community' (Wirth 1928: 284–5). Physical distance between groups was thought to be 'a product of [urban] growth rather than of deliberate design' and theorized to be ultimately beneficial to all groups since it allowed each to preserve its 'own moral codes' and to find its proper niche in a symbiotic geo-graphical mosaic.[16]

The 'underclass' problematic similarly contributes to the *naturalization of racial division* by demoting it from primary cause to correlate (when it acknowledges it at all) and from structuring social mechanism to be unhinged to an axiomatic feature of the metropolitan order of things. The residential separation of African-Americans from whites 'has been with us so long that it seems a natural part of the social order, a normal and unremarkable feature of America's urban land-scape' (Massey and Denton 1993: 17). So unremarkable that *The Urban Underclass* volume (Jencks and Peterson 1991) contains one chapter on 'class' segregation 'among' blacks but none on 'racial' segregation 'between' whites and blacks (or Latinos). And that Jencks and Peterson declined to publish in it the paper presented at the 'Conference on the Truly Disadvantaged' by the leading student of urban segregation in the USA, Douglas Massey, arguing that the residential seclusion of African-Americans is, along with rising joblessness, a major cause of the growth of the so-called 'underclass'.

Social analysts in the 1960s were not so squeamish when it came to recognizing the overriding role of ethno-racial power relations in struc-turing urban inequality and marginality. 'You will find two things involved in one way or another in every gesture and every word spoken in that ghetto', remarked Michael Harrington (1962: 74) in his depiction of Harlem's plight: 'the double indignity of racial discrimination and economic oppression, that unique amalgam which is Negro poverty in the world of American poverty'. Kenneth Clark was no less blunt in his indictment of the 'conjugation' of class division 'and' caste exclusion imposed upon ghetto residents. His diagnosis of nearly 40 years ago remains strikingly current:

> The poor are always alienated from normal society, and when the poor are Negro, as they increasingly are in American cities, a double trauma exists – rejection on the basis of class and race is a danger to the stability of society as a whole.
>
> (Clark 1965: 21)

For economists John Kain and Joseph Persky writing in a 1969 issue of *The Public Interest* on 'Alternatives to the Gilded Ghetto', it was equally clear that the forcible segregation of urban blacks was the para-mount force behind the parlous state of their communities and the correlative 'distortion in metropolitan development'. From a comparison of the different patterns of residential clustering near work places of blacks and whites, they concluded that 'the inference is inescapable: *central cities are poor largely because they are black, and not the converse'* (Kain and Persky 1969: 75, original emphasis). Anticipating many of the 'discoveries' of later underclass explorers, Kain and Persky argued that confining blacks to separate all-black districts truncated their 'access to the job market' by limiting informal work search methods to the ghetto and by locking them away from suburban job troves (given the cost and radial layout of public transit systems). In addition, segregation consigned African-Americans to massively inferior schools and depressed their expectations and aspirations by concentrating 'drug addiction, violent crime, and disorganization' within their neighbourhoods. The remedy they advocated for the host of social and fiscal ills brought upon large cities by rigid racial segregation was 'a major dispersal of the low income population, particularly the Negro'. And 'ghetto dispersal' was not simply the 'preferable long-term solution', argued Kain and Persky (1969: 75, 87): it was the only solution 'consistent with the stated goals of American society'.

What explains the camouflaging of the (racial) ghetto in the garb of the (poverty) slum as we moved into the 1980s? Why has segregation been accorded the status of 'a minor footnote in the ongoing debate on the underclass' when students of the ghetto in the 1960s granted it pride of place (Massey and Denton 1993: 16)? Such conceptual stenosis cannot be due to the dilution of ethno-racial division in the metropolis: patterns of black–white segregation in major metropolitan areas have proved exceedingly persistent and remain nearly as entrenched today as they were a half-century ago. So much so that demographers found it necessary to coin the concept of 'hypersegregation' to spotlight the extraordinary resiliency and all-enveloping character of black segregation in present-day America (Massey and Denton 1989).

The elision of the ethno-racial dimension of urban relegation in the tale of the 'ghetto underclass' is neither accidental nor innocent. It is emblematic of the *mounting suppression of race in policy-oriented research* over the past two decades as the 'War on Poverty' initiated by Lyndon Johnson gave way to the 'War on Welfare' launched by Ronald Reagan and pursued by his successors (Handler 1995; Katz 1995; Wacquant 1997). Following the brusque rightward turn of American politics in reaction to the social transformations ushered by the popular contestation of the 1960s, policies aimed at attacking racial inequality have been disqualified and shelved – save for cosmetic measures, such as Affirmative Action, designed to placate the politically active and privileged segments of subordinate groups and soothe the racial bad faith of white liberals. With the abandonment of 'the integrationist dream' (Orfield 1987), race has been expelled from the national agenda and segregation placed off-limits of both discussion and intervention.[17] State programmes have shifted from combatting ethno-racial and class disparities to accommodating their consequences under a two-prong strategy of 'benign neglect' in the higher sectors of the social structure and 'malign neglect' at its bottom (Wacquant 1996).

The ablation of race from the 'ghetto' is the conceptual retranslation, in the specialized *problématique* of policy-geared research, of the strict taboo that weighs on segregation in the political sphere. The conceptual recoil from race in the 'underclass' debate comes not because race has become less powerful a causal factor in the determination of life chances in the lower regions of American social space but, rather, because it is not a proper topic to broach openly for scholars who intend to be 'relevant' and 'influence' the current concerns of state elites.[18] Its rationale is not intellectual but tactical; it reflects not cognitive contraints but self-imposed political censorship as public debate on the topic drifts further and further rightward.

Much as 'groups', 'taxes', 'big government', 'crime', 'the War on Drugs' and 'welfare reform' have functioned as a coded idiom wherewith politicians can stoke and enlist the forces of racial and class reaction in the political field (Chambliss 1994; Edsall and Edsall 1991), 'underclass' and other putatively deracialized terms derived from the income-based conception of the 'ghetto' have served to refer to undeserving and unruly blacks without resorting to visibly 'coloured' language.[19] In sum, Jargowsky and Bane, and those who have borrowed or built on their reduction of ghetto to slum, have *made a conceptual virtue out of a political necessity*: they diligently effaced from their analytical framework the one cause that the American state stubbornly refuses to acknowledge, confront and mitigate when dealing with disparity and destitution: race. Equating the ghetto with extreme poverty *sans* mention of its ethno-racial underpinnings thus partakes, if not a scholarship of backlash (Steinberg 1995), certainly of a *scholarship of retreat and acquiescence* to the existing, hypersegregated structure of American city and society.

It is important to avoid succumbing to the logic of the trial and not to read this critique of the uncontrolled slippage towards a falsely deracialized notion of 'ghetto' as an indictment of the particular scholars cited. For this drift does not stem from their personal biases or shortcomings. Rather, it expresses the censorship effect resulting from the *structural subordination* of the field of policy research to the political and journalistic fields.[20] As an intermediate, mongrel, domain of inquiry, the raison d'être of public policy studies is to transliterate the current demands of state managers (as selectively amplified by the media) into the purportedly neutral and rational language of social research so as to supply the latter with seemingly scientific warrants for their policies. To do this, policy-oriented scholarship must of necessity accept and import into its own frameworks the categories, concerns and prejudices of the administrative elites charged with managing the 'problem populations' trapped in the 'ghetto'. It, therefore, comes as no surprise that its analytic tools should fill the empty shell of sociological concepts with the bureaucratic and ordinary common sense constitutive of the political *doxa* of the moment.

It is also not by happenstance if it takes a veteran historian, that is, a scholar whose intellectual as well as professional stakes are the furthest removed from the dictates of the public policy field, to express in plain terms the open secret of the past decade of debates on race and poverty in the American metropolis:

> As conditions worsened, a new group of scholars, journalists, and think-tankers, largely neoconservatives, suddenly discovered what everyone had warned about in the 1960s – that not only does the ghetto constitute a threat to its own people but it disturbs the general tranquility of our cities. These authors usually do not use the word *ghetto,* which smacks of race, but rather they embrace the trendy term *underclass,* which seems color blind. Yet in identifying this underclass in 800 computerized Census tracts, they found that nearly every one of the infected areas is black or Hispanic. Uncomfortable with the explosive connotations of race, they invented their own definition of underclass neighborhoods.
>
> (Wade 1990: 11)

Much as, in the 1930s, segregation was not a key term in the sociology of race relations 'primarily because it had not yet become a political or legal issue' (McKey 1993: 132), today segregation must again recede or disappear from the social study of urban inequality and marginality because it is a politically untouchable and intractable issue. Over fifty years after they wrote them, America is still, to borrow the piercing words of St. Clair Drake and Horace Cayton (1945: 765–6, 206), 'frozen and paralyzed before its Negro problem', incapable of recognizing that the so-called new urban poor not only bear the cross of economic dispossession but also 'wear the badge of color'.

Notes

1. I have tried elsewhere to clarify the terms and stakes of this debate by means of a critical genealogy of the 'underclass' in the social and scientific imagery of America, a dissection of the preconceptual commitments of research on the ghetto, and by an empirical comparison of the contrasted make up and evolution of the French 'Red Belt' and the US 'Black Belt' (see Wacquant 1996, 1997).

2. This excursus is not meant as a full recapitulation of the shifting and contested uses of the terms ghetto, slum, enclave, quarter, colony, tenement, and so on, over the past century. Its triadic division describes only the predominant tendency of each epoch with the aim of sketching the backdrop to the recent drift away from an ethno-racial conception of the ghetto. Ward (1989) offers a broad-ranging account of the twists and turns in the history of 'ghetto' and 'slum' in America while Philpott (1978) explores this duality in great depth in the paradigmatic case of Chicago.

3. Cf. the designation employed by Park et al. (1925) in their famous concentric map of the 'natural areas' of the city. The term 'Little Africa' was also used in some cities to refer to segregated black settlements (Wade 1990).

4. In *The Ghetto*, Wirth (1928: 6) assimilates to the ghetto the 'Little Sicilies, Little Polands, Chinatowns, and Black belts in our large cities', along with 'vice areas' – all of which are said to be 'natural areas' fulfilling a 'function' in the broader urban organism.

5. See, respectively, Osofsky (1971), Spear (1967) and Philpott (1978), Katzman (1973) and Kusmer (1976). For modifications and extensions of the 'ghetto synthesis' in historiography to other cities and regions of the United States, see Kusmer (1995) and Trotter (1995).

6. Recall that, when the term 'ghetto' gained currency to refer first to Jewish and later to other immigrant neighbourhoods, newcomers to America of non-English origins were commonly racialized: Jews, Germans, Italians, Poles and Irish were perceived as distinct cultural-cum-biological groupings, each with its own mores and hereditary characteristics.

7. Among others, Devine and Wright (1993), Hughes (1990), Jargowsky and Ellwood (1990), Jencks and Peterson (1991), Kasarda (1992), Mead (1992), Wilson (1991a, 1994, 1996).

8. For a lucid explication of the difference between relational and gradational (or monadic) attributes of inequality, see Wright (1994).

9. This is recognized by Wilson (1996: 254–6), who lists two full pages of conceptual and methodological critiques exposing the utter inadequacy of the 'poverty line' as a research tool but then goes on to use it throughout the book as basis for his key concepts of 'ghetto' and 'new poverty'.

10. This is why analysis on 'the growth of the underclass' and the spread of the 'ghetto' (redefined as extreme-poverty tracts) typically go back only to 1970, the first year for which the Census Bureau computed poverty rates by area.

11. Certainly, the 'current usage' Jargowsky and Bane invoke in 1991 is not that of social scientists: according to the entry on 'ghetto' in the 1988 edition of the *Dictionary of Race and Ethnic Relations* (Troyna 1988), 'most commentators agree that, technically a ghetto should comprise a high degree of

homogeneity' or a population presenting 'common ethnic and cultural characteristics' as well as 'living amidst poverty, in relation to the rest of the city's population' (the entry in the 1996 edition is unchanged). The *Oxford English Dictionary* similarly lists segregation and ethnic homogeneity among the defining features of the ghetto.

12. The only significant variation was among whites residing in 'college towns such as Madison, Wisconsin [sic], and Texas towns where many of the whites were probably Hispanic' (Jargowsky and Bane 1991: 243, note 17).

13. In a footnote that reads every bit like a Freudian slip, Jargowsky and Bane (1991: 238, note 7) overturn the scaffolding of their non-racial conception of the ghetto when they inadvertently concede: 'Race and poverty are both involved in creating ghetto neighborhoods'. The same analytical equivocation is in William Julius Wilson's work (1996).

14. Among the precious few exceptions to this collective myopia, one must cite Charles Johnson's (1943) *Patterns of Negro Segregation* (which served as basis for the chapter on 'Social Segregation and Discrimination' in Myrdal and Sissela's *An American Dilemma* (1944)); the work of legal scholars in the 1960s and of post-civil-rights historians of African-American urbanization; the stream of studies of racial disparities in urban housing and education by Gary Orfield (for example, 1983); and the master-book of Massey and Denton (1993), *American Apartheid.*

15. An indicator of the residual status of segregation in Wilson's analysis is the fact that it does not figure in the index whereas 'welfare' has 18 entries, 'poverty' 13, 'family' 11, and 'violence' four.

16. The only difference between the human and the plant community is that members of the former are 'more mobile, and through locomotion can seek those areas in which they can most satisfactorily gratify their fundamental interests and wishes'. Shorn of its material basis in segregation, the ghetto becomes 'not so much a physical fact as a state of mind' benignly rooted in 'the absence of intercommunication' (Wirth 1928: 283–5, 287).

17. A similar suppression of race has affected recent research on criminal justice and cross-pollinated with 'underclass' scholarship. Jerome Miller (1996: 59) notes that Wilson and Jencks have accepted econometrician Alfred Blumstein's controversial thesis on the 'color blindness' of the crime control apparatus at face value despite mounds of field, organizational and statistical studies indicating that ethno-racial bias is built into the very procedures, categories and activities of the police, courts and prison systems and, if anything, has *increased* in recent years with the unleashing of the 'War on Drugs' (Tonry 1995).

18. The latest round of 'welfare reform' should encourage scholars with policy ambitions to a modicum of sobriety (if not healthy scepticism and outright cynicism). It demonstrates, experimentally as it were, that politicians are *never* influenced by 'the force of true ideas' (to recall Spinoza's expression) and could not care less about rigorous scientific investigation into 'social problems'. Rather, they select from existing scholarship those arguments and research findings that support the policies they favour and simply ignore others. In short, far from being 'influenced' by policy researchers, they *use* them.

19. 'Terms such as "poverty", "the inner city", and "the truly disadvantaged" intentionally camouflage the real nature of their agenda. Thus we have the spectacle of a national debate over race that has been cleansed of any mention of race.' (Steinberg 1995: 214)
20. See Bourdieu (1996) for a cogent if sketchy analysis of the structural relations of dominance and subordination among the fields of politics, journalism and the social sciences.

4

Terms of Entry: Social Institutions and Immigrant Earnings in American, Canadian and Australian Cities[1]

Jeffrey G. Reitz

How is the impact of immigrants on a society affected by the structure of that society's own institutions? How is institutional restructuring altering the impact of immigration? These questions are important to immigrant-receiving societies such as the USA, Canada and Australia, because in all three countries the processes of global economic change and other forces are affecting both immigration and institutional change. Are institutional changes such as privatization, freer markets and streamlined social welfare, which have been undertaken in part as national competitiveness strategies, likely to facilitate a positive impact of immigration? Or does such structural change hinder the contribution of immigrants?

A glimpse of the effects of institutional structure and change on the impact of immigration can be gained by comparing the different position of recent immigrants in the USA, Canada and Australia. The position of immigrants in these three countries has been quite different, primarily because of differences in the basic structure of institutions most important to the economic functioning of the society. These institutions are not only different in the three countries, they are changing in different ways and at different speeds.

The impact of immigration on a society can be analyzed in terms of the economic status of the immigrants, the place they occupy in the social and economic hierarchy of society. From this standpoint, the impact of recent immigration is substantially less positive in the USA than it is either in Canada or Australia. This is because in the USA the entry level of most immigrant groups is substantially lower than it is in Canada or Australia. As a matter of fact, in certain US urban areas such as New York, Chicago, or Los Angeles where immigrants are most heavily concentrated, immigrants enter the occupational and earnings hierarchy at levels even lower than the national norm. Presumably the impact in these locations is even more negative.

The following analysis will show that institutional structure is the most important cause of these differences, when compared with other possible causes such as differences in immigrant selective characteristics, or differences in discriminatory treatment within institutions. Even more interesting, if one considers the relative importance of three institutional areas – namely education, labour market structure and social welfare – educational institutions and changes in educational institutions are most important in determining immigrant entry status. This is particularly important for Canada and Australia, given that education is the area where these two countries, and especially Canada, have been changing most rapidly toward the US model. Institutional convergence toward the US model may lead to a reduction in the positive impact of immigration in Canada and also in Australia.

The issue of immigrant status

Immigration, or more generally international migration, not only continues to be a significant issue but is very likely to become one of the most salient features of the new global economy which is emerging. World-wide change is creating pressures for increased exchanges of all kinds including those involving labour supply. The flow of refugees is also significant and unfortunately is likely to remain so. Specific numbers of immigrants from particular sources vary over time, but the fact of immigration as a significant social and economic phenomenon will continue.

The traditional immigrant-receiving societies of the USA, Canada and Australia continue to receive the most immigrants. Borjas (1988) estimated that these three countries were recipients of two-thirds of international migrants (a rough estimate because of poor and noncomparable data from some countries). In the USA, the numbers of immigrants increased steadily during the last three decades since the watershed immigration reforms of the 1960s. Recent policy changes will increase the numbers still further. In per capita terms, immigration to the USA is still small compared to recent immigration to Canada or to Australia. At 700 000 or so annual immigrants to the USA, the flow still constitutes only about 0.2–0.3 per cent of population, whereas the 250 000 immigrants to Canada constitutes closer to 0.9 per cent. Immigration to Australia has been higher than in Canada in per capita terms, though changes in the past few years have reduced per capita immigration to Australia down to US levels.

At the same time, all industrial countries participate in increased labour migration. Migration to European countries, particularly Britain, France and Germany, has some quantitative significance. In Japan migration has received attention within the country quite out of proportion to the numbers which while small are not negligible (perhaps 250 000 in total in Tokyo, for example; nationally this is only a trace, on an annual per cent-of-population basis).

The supposition that higher immigrant status leads to a more positive impact has acquired almost the status of conventional wisdom; most immigration policy is ostensibly based on it. There is an apparent international competition for the best-educated immigrants, on the basis that such immigrants are expected to be most beneficial. An economic argument for a positive impact of the best-placed immigrants involves several considerations. Immigrants earning high incomes make a positive net contribution to government balance sheets because they pay higher taxes, require no education or job training, demand few social services and no unemployment compensation. They also create stronger consumer demand, and their propensity for self-employment is a factor in job creation. Immigrants entering near the bottom of the social and economic hierarchy are often perceived as less positive in their impact. Any benefits to employer groups who use less skilled immigrants as a cheap labour supply would be offset by the negative impacts on domestic labour groups whose position is undercut.

The economic position of immigrants ramifies to determine also the social, cultural and political impact. Economically well integrated immigrants are likely to find that social, cultural and political integration follows fairly easily. Economically exploited immigrants may become embroiled in conflicts, or find that their cultures are negatively stereotyped and thus, political integration suffers. The impact of immigration is affected by other factors as well, of course, such as the total numbers of immigrants, and the way in which immigration affects the economic allocation among the native-born. But the economic success of immigrants is an important criterion for a positive impact.

There has been a growing concern about the declining position of immigrants. This concern is strongest in the USA, but exists in Canada and Australia as well. The educational levels of most recent non-European immigration is higher (though not always, particularly not for Mexicans in the USA and certain other groups), but in many groups the educational levels have been declining. These concerns have been underscored in studies by Borjas (1985) and Chiswick (1986), which show that the economic performance of the non-European groups also has been lower even in relation to education, and that earnings net of education also have been declining. In Canada and Australia, the effect of immigration reforms was different because newer non-European immigrants were better educated than the earlier European immigrants, many of whom were southern Europeans with very limited formal education. Yet some analyses in Canada have shown declining economic performance of recent immigrants as well (see Devoretz 1995).

Variations in immigrant status: cross-national and inter-urban[2]

By the criterion of immigrant status, the impact of recent immigration to the USA has been substantially less positive than has recent immigration in either Canada or Australia. This is because immigrants to the USA from virtually every origin group have distinctly lower relative occupational status and earnings than those in Canada or Australia. Furthermore, immigrant inequality is particularly great in those USA urban areas where immigrants are most concentrated. Such inter-urban variation is less in Canada and least in Australia.

The more extreme immigrant inequality in the USA is partly a function of the different composition of immigrant groups – the fact, for example, that in the USA there is a fairly large number of illegal Mexican immigrants who often have very little education and do menial work often for very little pay in large urban centres in the American southwest.[3] At the same time, Australia has been somewhat slower than the USA or Canada to admit immigrants from non-European sources who might suffer racial disadvantage.

However, the cross-national difference in immigrant status holds even when one compares the position of the same immigrant groups. It is useful to compare first the position of recent immigrants from Europe, in Table 4.1, Panel A. While the earnings of recent white male immigrants to Canada and Australia are on par with the earnings of their native-born white counterparts, in the USA these same immigrant groups earn only 90 per cent of the earnings of the native-born white (non-Hispanic) males. Recent white female immigrants to Australia earn 65 per cent of what the benchmark native-born white males earn, and in Canada they earn 50 per cent, but their counterparts in the USA earn only 44 per cent of what the native-born white male earns.

The lower position of immigrants to the USA is particularly evident in immigrant reception cities such as New York, Chicago or Los Angeles. While European-origin male immigrants nationally earned 90 per cent of the earnings of the benchmark group, in the cities with larger immigrant concentrations they earned only between 75 and 80 per cent of native-born white male's earnings. The national figure for white females of 44 per cent declines to between 30 and 40 per cent in the major urban immigration centres. This inter-urban variation is far less significant in Canada, where immigrants to Toronto and Montreal do only somewhat less well than those in Vancouver. Immigrants to Australia not only do better; their situation is even more uniform across cities.

Table 4.1 Entry-level earnings of recent immigrants in the urban labour force, for major urban areas by origins, gender, and host country, *c.* 1980

Men			Women			
Urban area	Relative mean earnings[1]	(N)	Urban area	Relative mean earnings[2]	(N)	Earnings relative to native-born white men[1]
A. White immigrants						
Vancouver	1.02	(299)	Melbourne	1.04	(227)	0.66
Sydney	1.02	(520)	Sydney	1.03	(309)	0.65
Washington DC	1.01	(326)	Vancouver	0.97	(186)	0.54
Melbourne	0.99	(327)	Montreal	0.96	(169)	0.57
Toronto	0.95	(869)	Boston	0.91	(288)	0.48
Detroit	0.95	(290)	Chicago	0.90	(630)	0.41
Montreal	0.93	(329)	Los Angeles–Long Beach	0.90	(578)	0.46
San Francisco–Oakland	0.90	(385)	Washington DC	0.88	(242)	0.45
Boston	0.80	(417)	Toronto	0.84	(673)	0.47
Los Angeles–Long Beach	0.79	(861)	San Francisco–Oakland	0.84	(247)	0.43
Newark	0.77	(434)	Philadelphia	0.80	(178)	0.38
New York	0.77	(2 373)	New York	0.76	(1 341)	0.43
Chicago	0.76	(1 010)	Newark	0.71	(287)	0.29
Total, Australia	1.00	(1 281)	Total, Australia	1.01	(829)	0.65
Total, Canada	1.00	(2 024)	Total, Canada	0.89	(1 361)	0.50
Total, USA	0.90	(10 567)	Total, USA	0.91	(6 608)	0.44

Table 4.1 continued

Men			Women			
Urban area	Relative mean earnings[1]	(N)	Urban area	Relative mean earnings[2]	(N)	Earnings relative to native-born white men[1]
B. Chinese immigrants						
Toronto	0.77	(258)	Toronto	0.90	(256)	0.50
San Jose	0.74	(111)	Vancouver	0.84	(171)	0.46
Vancouver	0.73	(202)	Los Angeles–Long Beach	0.78	(446)	0.40
Chicago	0.71	(128)	Boston	0.71	(103)	0.38
Houston	0.67	(100)	San Francisco–Oakland	0.66	(499)	0.34
Los Angeles–Long Beach	0.60	(531)	New York	0.61	(652)	0.34
Boston	0.55	(118)				
San Francisco–Oakland	0.51	(587)				
New York	0.44	(785)				
Total, Canada	0.77	(658)	Total, Canada	0.86	(584)	0.48
Total, USA	0.63	(3 470)	Total, USA	0.83	(2 763)	0.40
C. Black immigrants						
Toronto	0.70	(200)	Toronto	0.84	(195)	0.46
Boston	0.61	(202)	Newark	0.79	(172)	0.32
Chicago	0.55	(162)	Boston	0.75	(165)	0.40
Newark	0.51	(181)	Washington DC	0.71	(262)	0.36
New York	0.49	(2 393)	Los Angeles–Long Beach	0.70	(155)	0.36
Washington DC	0.49	(281)	New York	0.68	(2 375)	0.38
Los Angeles–Long Beach	0.48	(182)	Miami	0.63	(280)	0.32
Miami	0.48	(354)				
Total, Canada	0.70	(341)	Total, Canada	0.81	(324)	0.45
Total, USA	0.54	(4 985)	Total, USA	0.82	(4 308)	0.39
D. Asian immigrants						
Detroit	0.92	(261)	Detroit	1.29	(166)	0.57
Sydney	0.86	(162)	Chicago	1.17	(1 017)	0.54
Melbourne	0.85	(123)	Philadelphia	1.14	(254)	0.54
Philadelphia	0.83	(319)	Newark	1.05	(185)	0.43
Newark	0.82	(197)	Sydney	1.02	(126)	0.64
Chicago	0.78	(1 243)	San Jose	0.94	(475)	0.44
Toronto	0.77	(717)	Orange County	0.93	(388)	0.41

56   *Globalization and the New City*

Table 4.1   continued

Men			Women			
Urban area	Relative mean earnings[1]	(N)	Urban area	Relative mean earnings[2]	(N)	Earnings relative to native-born white men[1]
Vancouver	0.75	(364)	Los Angeles–Long Beach	0.90	(2 035)	0.46
New York	0.72	(2 302)	Houston	0.90	(327)	0.41
Houston	0.70	(534)	Montreal	0.90	(118)	0.53
Los Angeles–Long Beach	0.69	(2 587)	Toronto	0.86	(631)	0.47
Boston	0.69	(203)	New York	0.84	(1 582)	0.47
Dallas	0.67	(257)	Vancouver	0.83	(306)	0.46
Montreal	0.66	(205)	Dallas	0.83	(159)	0.39
Washington DC	0.64	(617)	Boston	0.82	(174)	0.43
San Jose	0.64	(543)	Honolulu	0.81	(581)	0.45
Orange County	0.64	(497)	San Diego	0.79	(367)	0.43
Honolulu	0.63	(603)	San Francisco–Oakland	0.78	(1 410)	0.40
San Diego	0.62	(380)	Washington DC	0.78	(509)	0.40
San Francisco–Oakland	0.58	(1 519)				
Total, Australia	0.84	(354)	Total, Australia	1.00	(267)	0.64
Total, Canada	0.76	(1 754)	Total, Canada	0.85	(1 396)	0.48
Total, USA	0.75	(15 507)	Total, USA	0.99	(12 356)	0.48

Notes: 1. Earnings relative to the earnings of the white, non-Hispanic male labour force.
2. Earnings relative to the earnings of the white, non-Hispanic female labour force.

Sources: 1980 US Census Public Use Microdata five per cent file (US Bureau of the Census 1983); 1981 Canadian Census Public Use Tape two per cent Individual File (Canada, Statistics Canada 1984b); 1981 Australain Census of Population and Housing one per cent File (Australian Bureau of Statistics 1984). For further details on these sources see Reitz (1998, Chapters 1 and 2).

The entire pattern of cross-national and inter-urban differences in the status of immigrant groups carries over to affect the racial minority immigrant groups too. In Table 4.1, Panel B, one can compare the entrance status of Chinese immigrants arriving in the major Canadian and USA cities in the 1970s. In Canada, recent Chinese immigrant males earned 77 per cent of the earnings of native-born white males, while their USA counterparts earned only 63 per cent of the earnings of the native-born white males. Recent female Chinese immigrants to Canada earned 48 per cent of the earnings of the male benchmark group, compared to only 40 per cent for their counterparts in the USA. And whereas in Canada the position of Chinese immigrants both in Toronto and Vancouver (where they are most heavily concentrated) is approximately the same as for the country as a whole, in the USA the position of recent Chinese immigrants in the urban areas in which they are most concentrated – New York and San Francisco especially – is substantially worse. In those two cities the earnings of the recent Chinese immigrant males was 44 and 51 per cent of the earnings of the native-born white males, while for the females it was 34 per cent in each case. In other USA cities, the position of the Chinese immigrants was somewhat better. Sometimes it was closer to the USA national average (in Los Angeles, for example) and sometimes it was even closer to the Canadian standard (in San Jose, for example).

The same cross-national and inter-urban comparison applies to black immigrants in the USA and Canada. In Canada, recent black male immigrants earned 70 per cent of the earnings of the native-born white male group, while in the USA their counterparts earned only 54 per cent. Among female immigrants the figures were 45 per cent for Canada and 39 per cent for the USA. And again in certain USA cities the position of black immigrants was even lower. Whereas in Toronto the position of blacks, both males and females, was comparable to the position of blacks nationally (70 per cent and 46 per cent, respectively), in Miami, New York, Washington and Los Angeles the relative earnings of black immigrants was worse than their position nationally (between 48 and 49 per cent for males and as low as 32 per cent for females). On the other hand, in Boston, black male immigrants earn 61 per cent of what whites earn, while women earn 40 per cent, closer to the national average, or even a bit above (though still lower than in Toronto).

In Australia, there is less immigrant inequality than in either Canada or the USA, even for Asian minorities, as Table 4.1, Panel D, shows. For Asian immigrants in Australia in 1981, males earned 84 per cent of what native-born white males earned, compared to about 76 per cent for Asian males in Canada and the USA. Female Asians earned 64 per cent of what native-born white males earned, compared to 48 per cent in Canada and the USA. This is partly because females in general earn relatively more in Australia. In Australia, like Canada but unlike the USA, there is less variation among urban areas, so the national data reflect the situation in major cities like Sydney, Melbourne and Perth.

In sum, recent minority male immigrant 'entrance status' (earnings relative to the native-born) in 1980/81 was about 15 per cent lower in the USA than in Canada, and 20–25 per cent lower in the USA than in Australia. An immigrant group which earns 70 per cent of the earnings of native-born whites earn in the USA, earns about 85 per cent of native-born earnings in Canada and over 90 per cent in Australia. Recent minority female immigrant pay status was 6–8 per cent lower in the USA than in Canada, and as much as 15 per cent lower in the USA than in Australia. Greater inequality in certain USA cities, such as New York, San Francisco, Los Angeles and Miami mean that racial minority immigrants there experience lower status than in other cities or countries, and for a longer period of time. Over time, of course, immigrants adjust and their earnings improve. However, racial minority immigrants find that their position improves more slowly than immigrants of European origins, and they do not appear to assimilate to the white average. Instead, they maintain a degree of disadvantage. So the cross-national and inter-urban differences continue to matter, and affect race relations and the impact of immigration.

Social determination of immigrant standing

What is the reason for the varying statuses and presumably varying impacts of immigration in different countries, or different places within countries? What is causing the changing and perhaps declining statuses of immigrants? The determinants of immigrant standing may be divided into three main categories: (a) the characteristics of the immigrants themselves, and their individual and group reservoirs of financial human, social and financial capital; (b) the treatment of immigrants and immigrant groups within the institutions of society, including the problem of discrimination; and (c) the structure of the institutions themselves. A consideration of the first two of these types of causes – immigrant characteristics based mostly on selection and racial discrimination – suggests that while these are important, they are unlikely to be most important in explaining variations across contexts. This forces us to consider the third category: the institutional causes.

Selection and self-selection of immigrants

The characteristics of immigrants are determined by policies of immigrant selection, and also by self-selection processes engaged in by the immigrants themselves. There can be little doubt that an important determinant of immigrant status and perhaps one source of its decline at least in the USA, is the selection and self-selection of immigrants. Borjas (1991, 1993) argues that the swing away from European immigrants has been most pronounced in the USA, and that because of the greater attention given to family-class immigrants, not only are the recent non-European immigrants more poorly educated, they are negatively self-selected to an increasing degree. Devoretz (1995) linked the declining performance of recent immigrants to Canada to declining skill levels of immigrants.

The American, Canadian and Australian policy revisions in recent years have been directed in part at raising the education level and other human capital of immigrants, and by emphasizing entrepreneurs, also raising their financial capital. The analyses by Borjas and also by Chiswick (1986, 1988) point to the increasingly prominent role of family-class immigrants in the total flow and mention also the depletion of the supply of suitable potential immigrants. Some of the 1990 American policy changes were directed specifically at this issue. The 1994 revisions announced in Canada also attempted to control family-class immigrants, particularly parents of immigrants. They also promised to increase attention given to human capital, such as language knowledge. Australian immigration policy has reduced immigration levels partly in an attempt to control unskilled immigration (see Baker *et al.* 1994).

However, immigration policy and the self-selection of immigrants cannot be the only, or even the chief, reason for greater inequality in the USA. In the first place, the Canadian and Australian policies are not necessarily more skill-selective, rather they are more occupationally selective. Canadian and Australian policies do give weight to education, increasingly over the years, but in fact they give more weight to occupational demand. Many of the occupations officially designated as in demand are far from highly-skilled (in one year, the occupation listed as most in demand was 'cook').

In any case, a direct comparison of the skill levels of immigrants to the three countries shows that the USA actually out-competes both Canada and Australia for highly-skilled immigrants in virtually every source pool. This has been documented in a comparison 1980/81 census data of Chinese and other Asian immigrants to Canada and the USA by Duleep and Regets (1992: 425–6). The three-country urban census data for 1980/81 show that Chinese immigrants in the USA during the 1970s averaged 13.2 years of education, while in Canada they averaged 12.7 years. Chinese immigrants in Australia are even less educated – only 11.3 years on the average. Despite its more *laissez-faire* policy, most immigrant groups are in fact better educated in the USA than either in Canada or Australia.

The reason for the USA success may relate partly to the ultra-selectivity of the smaller, skilled component of the immigration programme. This programme includes a very elite group of professionals and the family members of these highly selected immigrants also would tend to be comparatively well educated. However, immigrant self-selection may be even more important. In the first place, the USA is still most often the preferred choice as an immigrant destination. Borjas (1988) also has provided data to support the hypothesis that the USA attracts the most ambitious and economically aggressive immigrants, because of the greater likelihood that immigrant success leads to extreme wealth in the USA. The forces of self-selection suggest that the capacity of governments to control the entrance status of immigrants using immigration policy is actually quite limited.

The success of the USA in the competition for skilled immigrants seems to contradict the point, previously noted for example by Borjas (1991), that the most important single feature of greater immigrant inequality in the USA is that the immigrant education gap has been on average about one to two years greater in the USA than it is in Canada, where immigrant educational levels have been more on a par with native-born.[4] However, this immigrant education gap is not due to less-educated immigrants in the USA, but rather to the higher levels of education of native-born Americans. It is well known that, for many years, the USA native-born population has pursued much higher levels of education than in Canada, while the Australians have been less educated. This points toward the importance of the development of educational institutions in the three countries, a subject to which I return later. Native-born educational levels are also relevant to inter-urban variations in relative immigrant earnings.

Discrimination against minority immigrants

The potential impact of discrimination against immigrants is an issue virtually everywhere, although its significance is very difficult to measure quantitatively. Some attribute the substantial earnings disadvantages of non-European immigrants, net of measured human capital such as education, to discrimination based on racial minority status. Net earnings disadvantages of black immigrants in the USA are about 20 per cent. This is comparable to what is observed for native-born African Americans, as Model (1991) shows (compare also to Jaynes and Williams 1989). However, some attribute this disadvantage to 'unmeasured human capital' such as the quality of education, or even less tangible factors such as ambition. Field trials of discrimination show that some discrimination occurs, but they do not measure its significance in explaining the earnings disadvantages. The actual importance of discrimination in determining overall immigrant disadvantage cannot be settled here. What we can say is that the available indicators suggest that *cross-national differences* in the extent of discrimination are probably unimportant.

Some, reflecting strong public opinion in Canada, have suggested that for historical reasons one might expect racial discrimination to be less in Canada. However, this expectation is not supported in comparisons of labour force data, discrimination field trials or even data on attitudes to minorities (cf. Reitz and Breton 1994). Attitudes toward immigrants and minorities in Australia do not appear to be substantially more positive.[5] Anti-Semitic incidents recorded by B'nai B'rith,[6] and discrimination field trials,[7] also do not support the hypothesis of less discrimination in Australia (see also Foster *et al.* 1991). The relatively higher net earnings of immigrants in Australia could be a function of less discrimination, as might be suggested based on the studies by Evans and Kelley (1986, 1991), or to more favourable selection based on unmeasured human capital, as Borjas (1991) suggests. However, the evidence on discrimination is debated in all three countries. None of those participating in this debate have suggested that rates of discrimination vary cross-nationally.

The cross-national similarity in the findings on the potential for racial discrimination probably reflects the fact that, while the three countries have different historical experiences with race, they share the same British and European cultural heritage. The populations of the three countries may as a result exhibit the same attitudes toward non-Europeans, and show similar predispositions to racial intolerance and exclusion in specific social spheres including employment. Hence, the potential for discrimination seems hardly likely to provide the explanation for lower immigrant standing in the USA compared to Canada or Australia.

Institutional sources of immigrant standing

If considerations of immigrant selection, and discrimination against immigrants within institutions, are insufficient to explain the differences in immigrant status, then we are led to consider differences in the structure of the institutions themselves. Three institutional areas have a direct bearing on social and economic standing: (a) education, training and the preparation for labour market participation; (b) labour market processes of earnings allocation; and (c) social welfare policies for adjustment to labour market outcomes.

The three countries differ with regard to each of these institutional areas. To Americans, education has come to symbolize the quest for individual mobility and American society has invested more heavily in education than Canada or Australia. Furthermore, at its highest levels American education is privately controlled to a significant degree, so the aggregate investment in education at that level is subject to market processes to a greater degree. Labour markets in the USA are less extensively regulated and American provisions for social welfare tend to be less generous. In each case, USA institutions reflect a consistent and overarching American emphasis on the value of *individualism*. The American sociologist Seymour Martin Lipset has described how individualism affects specific institutional differences between Canada and the USA in his book, *The Continental Divide* (1989), including education, labour markets and social policy. Australia was not included in Lipset's analysis. In some respects, Australia seems more like Canada, while in other respects, it may be more like the USA.

To point out that USA institutions reflect individualism does not entail any assumption that culture is the source of the difference. Lipset's interpretation is essentially cultural. His hypothesis is that USA individualism was founded in the American Revolution, and is expressed in the Declaration of Independence and in the Constitution emphasizing 'life, liberty and the pursuit of happiness'. Canada was formed in a pro-British and somewhat elitist reaction, where the good of the collectivity – as defined perhaps by elites – was seen as of greater importance than giving free range to the impulses of every individual. Individualism is a social value and, therefore, is an item in the cultural sphere. Individualism also reflects common aspects of social institutional differences which may reinforce one another and which also may reinforce the culture itself.

Of the three institutional areas, perhaps labour markets have received most attention as affecting both the recruitment and settlement patterns of immigrants, and their relative earnings. The extent to which social welfare protects immigrants from extreme poverty also has been discussed. American immigration policy itself also reflects the individualist orientation, as much as American labour markets or social policies. The Statue of Liberty inscription 'give me your tired, your *poor*' underscores this. Immigrants are to be admitted on a less restricted basis, on the assumption that once landed, they are on their own to sink or to swim. In Canada or Australia, greater emphasis on immigrant selection may reflect in part the assumption that less qualified immigrants might become a greater social burden because of the greater collective social protection in labour markets or in access to public services.

The analysis that follows here will focus mostly on education, however. We will see that native-born educational levels are closely associated with cross-national and inter-urban variations in immigrant inequality. Changes in native-born educational levels produce changes in immigrant standing. However, following this discussion of education, comments regarding the importance of labour market structure and social policy will place the role of educational institutions in context.

Educational institutions

The greater immigrant education gap in the USA is due not to the selection of less-educated immigrants but primarily to the more rapid expansion of USA education for the native-born in the postwar period. Table 4.2 contains data on the growth in levels of educational attainment in the three countries. There has been significant expansion in all three countries, but this expansion occurred earlier and more rapidly in the USA. For example, the proportion of Americans completing secondary school rose from about 60 per cent to 85 per cent over the period from 1960 to 1980, after which time it levelled off. The proportion attending university doubled from 11 per cent to 22 per cent during the same period, and again levelled off.

A parallel expansion occurred somewhat later in Canada. There, secondary school completion rates lagged substantially behind the American rates but the gap closed in the 1970s and continued to close in the 1980s. University completion rates in Canada were only about one-third of the American rates in 1960, but rose to about half in 1970 and to about 70 per cent during the 1980s. Meanwhile, overall rates of post-secondary enrolment in Canada rose very rapidly during the 1980s, to virtual parity with the USA.

Educational expansion has occurred most slowly in Australia, and the gap with North America is only beginning to close in the 1980s. Good data on education in Australia is not readily available until recent years. Major expansion of Australian higher education is only now becoming a major priority for the country (Dawkins 1988).

These cross-national differences mean that there remain substantial differences among the three countries in the levels of education of the

Table 4.2 Education of population: USA, Canada and Australia, 1960–90

Year[1]	Age-specific enrolment/attainment rates (young adult cohort)									Education of population over 25 years					
	Per cent completing secondary school			Post-secondary enrolment ratios[5]			Per cent completing university degree			Per cent completing secondary school			Per cent completing university degree		
	USA[2]	Can.[3]	Aus.[4]	USA	Can.	Aus.	USA[6]	Can.[7]	Aus.[8]	USA[9]	Can.[10]	Aus.[11]	USA[12]	Can.[13]	Aus.[14]
1960	61.7	28.2	–	32.1	16.0	13.1	11.1	3.6	–	41.1	22.1	–	7.7	3.4	–
1965	–	–	–	40.2	26.4	16.0	–	–	–	49.0	–	–	9.4	–	–
1970	73.8	38.9	–	49.4	34.6	16.6	16.3	7.8	–	52.3	27.1	–	10.7	5.3	–
1975	–	61.7	–	57.3	39.3	24.0	–	13.3	–	62.5	39.2	–	13.9	7.6	–
1980	84.5	71.7	56.6	56.0	42.1	25.4	22.1	14.9	10.3	66.5	52.6	43.5	16.2	9.6	6.7
1985	86.1	72.0	59.3	57.9	53.6	27.6	22.2	14.6	11.8	73.9	56.2	46.2	19.4	11.1	8.0
1990	85.7	77.0	62.9	65.6	61.7	31.3	23.2	16.0	11.9	77.6	63.0	54.5	21.3	12.8	9.7

Notes:
1. Approximate years; see notes. Canadian census data are for one year later than indicated; Australian data are for years indicated in notes.
2. Per cent of persons aged 25–29 completing secondary school; US Bureau of the Census (1993 Table 230: 152; 1988, Table 215: 133).
3. Per cent of persons aged 25–34 with secondary school graduation certificate; 1961 (Canada, Statistics Canada, 1963, Table 102, includes grades 12 and 13 and are for persons aged 25–29); 1971 (Canada, Statistics Canada, 1974, Table 5); 1976 (Canada, Statistics Canada, 1978, Table 29); 1981 (Canada, Statistics Canada, 1984a, Table 3); 1986 (Canada, Statistics Canada, 1989, Table 2); and 1991 (Canada, Statistics Canada, 1993, Table 2).
4. Per cent of persons aged 25–34 attending highest level of secondary school available; Australian Bureau of Statistics (1982, Table 1.5: 5, 1982 data reported for 1980; 1985, Table 1.10: 11; 1990, Table 5: 10).
5. Ratio of the number enrolled in all post-secondary schools and universities (including vocational schools, adult education, two-year community colleges and correspondence courses) to the number of persons in the aged 20–24; UNESCO (1975, for 1960–65; 1985, for 1970–75; and 1993, for 1980–88). The 1990 figures are for 1988; after that date the Canadian data changed its inclusions.
6. Per cent of persons aged 25–29 with four years of college or more. See note 2.
7. Per cent of persons aged 25–34 with university bachelor's degree. See note 3.
8. Per cent of persons aged 25–34 with post-school degree. See note 4.
9. Per cent of persons 25 years or older completing four years of high school. US Bureau of the Census (1993, Table 233: 154).
10. Per cent of persons 25 years or older with secondary school graduation certificate. See note 3.
11. Per cent of persons 25 years or older attending highest level of secondary school available. See note 4.
12. Per cent of persons 25 years or older completing four years of college or more. See note 9.
13. Per cent of persons 25 years or older with university degree. Canada, Statistics Canada (1989, Table 1); Canada, Statistics Canada (1993, Table 1).
14. Per cent of persons 25 years or older with post-school degree. See note 4.

population. In 1990, the proportions of the adult population over 25 with secondary school diplomas was 77.6 per cent in the USA, 63.0 per cent in Canada and 54.5 per cent in Australia. The university degree completion rates for the adult population was 21.3 per cent in the USA, 12.8 per cent in Canada and 9.7 per cent in Australia. In the 1980 census samples used here, the American labour force averaged 13 years of education, compared to less than 12 in Canada and just over 11 in Australia. It is these differences which give rise to the greater immigrant education gap in the USA, placing immigrants there at a competitive disadvantage.

The effect of the higher USA native-born educational levels in producing lower immigrant earnings compared to Canada can be estimated either by substituting Canadian native-born educational levels in the USA earnings analysis for specific immigrant groups compared to native-born whites. If this is done, the 14 per cent difference in the relative position of recent Chinese male immigrants in the two countries is reduced to 5 per cent. (Alternatively, we may substitute American native-born educational levels into the Canadian earnings analysis, in which case the difference in the position of Chinese male immigrants in the two countries is reduced to 4 per cent.) For recent Chinese female immigrants, the 8 per cent lower earnings position in the USA is reduced to only 3 per cent if Canadian native-born educational levels are substituted into the American earnings analysis. The results of this analysis are similar for recent black immigrants. The 16 per cent cross-national difference in the relative earnings of recent black male immigrants in the two countries is reduced to 9 per cent if Canadian educational levels are substituted into the American analysis (or to 7 per cent if the American educational levels are substituted into the Canadian analysis). The 7 per cent difference in relative earnings of recent black female immigrants is reduced to 2 per cent when native-born educational levels are assumed to be equal.

The impact of native-born educational levels on the Australian/American comparison is even more dramatic. Whereas recently arrived Asian-born males in the USA earn 9 per cent less compared to native-born white males than their Australian counterparts, if USA native-born males had Australian educational levels then the Asian immigrants would enter at an earnings position 7 per cent *higher* in the USA. And whereas recently-arrived Asian-born women in the USA have relative earnings 16 per cent less compared to their Australian counterparts, if Australian native-born male educational levels are substituted into the

Table 4.3 Mean years of education of native-born whites in the urban labour force by age cohort, gender and country, *c.* 1980

Gender	Country	Age cohort[1]						Inter-cohort gain in years of over 50+ cohort
		25–34	(N)	35–49	(N)	50+	(N)	
Men								
	USA	14.29	(32 222)	13.82	(31 782)	12.82	(24 714)	1.47
	Canada	12.73	(13 083)	11.70	(11 618)	10.68	(7 641)	2.05
	Australia	11.97	(1 103)	10.98	(1 010)	10.22	(706)	1.75
	USA lead over Canada	1.56		2.12		2.14		
	USA lead over Australia	2.32		2.84		2.60		
Women								
	USA	14.06	(22 655)	13.21	(21 044)	12.45	(15 846)	1.61
	Canada	12.64	(9 764)	11.39	(7 797)	10.81	(4 626)	1.83
	Australia	11.74	(629)	10.62	(670)	10.24	(297)	1.50
	USA lead over Canada	1.42		1.82		1.64		
	USA lead over Australia	2.32		2.59		2.21		

Note: 1. Persons under 25 omitted from this analysis.

Sources: See Table 4.1.

USA analysis, then the relative disadvantage of the Asian-born women in the USA declines to only 6 per cent.

Changes in educational levels in the three countries are producing changes in the relative position of immigrants. The rapidly rising educational levels of the native-born in Canada, rising more rapidly now than in the USA, are having the effect of creating increased immigrant inequalities in Canada. The Canadian/USA convergence in educational levels is reflected in cohort-specific comparisons in Table 4.3. For males, the USA educational lead over Canada is over two years for persons over 50 years of age, but only 1.5 years for the younger cohorts. For females the cross-national difference also declined, but more slowly. These differences would have continued to decline for the youngest cohorts of the 1980s and early 1990s.

Table 4.4 Mean years of education of native-born white men in the urban labour force, for major urban areas in the USA, Canada and Australia, *c.* 1980

14.00 years or more	Mean	(N)	13.00 to 13.50 years	Mean	(N)
Washington DC	14.73	(2 732)	Dallas	13.49	(3 238)
San Jose	14.40	(1 220)	Riverside–San.	13.35	(1 011)
San Francisco–Oakland	14.30	(2 936)	Bern.–Ontario		
			New Orleans	13.33	(908)
New York	14.05	(5 650)	Philadelphia	13.30	(4 687)
Los Angeles–Long Beach	14.05	(4 986)	Kansas City	13.22	(1 505)
			Milwaukee	13.21	(1 554)
Denver	14.05	(1 863)	Columbus	13.20	(1 233)
Orange County	14.00	(2 092)	Buffalo	13.15	(1 363)
			Tampa	13.12	(1 399)
			Cleveland	13.10	(2 019)
			St. Louis	13.08	(2 266)
			Ft. Lauderdale	13.06	(931)
			Detroit	13.05	(4 196)

13.50 to 13.99 years	Mean	(N)	Less than 13.00 years	Mean	(N)
Newark	13.98	(1 754)	Cincinnati	12.94	(1 297)
Sacramento	13.89	(1 089)	Pittsburgh	12.91	(2 654)
San Antonio	13.87	(580)	Baltimore	12.91	(2 140)
Miami	13.80	(765)	Indianapolis	12.84	(1 347)
Boston	13.78	(2 451)	Toronto	12.40	(10 088)
Seattle	13.77	(1 986)	Ottawa-Hull	12.36	(3 558)
Houston	13.73	(2 616)	Calgary	12.23	(3 063)
Nassau	13.69	(2 783)	Vancouver	12.15	(5 041)
Salt Lake City	13.68	(1 051)	Edmonton	11.88	(3 379)
Minneapolis–St. Paul	13.58	(2 623)	Hamilton	11.69	(2 185)
			Winnipeg	11.63	(2 670)
San Diego	13.56	(1 887)	Québec	11.47	(3 143)
Chicago	13.55	(6 378)	Melbourne	11.46	(4 607)
Phoenix	13.54	(1 514)	Sydney	11.37	(5 754)
Atlanta	13.51	(1 795)	Adelaide	11.34	(1 602)
Portland	13.51	(1 503)	Montréal	11.16	(13 038)
			Perth	11.01	(1 476)
			Brisbane	10.91	(2 061)

Sources: See Table 4.1.

The earnings effects of the Canadian/US educational convergence are probably not yet as obvious as they will become. This is because of a market lag. The more rapid rise in the educational levels in Canada may have created a temporary comparative abundance of new highly educated workers in the Canadian labour market. A comparative study by Richard Freeman and Karen Needels (1993) showed that because the supply of university-educated workers increased during the 1970s and 1980s in Canada more rapidly than in the USA, their wage advantage over high school graduates increased less rapidly. Over time, as the increase in the university educated component of the workforce levels off in Canada, the earnings advantages of the university educated would be expected to improve. Unless immigrant education levels keep pace with the upgraded native-born population, the entrance status of new immigrants to Canada will fall back.

Given the more recent increase in the educational levels of Australian workers, immigrants there will continue to be comparatively well placed in the labour market for a longer period of time. However, eventually skill levels of the Australian workforce are expected to rise toward North American standards. When that happens, unless there are offsetting improvements in the recruitment of immigrants, the entrance level of immigrants will decline accordingly.

Immigrants, education and inter-urban variations

Inter-urban differences in native-born white educational levels are very important in the American case. The next series of tables shows that these variations in native-born education are in no small measure responsible for the most extreme immigrant inequalities in cities like New York and San Francisco. In Table 4.4, we can see how native-born educational levels vary across cities in the three countries. Educational levels are not only highest in the USA; they reach extremes in places like New York, San Francisco, Washington, Boston and San Jose. These variations are no doubt a result of local labour market demand. Urban areas with the highest educational levels tend to be those with the strongest local economies. Their economic strength attracts the most highly skilled workers. Some are internal migrants selectively recruited from less attractive locations within the USA; others are local natives who seek higher education and then remain in their hometowns because of the opportunity.

However, the effect of local conditions on immigrant educational levels is quite different from the effect on native-born education.

Urban areas with strong economies not only have high native-born educational levels but also attract large numbers of immigrants. Table 4.5 shows that high-education cities also are prime immigrant reception areas in the USA. Immigrants from each group with the exception of Mexicans and Cubans are concentrated in high education cities to a greater extent than is the population as a whole. The blacks and Chinese are the most extreme, but the same is true for all other groups. Whereas about 20 per cent of the native-born workforce (male or female) lives in high-education cities, the proportion of recent immigrants in such cities is about 60 per cent for blacks and about 55 per cent for Chinese. For all Asians the proportion is about 40 per cent. Even the Mexicans and Cubans are over-concentrated in medium-education cities (Mexicans in southern California and Texas; Cubans in Miami) and are not as often found in the low education cities as is the native-born population.

The effect of high native-born education on the immigrants in certain urban areas is compounded by a strong tendency for large ethnic communities to have comparatively *low* educational levels. Bartel (1989) already showed the relatively low educational levels of immigrants in urban areas of high immigrant concentration for large origin aggregates in a previous study. The data in Table 4.6 repeat the analysis for more detailed origin categories, and extends the analysis to include Canada and Australia. In the USA, for every group but the Koreans and Vietnamese, the larger the immigrant group the lower the education level. The most plausible explanation for this pattern involves chain migration among family-class immigrants. The least educated immigrants are most likely to want to settle near family members, seeking support. This would explain the Vietnamese exception, since that group was settled largely as a result of a government programme, rather than individual decision-making. The 1980 data reflect the earliest settlement patterns of these Vietnamese in the USA.

The result of these different patterns of recruitment is a polarization between the educational levels of immigrants and native-born. In certain USA cities where immigrants are heavily concentrated, there is a tendency both for native-born education to be *high* and for immigrant education to be *low*. The pattern, which Sassen (1991) has erroneously attributed to supposedly distinctive labour market structures of very specific so-called 'global cities', actually reflects processes of differentially selective recruitment.[8] These patterns of inter-urban variation are less pronounced in Canada, and virtually absent in Australia. Consider the Canadian data in Tables 4.4–4.6 first. Native-born educational

Table 4.5 Recent immigrant concentration in high-education urban areas by origin, gender and host country, *c.* 1980[1]

Origins and gender	Per cent residing in urban areas at each mean,[2] native-born white mean level of education by origins and gender, USA only				Years of education of native-born white labour force in urban area of residence, by origins, host country, gender		
	High 14.00+	13.50– 13.99	13.00– 13.49	Low <13.00	USA	Canada	Australia
Men							
Native-born white	19.8	32.2	31.6	16.4	13.48	11.85	11.26
Immigrant, Total	52.8	31.5	11.1	4.5	13.82	12.06	11.27
White	43.8	31.1	17.8	7.2	13.73	12.04	11.25
Black	59.1	27.0	10.0	3.9	13.88	12.02	–
Asian, Total	52.9	29.9	12.2	5.0	13.84	12.09	11.30
Chinese	63.8	23.3	9.8	3.0	13.92	12.16	11.33
Non-Chinese Asian	49.8	31.8	9.8	3.0	13.81	12.05	11.30
Filipino	53.6	34.6	6.9	4.9	13.78	–	–
Asian Indian	39.0	34.0	18.7	8.3	13.71	–	–
Korean	58.1	23.9	11.4	6.5	13.84	–	–
Vietnamese	45.2	33.2	18.2	3.4	13.82	–	–
Japanese	61.9	27.1	8.1	2.9	13.89	–	–
Other Asian	46.4	35.7	13.7	4.2	13.80	–	–
Mexican	58.8	33.8	7.0	0.4	13.87	–	–
Cuban	15.2	67.7	7.8	9.3	13.69	–	–
Other Latin American	63.7	24.9	5.6	5.8	13.88	12.03	11.36
Women							
Native-born white	21.0	32.3	30.9	15.7	13.5	11.87	11.26
Immigrant, Total	54.3	30.7	10.4	4.6	13.8	12.10	11.26
White	42.6	32.7	17.7	7.0	13.7	12.09	11.25
Black	66.1	24.0	7.1	2.8	13.9	12.09	–
Asian, Total	52.9	31.5	11.1	4.5	13.9	12.12	11.30
Chinese	66.6	23.3	7.6	2.4	14.0	12.17	11.29
Non-Chinese Asian	49.0	33.9	12.1	5.1	13.8	12.08	11.30
Filipino	52.2	34.9	8.2	4.7	13.9	–	–
Asian Indian	40.9	35.6	16.9	6.7	13.8	–	–
Korean	52.2	28.8	13.2	5.8	13.8	–	–
Vietnamese	45.2	33.0	18.2	3.6	13.8	–	–
Japanese	49.1	39.9	7.1	4.0	13.9	–	–
Other Asian	48.1	35.0	13.1	3.8	13.8	–	–
Mexican	64.9	29.0	6.0	0.2	13.9	–	–
Cuban	15.1	67.4	7.5	10.0	13.7	–	–
Other Latin American	67.0	21.8	5.2	6.0	13.9	–	–

Notes: 1. For more detail, see Reitz (1998: 50, 100).

2. The entries below show the means, across each category of origins, host country and gender, of the measured level of education of the native-born white labour force, which is itself a mean value.

Sources: See Table 4.1.

Table 4.6 Effects[1] of recent immigrant community size (logged) on years of education for urban labour force by host country, origins and gender, *c.* 1980

Immigrant origins	USA		Canada		Australia	
	Metric B	(N)	Metric B	(N)	Metric B	(N)
Men						
White	$-0.544^{(2)}$	(10 567)	$-1.852^{(2)}$	(2 024)	$0.783^{(4)}$	(1 261)
Black	$-0.563^{(2)}$	(4 985)	-0.481 ns	(341)	–	
Asian, Total	$-0.766^{(2)}$	(15 507)	$0.925^{(2)}$	(1 754)	$2.068^{(2)}$	(343)
Chinese	$-2.116^{(2)}$	(3 470)	$0.799^{(4)}$	(658)	2.533 ns	(78)
Non-Chinese Asian, Total	$-0.151^{(3)}$	(12 037)	$0.853^{(3)}$	(1 096)	$2.266^{(2)}$	(265)
Filipino	$-0.415^{(2)}$	(3 094)	–		–	
Asian Indian	$-0.979^{(2)}$	(3 049)	–		–	
Korean	0.028 ns	(2 105)	–		–	
Vietnamese	$0.499^{(3)}$	(1 570)	–		–	
Japanese	$-0.632^{(2)}$	(1 117)	–		–	
Other Asian	$-0.497^{(4)}$	(1 102)	–		–	
Mexican	$-0.327^{(2)}$	(15 049)	–		–	
Cuban	$-0.548^{(2)}$	(1 869)	–		–	
Other Latin America	$-1.027^{(2)}$	(7 079)	-0.517 ns	(251)	$2.780^{(4)}$	(76)
Women						
White	$-0.355^{(2)}$	(6 608)	$-1.511^{(2)}$	(1 361)	0.640 ns	(820)
Black	$-0.348^{(2)}$	(4 307)	0.032 ns	(322)	–	
Asian, Total	-0.082 ns	(12 287)	$1.343^{(2)}$	(1 396)	$1.362^{(4)}$	(261)
Chinese	$-1.737^{(2)}$	(2 761)	$0.772^{(4)}$	(584)	-1.329 ns	(57)
Non-Chinese Asian, Total	$0.633^{(2)}$	(9 526)	$1.186^{(2)}$	(812)	$1.766^{(4)}$	(204)
Filipino	-0.055 ns	(3 727)	–		–	
Asian Indian	$-0.819^{(2)}$	(1 676)	–		–	
Korean	$0.478^{(2)}$	(1 902)	–		–	
Vietnamese	$0.965^{(2)}$	(1 102)	–		–	
Japanese	0.263 ns	(467)	–		–	
Other Asian	$1.121^{(2)}$	(652)	–		–	
Mexican	$-0.504^{(2)}$	(5 794)	–		–	
Cuban	$-0.443^{(3)}$	(1 530)	–		–	
Other Latin America	$-1.009^{(2)}$	(5 027)	$-1.123^{(4)}$	(205)	$-3.140^{(4)}$	(33)

Notes: 1. A separate regression equation, with recent immigrant community size as the only independent variable, is estimated for each origin–gender group in each country. The metric regression coefficients represent the change in mean years of education in the immigrant group for each ten-fold increase in the number of immigrants arriving in the urban area.
2. $p < 0.001$.
3. $p < 0.01$.
4. $p < 0.05$.
5. ns = not significant.

Sources: See Table 4.1.

levels vary less among the urban areas in Canada. The extremes are Toronto and Montreal, and they are only one year apart on the scale, as can be seen in Table 4.4. Moreover, the concentration of immigrants in high-education cities is substantially less in Canada than in the USA. The right hand side of Table 4.5 shows this cross-national variation. In the right hand part of the table, the figures show the extent to which the mean educational levels of the native-born in cities where immigrant groups are located differs from the mean native-born educational levels across all cities. For black immigrants, the difference is about +0.5 years for blacks (male or female) in the USA (meaning that black immigrants to the USA are concentrated in cities with native-born educational levels 0.5 years above the urban average), but only +0.2 for blacks in Canada. For Chinese immigrants, the number is about +0.4 in the USA, and +0.3 in Canada. Table 4.6 shows that immigrant concentrations in Canada less often lead to lower educational levels. Blacks are an exception, reflecting largely the situation in Toronto. The immigrant educational polarization found in USA cities is far less prevalent in Canada.

In Australia, there is even more inter-urban uniformity in the educational levels of both native-born and immigrants. Native-born educational levels in the five Australian cities, as shown in Table 4.4, vary only within 0.4 years. These five cities are bunched together at the bottom of the education hierarchy across the three countries. And although Sydney has the highest native-born educational levels, and the largest concentrations of recent immigrants, the observed tendency for immigrants to be concentrated in high education cities in Australia is actually substantially less than in either the USA or Canada. For example, Table 4.5 shows that among Asian immigrants to Australia, the average educational level of the native-born in the cities where they are concentrated is only 0.04 years above the average educational levels of the native-born across all Australian cities. And in any case, the educational levels of immigrants in those cities with the largest concentrations of immigrants in most cases are actually higher than in cities where immigrants are less concentrated. Table 4.6 shows that only for Latin American migrants are those in the larger urban settlements actually lower in education.

The different relation between immigrant community size and educational levels in the three countries may be partly a consequence of different immigration policies. If the negative relation between the two variables in the USA reflects the effect of chain migration and networks of immigrant recruitment, then the immigration emphasis on family-class immigration may be one reason. Immigrants selected on the basis of family ties rather than labour market characteristics are more likely to choose areas of settlement on the basis of such ties and if such immigrants are less educated (as the study of immigrant classes in the USA by Sorenson *et al.* 1992 shows) then the result is a concentration of less educated immigrants in large ethnic communities. The greater prominence of occupational skills and labour market factors in the immigration policies of Canada and Australia might mean that settlement patterns are less influenced by family-based social networks. Even if such policies do not produce more highly skilled immigrants, the fact that fewer immigrants in Canada and Australia may have the option to settle with family members, means that local labour demand influences the settlement decisions of a larger number of them in Canada or Australia.

Labour market institutions and restructuring

The heavy emphasis on labour market structure in USA research on immigrant status suggests the potential importance of this variable in a comparative context. Large 'secondary labour markets' and unprotected or non-unionized jobs – leading to a wide gap between rich and poor in that country – may leave immigrants vulnerable to exploitation and disadvantage, as Piore (1979), Portes (1981) and others argue is the case in the USA. An influential version of this argument, presented by Sassen (1991), suggests that in 'global cities', corporate super elites have a heightened capacity to exploit immigrants in personal services, a capacity arising from extreme affluence and also from a global reach which frees them from the constraints of national boundaries and governments.

Higher rates of unionization in Canada (Kumar 1993) might help protect immigrant minorities, but the biggest differences in this respect might be expected in Australia. Not only higher unionization rates, but also the Australian industrial relations system, with its wage bargaining system which is still comparatively centralized despite recent changes (Bamber and Lansbury 1993), has prevented the development of a marked dual labour market to the extent seen elsewhere (Kalleberg and Colbjørnsen 1990). Various sources confirm that earnings inequality is greatest in the USA, less in Canada and least in Australia. These cross-national differences are very likely related to levels of unionization and labour market regulation. The consequence may be higher relative earnings for immigrants to Australia, as is suggested by the work of Lever-Tracy and Quinlan (1988), and also Bertone and Griffen (1992).

Inter-urban variations in labour market structures within the USA are not related to educational polarization, but nevertheless do have small independent effects on immigrant earnings. Not only are USA labour markets more individualistic than those in Canada and Australia, but inter-urban variations within the USA produce extremes in certain cities. Inter-urban variations in labour market structure play a role in the inter-urban differences in immigrant standing. Waldinger and Bozorgmehr (1993) suggested as much in a comparison of immigrants in New York and Los Angeles. Analysis for this study (see Reitz 1998, chapter 5, pp. 189–98) showed that in certain cities, immigrants are located in labour market segments where work is comparatively poorly paid. However, labour market *location* does not explain inter-urban variations in immigrant earnings, because where immigrant intensive industries and secondary labour market segments are small (cf. Defreitas 1988), immigrants are poorly paid anyway. Rather, labour market structure affects overall earnings inequality and overall earnings inequalities do indeed affect immigrant standing.

The size of the effect of the earnings distribution on the position of immigrants within USA urban areas suggests that while important, this variable is far less important than education as a source of variations in immigrant inequality. The analysis (see Reitz 1998: 198–202) based on inter-urban variations in the USA, suggests that differences in earnings inequality of the magnitude of the USA/Canada/Australia differences would be expected to produce differences of about one per cent or at most two per cent in the relative earnings position of immigrants. This is dwarfed by the effects of educational institutions, which were calculated above to produce differences in the relative earnings of immigrants between the USA and both Canada and Australia in the order of 10 per cent and more.

Social welfare and the safety net

The relevance of social welfare institutions or public health care to the well being of immigrants is a political issue in all three countries. In the USA, recent welfare reforms have reduced benefits for legal immigrants. In Canada, the Reform Party has expressed concerns about immigrant use of welfare and similar issues are raised in Australia. Generally, income redistribution through taxation and welfare transfers is less in the USA than in Canada or Australia, according to the Luxembourg Income Study data (Atkinson *et al.* 1995). Public assistance recipiency rates for USA native-born whites are six per cent, compared to about 10 per cent in Canada and Australia. These are significant differences, although overall impacts on average incomes are not great.[9]

However, whereas studies in the USA show welfare use by immigrants to be higher than by the native-born (between 10 and 11 per cent among Asian and black immigrants, for example, Borjas and Trejo 1991; Jensen 1988). Canadian and Australian research has generally found the reverse, namely lower rates of immigrant welfare use (Akbari 1989; Baker and Benjamin 1995; Whiteford 1992), even within specific origins groups. Despite a weaker social safety net in the USA, welfare payments to immigrants are greater, reducing cross-national differences in inequality.

This finding also suggests how the welfare burden of immigrants is in fact imposed by the institutional environment, as much as by the characteristics of immigrants themselves. Despite *higher* levels of education of immigrants from all sources in the USA, American institutions assign them *lower* status. They more often fall into poverty and require welfare assistance. The 'welfare burden' turns out to be a burden imposed by American institutions on immigrants, rather than the reverse.

Conclusions and implications

Three broad conclusions can be drawn from the study. First, the institutional dimension of society is an important determinant of both cross-national and inter-urban variations in immigrant inequality. The design of the institutions themselves: setting the institutional rules; deciding which individual resources will matter; and how much, is as important to the welfare of minorities as whether the rules are applied without discrimination, or the ease of minority-group access to specific resources. This is true for immigrant minorities, just as it is true for various native-born ethnic, racial and other groups. The term 'institutional discrimination' refers to a similar phenomenon, that institutional rules can have discriminatory effects. Institutional rules are discriminatory if they produce unequal results for racially defined groups that cannot be justified by productivity considerations. Here we do not evaluate whether the institutionally determined unequal outcomes are discriminatory. However, the fact that institutional variation across societies produces varying outcomes for minorities certainly raises the question of what is the justification for specific institutional arrangements.

The debate over institutional restructuring should take account of how institutional change affects the impact and welfare of immigrants.

Any particular institutional change may set in motion a chain of events, with complex implications for broader national objectives such as competitiveness or economic efficiency. The fact that immigrant status and impact is affected is only one of many potential implications, but its importance certainly should be factored into the calculation. If specific changes lead to lower immigrant status, a reduced economic benefit and greater racial polarization, these negative outcomes to some extent offset any perceived position outcomes.

Second, among three institutional areas assessed here, educational institutions are more important than either labour markets or the social welfare system in affecting immigrant status and inequality. These findings are a reminder of the strategic significance of education for the social and economic allocation in society. Regarding immigrants, the emphasis in many analyses has been on labour market structures as the strategic force, but the findings here suggest that labour market institutions while not unimportant are far from the most important institutional sector.

A larger social investment in education is very likely positive for a society, but the extent of the actual return is not really known. 'Returns to education' are normally measured in terms of earnings implications for individuals. These returns are the result of institutional arrangements, and their specific relation to actual productivity is largely a theoretical assumption – the basis for human capital theory – and not a proven fact. The social theory of 'credentialism' suggests that employers' preferences for educated workers is based on considerations other than the productivity associated with the specific vocational preparation implied by the education itself. Furthermore, educational aspirations of individuals are determined not only by expected earnings benefits but also by social competition for status. Educational credentials may accumulate and influence employer decisions apart from any productivity implications.

The comparatively massive accumulation of human capital by native-born American whites gives them a substantial advantage over immigrants including immigrant minorities. In the USA, privately provided higher education responds to the demand for education based on both economic and social pressures. The value of individualism and mobility, the perception that education provides an arena of meritocratic competition where those from the bottom have an opportunity to improve themselves, social and inter-racial competition, all may have fuelled this development.

In Canada, higher education is publicly funded and the aggregate investment in post-secondary education is essentially a political decision.

Canada has in recent decades implemented educational development toward the American standard partly because the proximity to the USA creates labour market pressures to which politicians as well as prospective students have responded. Native-born Canadians are rapidly becoming educated to the standard set in the USA, and the implications are the status of newly-arriving immigrant minorities can be expected to decline unless there are corresponding improvements in the educational levels of the immigrants themselves.

Australia has been relatively isolated from such pressures, and has provided educational investments at a lower level, following more closely a European pattern. In Australia, the comparatively lower levels of native-born education mean that immigrants from all groups will for a longer time find it easier to become well established.

Whatever educational institutions are devised, rising educational levels impose a need for individual employers to guard against educational inflation. Over-use of educational credentials as a job qualification artificially inflates an employer's potential payroll and may reinforce social boundaries arising from the unequal distribution of educational credentials in society. 'Skill-based not school-based hiring' means ensuring that domestic qualifications are not unjustifiably deferred to, as much as it means ensuring that foreign qualifications are properly recognized. If workers are hired on the basis of actual skills acquired during their school experience, rather than on the basis of the mere possession of a requisite 'sheepskin', employers' costs will be controlled and immigrants will be spared dysfunctional disadvantage. The social costs of credentialism include increasing inequality affecting certain minority immigrant groups. The issue will become more important for Canada in the near future and eventually will make itself felt in Australia as well. For the immigrant generation itself, on-the-job training opportunities are an important key.

As educational levels rise, accessibility also becomes a more important issue. Rising educational costs creates pressures for privatization. At the post-secondary level this can mean tuition fee increases in publicly funded universities as well as the actual growth of private universities. University tuition fee increases create greater potentials for inequality based on one's family's ability to pay – based, that is, on social class background. Accessibility can be affected by privatization, not only because private schools (or public schools with user fees) may be more expensive, but also because public schools may lose the political support of those using private schools.

In Canada, educational levels have risen but support for public education may be declining. Up to the present time minorities have enjoyed access to public education at all levels. The majority of student populations entering two major Toronto universities (the University of Toronto and York University) is now from non-European backgrounds. However, the question for the future is whether the rising costs of education in a more individualistic environment may create new barriers to educational opportunity.

While labour market structures do influence immigrant earnings, this is perhaps not as strongly as many have previously suspected. Immigrants to the USA often are concentrated in disadvantaged labour market locations, but the absence of these labour market segments does not reduce their disadvantage. Weak labour market structures affect immigrants by creating greater overall earnings disparities which drive down relative earnings for all of the less skilled.

Labour institutions that protect labour in Canada have the additional positive effect of increasing the likelihood that immigrant parents have the resources to ensure educational opportunities for their children. In Australia, labour institutions and the national wage arbitration system also have protected immigrants. The current trend toward the dismantling of these institutions so far has been limited, but is continuing. Earnings inequalities in Australia are now increasing more rapidly than in the Canada or USA.

Finally, the impulse in a recession to cut back social services such as health care and unemployment insurance does not in itself affect immigrant groups more than others. However, if immigrants do experience disadvantage because of educational disparities or because lack of labour market protection aggravates employment and pay discrimination, then they may be affected by the strength of the social safety net.

The third conclusion is that, to the extent that the institutions in all three countries converge toward the American pattern, the effect is to create greater immigrant inequality and presumably a less positive impact for immigration. While most controversy has attached to the importance of institutional restructuring in the areas of labour markets and social welfare, the restructuring of educational institutions may prove to be of greatest importance in the long run. However, cohort-specific effects of educational institutions are felt more slowly.

Institutional restructuring in all three countries stresses the value of individualism. The rationale for institutional individualism is that individualism is identified with reliance on market forces, which are expected to increase productivity and efficiency. This line of thinking is particularly strong in the USA where individualism is most salient as a value, but it holds sway in Canada and Australia as well. Individualism is identified with market-driven criteria and the challenge of the market competition is the concern of the current historical era.

However, individualism also leads to greater inequality, and extreme disadvantage may weaken work commitment and rebound to undermine competitiveness. Recent economic research (Persson and Tabellini 1994) has examined the negative correlation between inequality and productivity, on a cross-national basis. There can be little doubt that the extremes of inequality in major USA urban areas, and the social malaise and conflict that accompanies that inequality, is far from an asset to that country in its attempts to address global competitiveness. By contrast, the primary competitors – namely the Japanese and the Europeans, particularly Germany – have societies characterized not by greater individualism by rather by greater social cohesion. Individualism may undermine productivity by reducing the social cohesion essential for effective organizational action.

These considerations imply that policy proposals emphasizing the need for individualism should be evaluated in the light of the possibility that extreme individualism may in some instances serve as an ideology of inequality as much as a strategy for competitiveness. As institutional restructuring proceeds, there may be increasing pressure to enact more selective immigration policies. This pressure arises from the desire to offset increasing inequality and to ensure a more positive impact for immigration. The pressures have been particularly strong in Canada and Australia where individualistic immigration policies clash with more collectivist institutional structures.

Tightening up immigration selection criteria is a logical approach to ensuring adequate educational levels of immigrant groups. However, there is no guarantee that Canada and Australia can achieve improvements in this way. Their policies are already more selective than the American policies, but their immigrants are less skilled. Furthermore, they are also under a somewhat conflicting pressure to reduce total immigration. Reducing total immigration means either reducing family-class immigration – which could deter the most skilled – or reducing the skilled category itself. One reason that Canada and Australia have been as successful as they have been in recruiting skilled immigrants is the size of their immigration programmes. In recent times, both Canada and Australia have mounted advertising campaigns to attract skilled immigrants, with Canada spending $2 million and Australia $1 million, while the USA spends nothing on such advertising (*Globe and Mail*, 7 June 1995: A4). USA immigration has been increased recently precisely to increase the skilled component.

The limits to immigration selectivity, and the continuing need for more immigrants, means that we cannot escape the issue of institutional structure itself and its implications for immigrants' status. Ultimately, it is necessary to recognize that the contribution of immigrants reflects social institutions, and that the place of immigrants in society is largely a function of the way society chooses to organize itself.

Notes

1. Material in this chapter is drawn from *Warmth of the Welcome: The Social Causes of Economic Success for Immigrants in Different Nations and Cities* (Boulder, CO: Westview Press, 1998) and is reproduced with permission.
2. Unless otherwise stated, data reported in this chapter are based on 1980 census public use sample data for the USA (five per cent A file; see US Bureau of the Census 1983), 1981 public use sample census data for Canada (two per cent individual file; see Canada, Statistics Canada 1984b) and Australia (one per cent individual file; Australian Bureau of Statistics 1984). The findings reflect the earliest stages of the 'new immigration'. The samples include members of the labour force aged 16–64 earning at least $100 and residing in an urban area over 500 000 population (79 urban areas in the USA are included, along with 9 in Canada and 5 in Australia); the benchmark group consists of native-born males of European (non-Hispanic) origins; recent immigrants are those arriving between 1970 and 1980. Origins are based on race and Hispanic origins for the USA, ethnic origins for Canada, and birthplace and parental birthplace for Australia. For further details about the sample, see Reitz 1998, Chapters 1 and 2.
3. The mean earnings of recently-arrived Mexican immigrant males in the urban areas of the southwestern USA was 46 per cent of the native-born white male earnings. The corresponding Mexican-origin females earned 62 per cent of what native-born white women earned and 30 per cent of the earnings of the native-born white males.
4. In Australia, immigrants are on average about one-half year better educated relative to the native-born, compared to the situation in Canada. This comparison holds for specific origin groups. For example, black immigrants in Canada have been as well educated as the native-born, while black immigrants in the USA are about 1.2 years less well educated. In the USA, Chinese immigrants have been about 0.2 years less educated than the native-born, while in Canada they are about 0.8 years better educated, and in Australia as much as 2.6 years better educated than the native-born.
5. Morgan Gallup polls in Australia show that the proportion who thought that there are too many immigrants was 68 per cent in May 1992. This is comparable to findings in the USA and Canada. For example, Gallup poll data show the proportion of Americans wanting less immigration rose from 33 per cent in 1965 to 61 per cent in 1993. Various sources indicate that the proportion of Canadians currently thinking there is too much immigration is in the range between 53 to 66 per cent (Reitz and Breton 1994: 77–8).

6. The number of anti-Semitic incidents recorded by the B'nai B'rith in each country is roughly in proportion to population size and, if anything, somewhat higher than expected in Canada and Australia based on the USA benchmark. For example, in 1991, the Anti-Defamation League of B'nai B'rith in the USA recorded 1879 anti-Semitic incidents, in 1991 the League for Human Rights of B'nai B'rith in Canada recorded 251 such incidents, more than expected based on a ten to one population ratio. The number recorded by the B'nai B'rith Anti-Defamation Commission in Australia was 207 in 1993 and 227 in 1994, rising rapidly in recent years. This again is more than expected based on total population ratios.

7. The Australian, Canadian, American and other discrimination field trials are compiled by the International Labour Office in Geneva, and described by Bovenkerk (1992). The Australian results (Riach and Rich 1991) are similar to the Canadian (Henry and Ginsberg 1984) and American (Turner *et al.* 1991) findings (see Reitz and Breton 1994, 82–3, for a detailed comparison of the Canadian and American data).

8. Evidence on the effect of labour market structure is discussed below.

9. Transfer payments reduce poverty by 5.7 percentage points in Canada, but 1.9 per cent in the USA. Raising 6 per cent out of poverty in Canada improves average wages only about 1–2 per cent.

5
Immigrants' Social Class in Three Global Cities[1]

Suzanne Model

In recent years, quantitative cross-national research has undergone refinements in data quality and in methodological precision (Charles and Grusky 1995; Erikson and Goldthorpe 1992). As a result, comparative studies of class inequality and of women's disadvantage are reporting exciting new findings (Rosenfeld and Kalleberg 1990; Wright 1997). Yet, few scholars of racial and ethnic stratification have exploited these refinements.[2] The work reported here is one of a series of analyses aimed at redressing this imbalance (Model 1997; Model and Fisher 1997; Model and Ladipo 1996; Model *et al.* 1999). The analyses ask: do immigrants with similar backgrounds obtain similar socio-economic rewards across destinations. This chapter compares the attainment of three job outcomes: unemployment; Goldthorpe class; and occupational status among eight groups of immigrants who have settled in London, New York and Toronto.

The expectation is that immigrant attainment will vary across destinations in predictable ways. Several observations support this hypothesis, some of less theoretical interest than others. For example, newcomers from the same sending country may choose to dwell in different places because of systematic differences in their human capital. If immigrants already differ in human capital, their post-migration attainments are likely to differ as well. This is not a very intellectually challenging possibility, however. Luckily, statistical techniques allow investigators to take into account at least some differences in immigrants' human capital. A second possibility is that disparities in the opportunity structure of receiving nations will produce discrepancies in their outcomes. For instance, immigrants will be more vulnerable to unemployment in nations with high rates of joblessness than in nations with low rates. This possibility, likewise, is not of great theoretical interest. Happily, multi-variate techniques can also control for cross-national variations in job opportunities (Kelley 1990).

Since investigators can estimate the magnitude of the gap between the dominant group and an immigrant group, holding constant both individual characteristics and economic opportunities, the more meaningful the question becomes: will multi-variate analysis reveal that immigrants from identical sending countries experience similar gaps vis-à-vis their respective dominant groups once individual and structural attributes are controlled?

In proposing an answer, it is useful to begin by identifying the causal factors that theory associates with the group membership coefficient, *ceteris paribus*. The three most frequently cited contributors are culture, selectivity and discrimination. With respect to culture, in the immigrant situation, an individual initially absorbs one tradition and is later transplanted into another. Thus, cultural differences among groups of different origins may translate into employment differences among those groups at destination. Yet, the present study compares individuals of similar cultural background across destinations, not individuals of different cultural backgrounds within a single destination. Thus, the cross-national design largely controls for culture.

A second source of variation at the individual level is 'selectivity'. This term refers to characteristics that distinguish 'movers' from 'stayers'. Selectivity can be positive – movers are more talented, ambitious and diligent than stayers – or negative. Because individuals from the same sending country may be differentially selected with respect to destination, examining individuals with similar origins across destinations does not control for selectivity. Of course, to the extent that such characteristics are measured, a multi-variate analysis can control for them; yet, to the extent that they are unmeasured, a multi-variate analysis transmits them as part of the group membership coefficient. Luckily, empirical research suggests selectivity will not confound the cross-national comparison below. Studies of immigrants to the USA, the UK and Canada uncover no evidence of unmeasured differences in the selection of immigrants from identical sending countries (Borjas 1993; Duleep and Regets 1992; Model 1997).

The final theoretical possibility is that variations in the receptions accorded immigrant groups at destination account for the discrepancies in their employment outcomes. In particular, the more discrimination directed toward a group, the more disadvantage its workers will suffer. When more than one labour market is under scrutiny, however, the researcher must not only consider the position of the immigrant group in the eyes of dominant group employers but also the proportion of the city's labour force accorded an even higher position. More specifically, other things equal, the larger the proportion of the local labour force more favourably ranked than the immigrant group, the more deleterious the immigrant outcome; the smaller the proportion of the local labour force more favourably ranked than the immigrant group, the more auspicious the immigrant outcome. Thus, to the extent that nations vary in the way their employers rate immigrant groups and in the size and origins of the groups they admit, the relative socio-economic status of members of a given group will vary cross-nationally.

To be sure, the 'other things equal' condition is a criterion that no statistical analysis can meet. Researchers cannot completely control for all the relevant measurable determinants of socio-economic success, nor can they control for any of the unmeasurable ones. Thus, the results of a multi-variate analysis are at best approximations of the relevant causal factors. Still, an awareness of which variables may be omitted and a sensitivity to the magnitude and direction of their effects minimizes the danger of hasty generalizations.

This study explores these ideas by comparing the unemployment rates, Goldthorpe class location, and occupational status of immigrants in three labour markets: New York, Toronto and London. The data come from the most recent Canadian and American censuses and from a set of British Labour Force Surveys. The results indicate that several groups do better in New York. The reason appears to be the smaller percentage of whites in New York, relative to Toronto and London. But in order to take advantage of this small percentage, an immigrant group must also rank above African-Americans in the eyes of New York's employers. A related finding is that New York employers rank a larger number of immigrant groups above African-American males than above African-American females. The implications of these and other aspects of the results are taken up in the chapter's conclusion.

Queuing theory

The name of the explanatory framework just described is 'queuing theory'. It was initially developed to explain the socio-economic differentials between black and white Americans. The notion of a labour queue builds on the idea that candidates for any desired good, theatre tickets for instance, will await service in a line rather than in a disorganized mass. A labour queue, however, differs from a ticket line in that the position of applicants is determined by their desirability to employers rather than by the order of their application or by their manners in public. Furthermore, queuing theorists assume that employers, not being clairvoyant, have some difficulty assessing applicants' desirability. A simple solution is to rate applicants on the basis of some easily observable characteristic, particularly if the employer associates this characteristic with job-related attributes such as aptitude, diligence, or reliability. In this way ascriptive group membership – sex, race, religion, and ethnicity – comes to the fore (Hodge 1973; Lieberson 1980; Thurow 1975).

Queuing theorists believe that, as long as the supply lasts, employers will hire into the best jobs workers of the heritage that employers rank most desirable. As the supply of such workers declines and/or the job opportunity becomes less attractive, employers will consider applicants with less desirable ancestries. And they will hire members of the least desirable heritage only when the supply of more favourably ranked groups is exhausted. By the same logic, when the work force must be reduced, members of the least desirable heritage are the first to be made redundant. These decisions result in the oft noted tendency of African-Americans being 'last hired, first fired'.

To be sure, the reality is more complex than this idealized picture implies. For example, when the employer is him or herself a member of a minority, s/he is likely to exhibit a preference for co-ethnic employees. This form of 'queue jumping' reflects the propensity to accord highest status to members of one's own heritage. Another complication is that workers also have job preferences. Immigrants are especially likely to cluster in particular industries or firms because of their pre-migration skills and/or because of their dependency on compatriots for job information (Waldinger 1986–87). Nevertheless, to the extent that members of a subordinate group depend on members of the superordinate group for a livelihood, queuing theorists expect subordinate group members to be victims of 'statistical discrimination', that is, of judgements based on stereotypes associated with their ancestry. Thus, a minority group's average employability and average occupational position will depend on the proportion of the available labour force that employers rank more highly. The larger that proportion, the poorer the outcome for members of the minority group.

Within the United States, the rank and relative size of contending groups have proved useful in explaining variations in the success of particular backgrounds in different labour markets. For example, Frisbie and Neidert (1977) have shown that, across southwestern cities, the smaller the proportion of non-Hispanic whites and the larger the proportion of African-American blacks, the higher the occupational status of Mexican Americans. This result obtains because, in the eyes of most employers, Mexicans hold an intermediate position between whites and blacks. When the white population shrinks at the expense of the black, Mexicans prosper.

To be sure, employers in different localities may perceive members of the same group differently. For instance, gatekeepers in the southwestern USA may accord Mexicans lower status than gatekeepers in the northeast. Still, group standing is probably more homogeneous within than across national borders. As for group size, it too will vary both within and across societies. Together, these observations mean that, in the present study, attention must be paid to the rank and the size of contending groups in New York, London and Toronto, if queuing theory is to serve as a basis for predictions about the relative position of immigrants in these cities. Group size, of course, is relatively easy to measure; group standing, on the other hand, is relatively difficult to measure. Still, a review of the relevant literature offers several clues, as the summary below reveals.

The labour queue in three global cities

In the effort to measure the relative standing of racial and ethnic groups, scholars have undertaken experiments, employer interviews and surveys. Regrettably, each of these methods is flawed. Experiments and interviews are invariably limited in their generalizability; their findings do not extend to the full range of employment opportunities. Social surveys are less subject to this shortcoming, but suffer from other problems. For example, respondents may behave quite differently in real life than in their self depictions. An additional problem with surveys is that people's opinions about minorities are multi-dimensional. A superordinate group may view minority group members as desirable employees but undesirable neighbours. Yet, some measures, such as the Bogardus Social Distance Scale, reduce the answers to several questions to a single number. Another difficulty, which presents an obstacle for all three methods, is the limitation of time and place. In the present instance, information is needed about the relative ranking of immigrant groups in New York, London and Toronto in the early 1990s. And, as the discussion to follow suggests, the position of some South Asian groups may be changing.

To begin with the British case, sociologist John Rex (1970) anticipated that immigrants from former colonies would encounter far greater discrimination than white European immigrants. He based this prediction on the negative qualities with which conquerors usually label their subjects, labels Rex assumed the physically identifiable ex-colonial could not easily shed. His expectations were confirmed in field experiments carried out during 1973/74, 1977/79 and 1984/85 in several major British cities. In these experiments, candidates differing only on ascriptive group membership applied for a variety of jobs. While 10 per cent of the Greek and Italian applicants experienced discrimination, one out of three West Indians and South Asians were turned away (Brown and Gay 1994).

Rex did not raise the possibility that status differentials might obtain *among* coloured ex-colonials, nor did the experimenters detect significant differences in the rates of rejection among non-white backgrounds. But, both the annual 'British Social Attitudes' survey and the 'Fourth National Survey of Ethnic Minorities' detect a mild tendency for the public to stigmatize South Asians more than Caribbean blacks (Jowell *et al.* 1992; Modood *et al.* 1997). For instance, between 1983 and 1994, the former survey recorded a 4 per cent increase in the difference between the percentage of respondents believing that Asians suffered 'a lot' of prejudice than believing that blacks did. These questions, however, allow multiple response. When the Fourth National Survey 'forced' respondents to select the single minority facing most prejudice, 57 per cent of whites chose some South Asian designation and only 14 per cent chose some black designation. Finally, when whites were asked which groups they harboured prejudice against, about a quarter selected Asians or Muslims. This term, however, excludes Chinese, whom only 8 per cent of whites admitted prejudicial sentiments toward.

These considerations raise the possibility that British opinions about non-whites are ambivalent and in flux. At least two different interpretations have appeared in the literature. One is that the decline in the status of Asians is actually a decline in the position of Muslims. Events such as the Rushdie affair and the government's tendency to vilify Arab leaders like Muammar Qaddafi and Saddam Hussein are among the factors that could explain a drop in the status of Muslims. From this perspective, Hindus and Sikhs enjoy increasing educational and economic 'success', at the same time that 'Islamophobia' (Runnymede Trust 1997) gains increasing respectability among the British public (Modood 1992, 1996). The other interpretation is that the British have new reasons for anger toward South Asians, motives based on Asian economic success, not on Asian religious proclivities. More specifically, improvements in the educational and occupational achievements of East Indians have intensified their threat to British whites. It is this 'new competition' from non-whites who previously followed ethnically segregated occupational pathways, that has exacerbated racism in the dominant group (Cross 1989; Robinson 1990, 1993). This analysis mirrors the thinking of Olzak (1992) whose research shows job competition to be a major cause of ethnic conflict. These two interpretations have different consequences for the relative rank of South Asians by religion, but both versions are consonant with the notion that Caribbeans face less hostility than emigrants from the subcontinent.

The literature thus motivates the present study to entertain the following working hypothesis with respect to the British labour queue: white European immigrants enjoy highest status, followed by the Chinese, Caribbean blacks, and South Asians. Among the latter, East Indians outrank Pakistanis or Bangladeshis. Unfortunately, the research literature offers no useable information on the relative position of Pakistanis versus Bangladeshis or on perceptions about immigrants from Africa, be they South Asian or black.

In addition to its British and French 'charter groups', Canada is home to a white population of diverse origins and to a non-white population both Aboriginal and immigrant (Marger 1997). Early in this century, official government policy paralleled that in the USA by championing 'Anglo conformity'. Assimilation was explicitly encouraged in schools, workplaces and civic organizations. After the Second World War, however, Anglo-conformity was replaced, first by 'cultural pluralism' and, more recently, by 'multi-culturalism' (Small 1995). Reinforcing these objectives, Canadian leaders have described their nation as an 'ethnic mosaic', that is, as a society that respects ethnic boundaries and treats all groups equally. Indeed, many Canadians believe themselves to be more tolerant of diversity than residents of the USA or the UK (Reitz and Breton 1994).

This 'ethnic mosaic', however, is more rhetoric than reality. In the words of John Porter (1965), Canadian society is a 'vertical mosaic'; that is, a nation in which some backgrounds enjoy higher prestige than others. A 1965 investigation of ethnic 'social standing' in English speaking Canada resulted in the following scores: English 82, Italians 43, Chinese 33 and blacks 25 (Pineo 1977). A 1974 national survey found Canadians ranked European nationalities highest, followed by West Indians, Chinese, Negroes and East Indians, in descending order (Berry *et al.* 1977). In a slightly different vein, the 1979 Toronto study,

'Ethnic Pluralism in an Urban Setting', asked respondents how much employers discriminate against particular backgrounds. The per cent of white natives expecting a particular group to experience 'a lot or some discrimination' from employers was Germans 17 per cent, Italians 38 per cent, Chinese 47 per cent, Portuguese 49 per cent, West Indian 76 per cent and Pakistani 78 per cent (Breton *et al.* 1990).

These rather dated studies are ambiguous regarding the position of West Indians relative to South Asians, but more recent research suggests the former hold the more favourable position. A 1985 experiment patterned on the British field trial described above found Toronto employers most likely to reject South Asians (44 per cent), followed by black Caribbeans (36 per cent) and applicants with Italian or Slavic accents (31 per cent). White Canadians were least likely to be rejected (13 per cent). A pattern of East Indians triggering the most antagonism is also evident in the past two decades of surveys by Reginald Bibby, which include a question about whether or not respondents feel 'uneasy' around particular minority groups. Although the proportion of all Canadians reporting such uneasiness steadily declined over time, in each survey year more respondents were uneasy about 'East Indians/Pakistanis' than about 'blacks'. The label 'Asians (Orientals)' stimulated even less antagonism (Bibby 1995).

These results suggest that non-whites are ranked similarly in Toronto and London. The most cordial reception is accorded white European nationalities, followed by Chinese, West Indian blacks and finally South Asians. Again, scholars have undertaken little systematic research on differences within this last category.

As for the USA, reliable information regarding the hierarchy of disadvantage is scanty despite that nation's long social science tradition. To be sure, scholars have measured responses to African-Americans, but systematic comparisons of minorities relative to one another have been lacking. The main source of information on rankings is the Bogardus Social Distance scale, an index developed in the 1920s. The scale combines responses to seven different dimensions of inter-group contact, ranging from intermarriage to citizenship. Unfortunately, the scale is rarely administered to nationally representative samples; frequently, college students comprise the respondents.

These caveats aside, the relative rank of most of the 30 groups traditionally included on the scale has changed little between 1926 and 1991. An exception must be made, however, in the case of political enemies. For instance, between 1926 and 1946, the Japanese fell from

24th to 30th position. Similarly, between 1946 and 1977, Russians dropped from 13th to 29th, yet, in 1991 they ranked 16th! Another exception concerns African-Americans, who moved from the lower third to the middle of the hierarchy as the century progressed. This improvement is reflected in the 1991 finding that respondents associated most non-whites with greater social distance than African-Americans. For instance, in the eyes of Illinois college students, Chinese, Japanese, Koreans and Asian Indians were all more distant than African-Americans (Schaefer 1995).

Contradicting these results are the responses of a national sample to a special module of the General Social Survey on which participants were asked to rank ethnic groups in terms of their 'social standing', which ranged from 9 (high) to 1 (low). Not surprisingly, native whites scored highest (7.03). Other relevant rankings include Italians (5.69), Chinese (4.76), Asian Indians (4.29), Negroes (4.17), Arabs (3.57), African Blacks (3.56), West Indian Blacks (3.56), Haitians (3.45), Puerto Ricans (3.32) and Iranians (2.99). Note that in these rankings, Asians rank above African-Americans, while other black ethnicities and Muslim nationalities rank lower.[3] A year later, another GSS module, this one devoted to 'ethnic images' likewise concluded that white Americans hold far more pernicious stereotypes of blacks than of Asians (Smith 1990, 1991). One way of reconciling the differences between the Bogardus studies and the findings of the GSS is that Americans feel more 'socially distant' from Asians than from blacks, but that they view Asians more favourably.

Unfortunately, American field tests for hiring preferences have been limited to comparisons among whites, blacks, and Hispanics (Turner *et al.* 1991). Employer interviews comprise an alternative source of information. These indicate that many employers believe immigrants display a stronger 'work ethic' than natives, especially when the natives are African-American males (Holzer 1996; Kirschenman 1991). For instance, a case study of attitudes toward black workers at a New York catering firm showed managers with a pronounced preference for West Indians over African-Americans, a preference that West Indians admit to cultivating (Arnold 1996; Waters 1993). Again, however, little is known about the generalizability of this opinion.

In short, some similarities in the 'hierarchy of discrimination' (Arnold 1984) obtain across all three cities, in particular the relatively high position of Chinese and the relatively low position of Muslims. On the other hand, US research is most consonant with the expectation that East Indians rank higher in the labour queue than West Indians do, while the reverse obtains in Canada and the UK. Thus, predictions based upon 'the hierarchy of discrimination' indicate that West Indians will do better in Toronto and London, and East Indians will do best in New York – provided, of course, that an identical proportion of each city's labour force is ranked above East and West Indians.

But this proviso does not hold. Rather, the proportion of whites – the most favoured group in all three locales – is largest in London (82 per cent), intermediate in Toronto (73 per cent), and smallest in New York (64 per cent). As a result, most non-white groups should stand higher in New York's labour queue than in Toronto's or London's. Indeed, a non-white group is likely to fare best in New York, unless that city's employers rank its members below African-Americans. This follows because the presence of African-Americans, 10 per cent of New York's labour force, is an important reason why New York contains a smaller proportion of whites than Toronto or London. Consequently, any New York group ranking lower in the hierarchy than African-Americans cannot benefit from the relatively smaller size of that city's white population.[4] Instead, inter-city differences in the success of groups falling below African-Americans in New York will depend on inter-city differences in rankings, not just on inter-city differences in the proportion of whites.

Which New York groups will rank lower in the queue than African-Americans? As already suggested, the relative ranking in the USA of the various black subgroups – African-Americans, black Caribbeans, and black Africans – is unclear. Survey data suggest that African-Americans hold an edge over West Indians; interview data suggest the opposite. As for Pakistanis and Bangladeshis, as Muslims, they also constitute a potential pariah group. For over a decade, American politicians have cast Arab nations in the role of enemy. Therefore, black Caribbeans, black Africans and Muslims are candidates for poor performance in New York, but, among these three, only black Caribbeans potentially have higher status in London and Toronto than in New York.

To sum up, a queuing perspective requires taking both dominant group perceptions and group size into account. Doing so leads to the prediction that most groups will do better in New York. Potential exceptions include black Caribbeans, whose outcome hinges on whether or not New York employers rank them higher or lower than African-Americans, and immigrants from Africa, Pakistan and Bangladesh. These last three groups are expected to do poorly, possibly equally poorly in all three settings.

Queue jumping

In order for queuing theory to apply, members of the subordinate group must depend on members of the superordinate group for job opportunities and the superordinate group must be free to act upon its preferences. Unfortunately, there are at least three situations in which these conditions will not obtain. These are, first, when gatekeepers comply with affirmative action directives, second, when subordinate group members work for co-ethnics and, third, when subordinate group members are self-employed. In the case of self-employment, rank in the labour queue is moot because the worker's outcome does not depend on the judgement of another individual. In the remaining two instances, however, not only does judgement matter, but that judgement is likely to propel the minority group member to the head of the queue. Affirmative action produces this result through the threat of state sanctions; co-ethnic employment produces this result through in-group preference. A fair test of queuing theory must take these complexities into account.

With respect to affirmative action, only the US and Canadian governments have enacted programmes of consequence. The USA initiated affirmative action about 20 years before Canada, while the UK still debates doing so (Edwards 1995). Furthermore, statistics indicate that Canada's 'Employment Equity Act' has yet to produce measurable results (Cardozo 1993; Lum 1995). On the other hand, the programme's effect in the USA is measurable; several scholars detect an advantage which they attribute to it (Beggs 1995; Donohue and Heckman 1991). Confirmation in America presents a methodological problem for the present analysis because both affirmative action effects and queuing effects could transmit an advantage to New York's immigrants relative to those in Toronto and London. One way to dilute the potential confounding associated with affirmative action is to limit the US side of the analysis to workers in the private sector. This approach has merit if public sector employment is the arena in which US affirmative action requirements are taken most seriously. Indeed, a variety of studies indicate that US minorities receive better treatment in public than private jobs (Waldinger 1996; Zipp 1994). Not surprisingly, this situation does not obtain in the Canadian or British civil services (Cabinet Office 1996; Cardozo 1993). Thus, a more accurate test of queuing theory involves omitting New York's non-white public employees from the analysis.

With respect to working for oneself or under the auspices of co-ethnics, these are strategies that some minorities rely upon to circumvent their low standing in the eyes of the dominant group. Research suggests that some of these 'ethnic economy jobs' offer better rewards than jobs in the mainstream economy; at minimum ethnic economy jobs are assumed to reduce a group's vulnerability to unemployment (Light *et al.* 1994; Phizacklea and Ram 1996). Again, the question in the present instance is how to control for this form of 'queue jumping'. The self-employed present no problem; the data sets used here contain information on this point and they can be deleted from the analysis. The co-ethnically employed are problematic, however, as few data sets contain information about the ethnicity of workers' superiors. As a result, a procedure developed by Logan *et al.* (1994) for identifying the co-ethnically employed through information on industry and employ-ment status is utilized here. In the first step of this procedure, each group's 'ethnic economy industries' are defined. These are industries in which the odds of ethnic group representation as entrepreneurs and as employees is at least 1.5. In the second step, all group members employed in those industries are coded 'ethnic economy employees'.

Using the 1990 PUMs (Public Use Microdata) and 1991 SARs from the British census respectively, Model (1997) already identified the rele-vant ethnic economy industries for New York and London. The present study extends this exercise to Toronto. Unfortunately, the Canadian census offers less industrial detail than the USA or UK censuses. Therefore, the imputation of ethnic economy employment in Toronto is less reliable than the imputation for New York and London. Still, in the absence of better data, this method of identifying the co-ethnically employed is the best available. The ethnic economy industries that the procedure associates with each group in the three cities are listed in the Appendix to this chapter. Note that foreign born whites are excluded from the table. They do not appear because their ethnic economy industries vary by ethnicity; that is, 'white ethnic economy industries' include Italian ethnic economy industries, Irish ethnic economy indus-tries and so on. Not only are these national origin groups not identifi-able in all three cities, but also white ethnic differences are not the focus of the present inquiry. Hence, no attempt is made to define foreign born whites' ethnic economy industries.

To conclude, at least three categories of queue jumpers merit atten-tion: beneficiaries of affirmative action, the self-employed and the co-ethnically employed. Since some means exist for identifying each of these groups, they can be eliminated from the analysis when this step seems advisable. As a result, some of the models below are estimated on the whole sample; others are run twice, once on the whole sample and once with potential 'queue jumpers' excluded.

Data and methods

The data sources for this study are, for Britain, a concatenation of Labour Force Surveys (LFS) covering the years 1987 through 1993; for the United States, the 1990 Public Use Microdata (PUMs) drawn from the census of that year; and, for Canada, the Public Use Microdata File Individuals (PUMFI) sampled from the 1991 census. Although a sample of records from the 1991 UK census is available, the LFS is used here because it offers the year of the immigrants' arrival in Britain and greater educational detail than does the census. Nevertheless, there are several shortcomings in the data. Many useful variables are unavailable, for example English language ability, work experience, urban/rural origins, parental social class and so on. Another factor that influences labour market outcome is 'period of arrival'. Most non-whites arrived in Britain at a time when modest schooling was the rule and opportunities for unskilled workers were considerable. Most non-whites arrived in Canada and the USA at a time when higher education was becoming an asset and opportunities for unskilled workers were diminishing. Capturing this 'period effect', which is not the same as the impact of age or years since arrival, requires longitudinal data. Still, it is unlikely that better data would yield great changes in the relative attainment of the groups in this study, and relative attainment is the primary focus of the analysis.

A more mundane difficulty is that many of the available variables are not coded in comparable fashion. Heritage was determined on the basis of information on place of birth, ethnicity or ancestry, religion and race. In this respect, the Canadian census creates a stumbling block because it lists only an undifferentiated 'South Asia' category in response both to questions of nativity and ethnicity. Thus, Pakistanis, Bangladeshis, Indians and Sri Lankans cannot be distinguished. The solution was to rely upon information about religion, which only the Canadian census provides. Persons whose religion was not Muslim but who listed 'South Asia' for both birthplace and for ethnicity were defined as 'Asian Indian'. Justification for this decision can be found in The Fourth National Survey of Ethnic Minorities in Britain, which reports that only 6 per cent of 'Indians' are 'Muslim' (Modood *et al.* 1997). As for Canada's 'South Asian Muslims', they were excluded from the present study because previous research shows substantial difference in their socio-economic attainment depending on whether they were born in Pakistan or Bangladesh (McMahon 1997; Model 1997; Model and Ladipo 1996). Finally, allowing the category 'South Asian' to serve as a proxy for 'Indian' ethnicity in Canada has the additional consequence of identifying as 'Indians' several hundred persons born in Africa. Sufficient numbers of this group can also be found in the LFS, though not in the PUMs. Their absence from the US data reflect African Indians' migratory history; they are a refugee population with special ties to the British Commonwealth (Robinson 1995). An unexpected discovery is that Britain's and Canada's 'African Indians' differ in their religious composition. Two-thirds of Canada's African 'South Asians' are Muslim compared with 15 per cent of Britain's African 'Indians'. Most of the Canadians are probably Nizari Ismaili, a prosperous Islamic denomination who revere the Aga Khan (Nanji 1983). Along with their Sikh and Hindu compatriots, Indian Muslims were evicted during the African independence movements of the 1970s.

British West Indian blacks constituted another category whose identification in the Canadian census proved troublesome. Canadians in this category were persons coded 'black/Caribbean' on ethnicity, 'Central America, Caribbean, Bermuda and South America' on nativity and 'English' on mother tongue. The remaining immigrant groups, whose heritages were relatively easy to identify, were foreign born whites, Chinese and black Africans. In addition, in New York, African-Americans were distinguished because of their significance in the New York labour queue. Although African-Americans do not appear as a category in the tables of the present chapter, the text explores how their attainment is intertwined with that of New York's immigrant groups. Finally, the benchmark to whom all the immigrants are compared in each city is native-born whites.[5]

Three dependent variables are used in this study: unemployment; Goldthorpe class; and occupational status. They were selected both because it is possible to construct them from the data at hand and because, as an explanatory framework, queuing theory is particularly applicable to discrete outcomes.[6] All three data sets inquire about unemployment during the survey week, so the construction of this measure is straight forward.

When Goldthorpe (1987) developed his class categories, he sought to capture differences in market position and employment situation. Nevertheless, the number of categories in his scheme has varied on both theoretical and empirical grounds. Recently a justification for aggregating these categories into three, ordered classes has appeared. Erikson and Goldthorpe write

...good grounds would appear to exist for introducing within the seven-class version of the scheme a three-fold hierarchical division which could be more or less equally well taken as ordering class position in terms of their prestige, socio-economic status, or 'general desirability' (1992: 45).

The advantage of the ordered scheme over an unordered, categorical scheme is that the former supports ordered logistic regression, which yields one set of parameters for all three classes. Multi-variate analysis of an unordered categorical scheme, however, requires multinomial logistic regression, which yields one set of parameters for each class category except the one designated as the benchmark. For these reasons, the three category, ordered version of Goldthorpe class serves as one of the dependent variables in the analysis below. To facilitate comprehension of the coefficients, the highest of these classes, the service class, is coded 3, the intermediate classes are coded 2 and non-skilled workers are coded 1.[7]

Finally, the internationally standardized occupational status index, or ISEI, is the measure of occupational status used in this study because it is specifically designed for cross-national comparisons. An ISEI score is available for each ISOC (International Standard Classification of Occupation), as are the occupational titles corresponding to each ISOC in the British and American data (Ganzeboom *et al.* 1992; Ganzeboom and Treiman 1996). Thus, merging ISEI codes into the LFS and PUMs is not difficult. Assigning Canadian occupations their proper ISEI score, however, is problematic. The PUMFI provides just 14 different occupational categories for the entire work force, hence, ISEI scores must be aggregated into 14 meaningful units. The procedure used here accepts Ganzeboom *et al.*'s (1992) assumption that 'the costs of being crude' are severe only when the number of occupations falls below six. Thus, weighted average ISEIs were computed for each of the 14 Canadian occupations. Calculating these averages required three pieces of information: the detailed occupational codes associated with each of the 14 categories (Statistics Canada 1994), the title of and number of persons in each detailed occupational code (Statistics Canada 1995) and the ISEI score for each occupational title (Ganzeboom and Treiman 1996). To facilitate the mapping process, Ganzeboom and Treiman's 'numerical dominance rule' was used. That is, when a detailed Canadian occupational code contained titles associated with more than one ISEI, the Canadian occupation was assigned the ISEI of its largest title. After each of the 14 occupations had been assigned all its component ISEIs, the ISEIs were weighted by the number of their incumbents. Each Canadian individual then was assigned an ISEI equal to the weighted average associated with her or his PUMFI occupation.

As for the independent variables, they are drawn from human capital theory because the goal of the analysis is to measure the effect of group membership on unemployment, Goldthorpe class and occupational status, controlling for human capital. The traditional human capital variables include age, age squared, education, marital status and years post-migration. The US and Canadian censuses offer this latter variable only as intervals, hence, each immigrant was assigned a value equivalent to the mean of this interval. An additional step was to recode the 'years post-migration' of each individual as deviations from his or her compatriots' group mean. This step standardizes for the disparities in arrival times across backgrounds.

The most problematic independent variable is schooling. The structure of education in Canada and the USA is similar, although the Canadian system offers more in the way of vocational preparation (Gaskell 1991). In the UK, education carries several salient distinctions that most data sets ignore, for instance public versus private schooling (Kerchkoff 1990). In this situation, cross-national comparability can only be approximated. The approach taken here follows previous studies by including two measures of schooling: age at which the respondent left school and a six-category 'educational credentials' variable in which 1 indicates no qualifications and 6 designates an advanced degree (Model and Ladipo 1996). Developing the first of these measures for Americans and Canadians required approximating the age of school leaving from the 'grades completed' variable in their respective censuses. The LFS provides age of school leaving directly. As the above synopsis indicates, a considerable amount of effort is required to prepare the materials for analysis; unfortunately, this effort does little to mitigate the shortcomings in the data.

Results

This section presents four different types of findings. It begins with a brief discussion of the data, emphasizing mean differences in the dependent and independent variables among groups and across cities. Then efforts to predict the three dependent variables are presented. Predictions of the latter two outcomes, Goldthorpe class and ISEI, are estimated twice, once on the full sample and once on mainstream economy employees, which is to say, absent the three types of 'queue jumpers' defined above. Since the unemployed do not have jobs and hence cannot have a status vis-à-vis 'queue jumping', only one sample can meaningfully estimate this dependent variable.

Table 5.1 contains descriptive information about the major variables in the analysis, separately for men and women by city. Any group for

Table 5.1 Means and standard deviations of major variables[a] by city and gender

Group	Men New York	Men Toronto	Men London	Women New York	Women Toronto	Women London
Native-born white						
Age	41.8	39.5	42.0	42.5	39.9	42.3
	(11.3)	(11.0)	(11.5)	(11.5)	(11.0)	(11.7)
Age left school	20.3	19.6	17.0	19.8	19.5	16.8
	(2.8)	(3.1)	(2.9)	(2.5)	(2.9)	(2.4)
% Unemployed	4.6	7.2	8.4	4.5	6.6	6.5
Goldthorpe class	2.35	2.23	2.40	2.35	2.29	2.23
	(0.75)	(0.77)	(0.71)	(0.66)	(0.62)	(0.75)
ISEI	50.9	47.1	47.8	52.7	50.1	46.8
	(16.9)	(13.1)	(16.3)	(13.7)	(11.0)	(15.2)
N	2 415	14 446	3 059	2 246	13 272	2 363
Foreign-born white						
Age	43.4	46.0	42.2	44.9	45.6	43.1
	(11.3)	(10.6)	(11.5)	(11.2)	(10.6)	(11.3)
Age left school	18.7	17.9	18.0	18.0	17.3	17.6
	(4.2)	(4.5)	(3.9)	(4.1)	(4.4)	(3.5)
Year of migration	21.9	24.5	23.5	23.3	24.5	23.3
	(15.3)	(11.2)	(14.0)	(15.3)	(11.1)	(13.4)
% Unemployed	5.4	7.8	10.0	7.5	8.4	10.4
Goldthorpe class	2.17	2.04	2.29	2.07	2.00	2.18
	(0.78)	(0.79)	(0.81)	(0.76)	(0.71)	(0.80)
ISEI	46.7	43.1	46.5	46.6	44.9	46.4
	(17.4)	(13.6)	(17.6)	(15.9)	(12.2)	(16.1)
N	1 678	7 443	421	1 314	6 094	403
Chinese						
Age	41.7	40.4	40.1	41.3	40.3	40.1
	(10.8)	(10.6)	(9.9)	(10.9)	(10.4)	(9.7)
Age left school	18.3	19.5	19.1	17.2	18.3	18.0
	(5.2)	(4.1)	(4.1)	(5.3)	(4.6)	(3.3)
Year of migration	13.1	11.2	16.7	12.5	9.9	16.2
	(10.6)	(8.8)	(8.8)	(10.1)	(7.9)	(9.1)
% Unemployed	5.4	8.6	9.4	4.7	10.3	9.8
Goldthorpe class	2.15	2.23	2.03	1.91	2.01	2.32
	(0.79)	(0.76)	(0.92)	(0.86)	(0.72)	(0.74)
ISEI	46.6	48.0	45.6	45.8	46.0	46.3
	(17.6)	(13.2)	(15.4)	(16.1)	(12.4)	(13.4)
N	2 965	1 517	148	2 595	1 400	105
East Indian						
Age	39.4	40.0	44.3	39.1	39.7	41.6
	(9.6)	(10.4)	(10.6)	(9.7)	(10.9)	(10.5)
Age left school	21.1	19.8	19.3	20.1	18.3	18.0
	(3.5)	(3.4)	(3.8)	(3.4)	(4.6)	(3.5)
Year of migration	9.9	10.4	20.4	9.4	10.1	17.3
	(7.3)	(7.9)	(8.4)	(6.8)	(7.4)	(8.0)

Table 5.1 continued

Group	Men			Women		
	New York	Toronto	London	New York	Toronto	London
% Unemployed	4.3	12.5	11.6	7.1	16.5	11.2
Goldthorpe class	2.39	1.95	2.18	2.24	1.80	1.82
	(0.78)	(0.80)	(0.79)	(0.76)	(0.67)	(0.77)
ISEI	54.2	43.2	46.6	49.7	41.6	42.0
	(18.3)	(13.2)	(15.8)	(17.3)	(12.7)	(15.1)
N	2 094	828	450	1 265	564	332
African Indian						
Age		41.8	38.2		40.2	38.0
		(10.1)	(9.0)		(9.5)	(9.5)
Age left school		20.4	19.0		19.3	18.0
		(2.6)	(3.1)		(3.6)	(3.0)
Year of migration		13.0	17.9		13.4	17.3
		(6.5)	(6.2)		(6.8)	(5.9)
% Unemployed		7.4	7.5		11.2	12.7
Goldthorpe class		2.36	2.35		2.20	2.24
		(0.71)	(0.72)		(0.64)	(0.70)
ISEI		49.2	48.9		48.7	47.3
		(12.0)	(14.6)		(11.3)	(12.5)
N		162	347		165	225
West Indian						
Age	40.6	40.8	46.7	40.9	40.5	44.1
	(10.6)	(10.2)	(10.9)	(10.7)	(10.2)	(10.4)
Age left school	18.0	18.9	16.4	18.2	18.7	16.5
	(3.5)	(3.1)	(2.4)	(3.2)	(3.1)	(1.9)
Year of migration	14.2	14.8	26.8	14.8	14.8	26.0
	(9.6)	(7.6)	(6.9)	(9.7)	(7.8)	(6.8)
% Unemployed	10.5	12.1	14.0	7.8	10.6	10.8
Goldthorpe class	1.91	1.85	1.87	1.94	1.99	1.99
	(0.77)	(0.76)	(0.71)	(0.80)	(0.70)	(0.89)
ISEI	40.8	40.1	36.9	41.8	44.2	38.0
	(15.1)	(11.8)	(12.5)	(15.7)	(11.9)	(14.6)
N	3 649	1 062	443	4 844	1 412	474
Black African						
Age	36.9	34.7	38.4	35.4	34.9	36.1
	(7.3)	(7.4)	(9.1)	(7.7)	(8.9)	(8.2)
Age left school	20.0	19.6	20.9	19.3	18.2	19.0
	(3.8)	(3.3)	(4.2)	(3.4)	(3.3)	(3.3)
Year of migration	10.3	6.9	13.4	9.7	7.9	12.9
	(6.9)	(6.1)	(9.3)	(7.0)	(7.0)	(8.1)
% Unemployed	6.2	14.9	15.8	11.2	25.0	10.8
Goldthorpe class	2.11	1.76	2.28	1.94	1.87	2.03
	(0.88)	(0.79)	(0.77)	(0.84)	(0.64)	(0.87)
ISEI	46.9	40.0	46.4	41.5	41.9	40.6
	(17.7)	(12.9)	(17.0)	(16.5)	(12.2)	(15.9)
N	538	190	114	300	94	112

Table 5.1   continued

Group	Men			Women		
	New York	Toronto	London	New York	Toronto	London
Pakistani						
Age	36.2		40.5			
	(8.3)		(10.1)			
Age left school	19.9		18.4			
	(3.7)		(3.8)			
Year of migration	8.3		19.1			
	(5.6)		(8.8)			
% Unemployed	6.5		23.0			
Goldthorpe class	1.96		2.20			
	(0.85)		(0.74)			
ISEI	45.5		44.6			
	(17.8)		(14.2)			
N	315		161			
Bangladeshi						
Age	34.4		41.6			
	(7.3)		(10.7)			
Age left school	19.2		19.0			
	(4.2)		(4.4)			
Year of migration	7.6		17.3			
	(5.2)		(10.6)			
% Unemployed	12.4		36.5			
Goldthorpe class	1.67		1.96			
	(0.79)		(0.85)			
ISEI	39.2		43.0			
	(15.7)		(16.9)			
N	92		137			

Notes: [a] Variables describe persons 25–64.
N's encompass persons providing an occupation.

Source: Tables 5.1–5.5: Britain – Labour force surveys (1987–93); United States – 1990 Public Use Microdata (PUMs); Canada – Public Use Microdata file individuals (1991).

which the number of usable cases fell below 90 was excluded from the analysis, which explains the absence of Pakistani and Bangladeshi women. In examining the dependent variables, it is useful to keep in mind that unemployment rates include everyone aged 18–64, ISEI scores pertain to all persons aged 24–64 who provided occupational information, and Goldthorpe class locations describe those in the ISEI subset who were employees. A useful point of departure is the difference in economic structures across cities. Unemployment is lowest in New York and highest in London, ISEI is highest in New York, while Goldthorpe class is distributed quite similarly across the three labour markets. Other relevant patterns include that the mean ISEI of women is higher than that of their male counterparts and that Londoners have the least education of the three urban groups. A less surprising finding is that the number of post-migration years is highest for London's immigrants. This distinction obtains because most non-whites entered Britain before the mid 1960s, while most non-whites entered Canada and the USA after that date.

Turning to trends within cities, note that on each dependent variable at least one non-white group has a more salutary outcome than native-born whites. On unemployment, for instance, New York's East Indian males and London's African Indian males have lower rates than their native-born white counterparts. On Goldthorpe class and ISEI, three immigrant groups sometimes outperform native whites: Chinese, African Indians and East Indians. The strong showing by East Indians, however, surfaces only in New York. As for the least salutary outcome, in cities where Bangladeshis are included, they fare very poorly; otherwise black Africans or West Indians register the greatest shortfalls. Another noteworthy pattern is that group rankings on the three dependent variables are not identical. To illustrate: in New York black African women rank lowest on ISEI but Chinese women rank lowest on Goldthorpe class.

In addition to variations across the three dependent variables, another source of group differences within cities is variation in human capital. On age, for instance, only one group is older than New York's native whites, that is foreign born whites. Two groups are older than London's native whites: foreign-born whites and West Indians. But most of the immigrant groups in this study are older than Toronto's native whites. Inter-city variations on schooling are also substantial. In London, all immigrant groups, save West Indians, average *at least* as many years of schooling as native whites of the same gender; often the immigrants report substantially more. In the other two cities, only two groups, East Indian and/or African Indians, have more schooling than their native white counterparts. Thus, cities differ in the size of the respective gaps between immigrants and natives on the dependent and on the independent variables. To disentangle the causally relevant factors, multi-variate analyses must be pursued.

Gainful employment is the primary means for survival in developed societies. Thus, when racial and ethnic minorities suffer higher rates of joblessness than equally qualified whites, the minorities are facing a fundamental threat to their life chances. As mentioned above, almost all the non-white immigrant groups in this study have higher unemployment rates than native whites. But they may also be younger and/or less educated than whites. The numbers in Table 5.2 reflect the

Table 5.2 Net effects of group membership on unemployment by city and gender[a]

Immigrant group	Men			Women		
	New York	Toronto	London	New York	Toronto	London
White	.0216	.1996**	.3343*	.5162**	.1783**	.3226
	(.1511)	(.0575)	(.1667)	(.1575)	(.0624)	(.1806)
Chinese	.1450	.4190***	.1656	.0583	.4866***	.6170*
	(.1278)	(.0961)	(.2861)	(.1436)	(.0948)	(.3096)
East Indian	.1191	.8245***	.6033**	.6768***	.9970***	.6829***
	(.1414)	(.1087)	(.1620)	(.1547)	(.1145)	(.1895)
African Indian		.3078	.1130		.6689**	.7466***
		(.2831)	(.2050)		(.2415)	(.2011)
West Indian	.5569***	.5649***	.5722***	.3748**	.4640***	.5142**
	(.1100)	(.0954)	(.1489)	(.1190)	(.0907)	(.1690)
Black African	.4207*	.8231***	1.4478***	.8203***	1.4319***	.7922**
	(.1942)	(.1982)	(.2629)	(.2224)	(.2246)	(.3027)
Pakistani	.3376		1.3978***			
	(.2321)		(.1861)			
Bangladeshi	.6484*		1.5964***			
	(.3288)		(.1616)			

Notes: [a] Logistic regressions were estimated on labour market participants aged 18–64. In addition to group membership, all models control for age, age squared, years of education, educational credentials, marital status and years since migration. The British model also contains 6 dummies for survey year; the excluded year is 1990. In all estimates, the excluded group is native born whites.
*p < .05, **p < .01, ***p < .001.

effect of group membership on unemployment when such human capital factors are controlled. In these regressions the omitted group is native-born whites. Thus, the numbers in the table represent the net difference on the dependent variable between the non-white group named on the far left and native-born whites. Asterisks indicate statistical significance.

Looking at the results within cities, it is interesting to observe that men and women of the same background do not necessarily have the same unemployment vulnerabilities. In New York, foreign-born white males and East Indian males do not suffer significantly higher unemployment than native-born white males with the same characteristics, but women of these two backgrounds have significantly higher rates than their native white counterparts. In Toronto, African Indian males are the only immigrants not incurring significantly higher chances of unemployment than native whites. As for Londoners, foreign-born white women, Chinese men and African Indian men are the three groups that escape a significant shortfall. Another generalization about these findings is that the male groups are slightly less vulnerable to unemployment than the female groups. These differences between men and women raise an intriguing question: do dominant group employers rank national backgrounds differently by gender?

Since there are no statistical tests for comparing coefficients of logistic regressions across models, inter-city comparisons of the effect of group membership are only impressions. Still, it appears that most backgrounds fare better in New York than in the other two cities. Exceptions include West Indian men, whose coefficients are nearly identical in the three locales, and white immigrant women, who suffer less unemployment in Toronto. Contrasting Toronto with London does not reveal any consistencies either within groups or within gender categories.

One factor that may mask regularities in immigrants' risk of unemployment is the presence in the sample of queue jumpers, or, more accurately, 'potential' queue jumpers. As explained above, queue jumpers are persons who do not depend on the dominant group for jobs and are, therefore, only indirectly subject to discrimination. When job seekers are combined with job holders, which is the strategy required in any analysis of unemployment risk, the proportion of the unemployed who are potential queue jumpers cannot be determined. Yet, causal processes relevant to queue jumping may contribute to unemployment vulnerability. For instance, inter-city differences in the size of a group's ethnic economy will translate into differences in the percentage of that group dependent on dominant group employers. This situation, in turn, will produce inter-city differences in group members' vulnerability to unemployment. These considerations imply that the results in Table 5.2 do a good job of depicting the experience of different groups across the three labour markets but a poor job of testing the ability of queuing theory to explain those results.

Multi-variate estimates of the remaining dependent variables, Goldthorpe class and ISEI, have the potential for more theoretically useful results because queue jumpers can be identified and eliminated from the analysis. Thus, Table 5.3 offers two sets of results for Goldthorpe class: Model 1, which contains all cases for which this dependent variable is defined, and Model 2 which excludes public

Table 5.3 Net effects of group membership on Goldthorpe class by city and gender[a]

Immigrant group	Model	Men			Women		
		New York	Toronto	London	New York	Toronto	London
White	(1)	-0.0697 (.0716)	-0.2044*** (.0327)	-0.3912** (.1347)	-0.3212*** (.0731)	-0.4225*** (.0352)	-0.4623*** (.1236)
Chinese	(1)	-0.1827** (.0617)	-0.1644** (.0603)	-1.4395*** (.2238)	-0.7003*** (.0629)	-0.8558*** (.0620)	-0.5894* (.2360)
	(2)	-0.0016 (.0728)	-0.2050** (.0705)	-0.6565* (.2984)	-0.2591*** (.0719)	-0.8665*** (.0707)	-0.5737* (.2463)
East Indian	(1)	-0.3299*** (.0687)	-0.9774*** (.0780)	-1.0718*** (.1364)	-0.9492*** (.0763)	-1.6923*** (.0937)	-1.2090*** (.1400)
	(2)	-0.3861*** (.0746)	-0.7809*** (.0910)	-0.9682*** (.1465)	-1.1680*** (.0887)	-1.2433*** (.1050)	-1.0814*** (.1474)
African Indian	(1)		-0.0150 (.1735)	-0.5556*** (.1503)		-0.3310* (.1679)	-0.3105* (.1529)
	(2)		0.0276 (.1848)	-0.5266** (.1728)		0.3195 (.1960)	-0.2741 (.1800)
West Indian	(1)	-0.4083*** (.0568)	-0.7925*** (.0648)	-0.9593*** (.1126)	-0.5668*** (.0539)	-0.7031*** (.0605)	-0.5375*** (.1099)
	(2)	-0.4185*** (.0594)	-0.7893*** (.0648)	-0.9665*** (.1155)	-0.6856*** (.0565)	-0.7041*** (.0606)	-0.4995*** (.1115)

Black African	(1)	−0.8493*** (.1050)	−1.3407*** (.1608)	−1.2035*** (.2412)	−1.0518*** (.1304)	−1.1971*** (.2277)	−1.1525*** (.2161)
	(2)	−0.8062*** (.1241)	−1.3387*** (.1609)	−1.1183*** (.2459)	−1.2655*** (.1511)	−1.1989*** (.2278)	−1.0626*** (.2249)
Pakistani	(1)	−1.0310*** (.1342)		−0.7235** (.2121)			
	(2)	−1.0406*** (.1611)		−0.6781** (.2245)			
Bangladeshi	(1)	−1.6125*** (.2441)		−1.5580*** (.2134)			
	(2)	−1.7113*** (.3155)		−1.1751*** (.2577)			

Notes: [a] Ordered logistic regressions were estimated on persons aged 25–64 reporting an occupation and describing their class position as employees. Model 2 omits persons working in 'ethnic economies' as defined in the text. In addition to group membership, both models control for age, age squared, years of education, educational credentials, marital status and years since migration. In all estimates, the excluded group is native born whites.

*p < .05, **p < .01, ***p < .001.

sector employees in New York and ethnic economy employees in all three cities.

Because class was coded so that greater values signify higher social class, most of the group membership coefficients are negative; that is to say, most immigrant groups are less likely than are native whites to belong to the most desirable category, the service class. There are exceptions, however: foreign-born whites, Chinese, and African Indians. Interestingly, the exceptions are more frequent in Model 2 than Model 1, a pattern which indicates that queue jumping does not always enhance social class position. This interpretation is especially applicable to New York's Chinese, who incur far smaller penalties in the mainstream economy than in their ethnic economy. Note that Table 5.3 contains no Model 2 coefficients for foreign-born whites; this is because of an inability to identify the ethnic economy industries of the many white ethnic groups included under this rubric.

The coefficients for Model 2 provide insight into the 'hierarchy of discrimination' within cities, though the figures must be interpreted with caution because many of the group differences in coefficients within the same city are not statistically significant. For men, the hierarchy is remarkably similar in the three labour markets. As pointed out already, Chinese and African Indian immigrants rank at the top. West and East Indians hold the middle. Black Africans, Pakistanis and Bangladeshis occupy the bottom. The most unanticipated of these rankings is the strong position of African Indians. In addition, East Indians were expected to surpass West Indians in New York, but the analysis shows that, in all three cities, West Indian and East Indian males experience deficits of about the same size.

Table 5.3 adds credibility to the interpretation that the labour queue varies by sex. In each of the three cities, East Indian women rank near the bottom, as opposed to East Indian men, who hold middle ground. But the women's labour queue also varies more by city than the men's. The most noticeable difference is that Chinese women rank above West Indians in New York but maintain a slightly poorer position than West Indians in the other two cities. Does this mean that Chinese women do better in New York?

Ordinary least square regression of occupational status provides the best answer to this question because this technique supports statistical tests for differences among cities. Table 5.4 contains these results. Again, all cases appear in Model 1; queue jumpers are excluded from Model 2. Comparing the two models again suggests that queue jumping is a mixed blessing. Evidently, New York's Chinese have higher status occupations in the mainstream economy, as do London's Pakistani and Bangladeshi men. The converse holds for New York's East Indian males, who incur a deficit only in Model 2. Interestingly, among women, the difference between Models 1 and 2 is generally small.

With respect to the 'hierarchy of discrimination', men's occupational status rankings parallel those for Goldthorpe class: African Indians and Chinese stand near the top, East and West Indians hold the middle, black Africans, Pakistanis and Bangladeshis sink to the bottom. But on Goldthorpe class, East Indian and West Indian men held roughly equal rankings in all three cities; instead, on ISEI, East Indian males have smaller deficits than West Indian males in all three labour markets. Statistical tests of this differential, however, reveal that only New York's East Indian males enjoy a significant advantage over West Indians; the difference in London is just short of significant, and the difference in Toronto is insignificant.[8] These results mesh far more closely with field experiments that show no difference between the two groups in Canada and Britain than with survey evidence, which shows South Asians rank lower than black Caribbeans in the two countries. Another difference between men's ISEI rankings and men's Goldthorpe rankings is that on the former New York's black Africans secure a ranking closer to the middle than to the bottom. They are less than a point below West Indians and over a point above Pakistanis. On the other hand, black Africans in Toronto and London appear near the bottom of the queue. In sum, the analysis suggests that New York penalizes some of these non-white immigrants less severely than the other locales.

Turning to the women's results, it is apparent that the gender gap on ISEI is greater than the gender gap on Goldthorpe class. This difference may arise because ISEI, as the more finely calibrated dependent variable, is more sensitive to gender discrimination. The central focus of the present study, however, is the hierarchy of discrimination. Table 5.4 shows that some patterns are the same for women and men: white immigrants and African Indians face relatively small penalties, followed by Chinese women. The deficits of black African women are consistently largest. But the middle of the women's hierarchy is different from the men's. Statistical tests show East Indian women rank equal to West Indian women in New York and London, but East Indian women fall significantly below West Indians in Toronto. Attention to the coefficients responsible for these results indicates only small differences among East Indian women in the three cities; the critical factor appears to be that West Indian women in Toronto incur relatively smaller penalties than elsewhere.

Table 5.4 Net effects of group membership on ISEI by city and gender[a]

Immigrant group	Model	Men			Women		
		New York	Toronto	London	New York	Toronto	London
White	(1)	−0.8246 (.4223)	−2.0252*** (.1635)	−1.6753* (.7045)	−2.7886*** (.4561)	−2.4437*** (.1570)	−1.6834* (.7166)
Chinese	(1)	−1.2965*** (.3673)	−0.3052 (.2950)	−3.5855** (1.1628)	−2.9845*** (.3861)	−3.1819*** (.2736)	−4.4390** (1.3026)
	(2)	−0.0401 (.4455)	−0.5542 (.3629)	−2.5284 (1.7170)	−1.9799*** (.4532)	−3.4759*** (.3218)	−5.3747*** (1.4833)
East Indian	(1)	−0.5961 (.3986)	−5.0518*** (.3900)	−3.1456*** (.7152)	−6.7268*** (.4649)	−8.0061*** (.4192)	−4.6358*** (.7986)
	(2)	−1.4822** (.4603)	−3.5253*** (.4871)	−4.6082*** (.8948)	−6.8255*** (.5760)	−5.5403*** (.4903)	−5.6923*** (.9023)
African Indian	(1)		0.0585 (.8604)	−0.5062 (.7682)		−1.1848 (.7592)	−1.3032 (.9059)
	(2)		0.3825 (.9806)	−1.3908 (1.0667)		−1.6915 (.8937)	−2.3797* (1.1149)
West Indian	(1)	−3.1235*** (.3532)	−4.9473*** (.3473)	−6.7590*** (.6970)	−6.4216*** (.3411)	−3.9846*** (.2730)	−7.1453*** (.6690)
	(2)	−3.2072*** (.3887)	−4.5727*** (.3569)	−6.9033*** (.7720)	−6.8782*** (.3667)	−3.8756*** (.2762)	−7.0061*** (.6872)

Black African	(1)	−4.6048*** (.6335)	−6.4744*** (.7951)	−8.6946*** (1.3466)	−10.5779*** (.8054)	−6.8460*** (1.0036)	−10.0157*** (1.3051)
	(2)	−3.7589*** (.7737)	−6.1925*** (.8190)	−8.2941*** (1.4715)	−11.7697*** (.9497)	−6.9035*** (1.0226)	−9.5987*** (1.3815)
Pakistani	(1)	−4.6933*** (.7941)		−3.4748** (1.1021)			
	(2)	−4.9252*** (1.0089)		−4.9622*** (1.3934)			
Bangladeshi	(1)	−7.8380*** (1.4054)		−5.7045*** (1.2000)			
	(2)	−7.9117*** (1.8870)		−6.6442** (1.5822)			

Notes: [a] OLS regressions were estimated on all persons aged 25–64 reporting an occupation. Model 2 omits persons working in 'ethnic economies' as defined in the text. In addition to group membership, both models control for age, age squared, years of education, educational credentials, marital status and years since migration. In all estimates, the excluded group is native born whites.
*p<.05, **p<.01, ***p<.001.

Tests of statistical significance are needed to ascertain the chances that sampling variation accounts for inter-city differences. These appear in Table 5.5, which compares results for Model 2 among cities. The numbers report the t-value for the difference in coefficients associated with living in the city listed first versus the city listed second. Thus, in the column headed London–NY positive values mean that Londoners obtain the higher ISEI, negative numbers mean that New Yorkers do. An absence of asterisks implies the inter-city difference is statistically insignificant.

With respect to men, the central finding is that three groups – East Indians, West Indians, and black Africans – enjoy higher occupational status in New York than in Toronto or London. Recall that New York's small white population was anticipated to provide immigrants with higher occupational status, provided those groups ranked above African-Americans. This caveat was appended because groups falling below African-Americans would be less able to benefit from that city's small white population than groups ranking above African-Americans. One way of testing this hypothesis is to examine the coefficient that African-American males attain in a Model 2 equation predicting ISEI. When added to the New York sample in Model 2, African-Americans obtain a coefficient of -4.9306 (0.4136). Additional statistical tests (not shown) indicate that New York's East Indians, West Indians, and black Africans experience more favourable occupational outcomes than African-Americans do; that is, the three groups enjoying a New York

Table 5.5 T-values for inter-city differences in ethnic coefficients predicting ISEI in Model 2

Immigrant group	Men			Women		
	London–NY	Toronto–NY	Toronto–London	London–NY	Toronto–NY	Toronto–London
Chinese	−1.40	−0.89	1.12	−2.19*	−2.69**	1.25
East Indian	−3.11**	−3.05**	1.06	1.06	1.70	0.15
African Indian			1.22			0.48
West Indian	−4.28***	−2.59**	2.74**	−0.16	6.54**	4.23***
Black African	−2.73**	−2.16**	1.25	1.35	3.49***	1.52
Pakistani	−0.02					
Bangladeshi	0.52					

*p<.05, **p<.01, ***p<.001.

advantage appear to rank above African-Americans in the labour queue. Pakistanis, on the other hand, hold similar, and Bangladeshi's hold lower occupations than do African-Americans. In other words, the two predominantly Muslim groups do not profit from the city's smaller white population, instead, they experience similarly poor outcomes in New York and London.

These observations offer strong support for a queuing interpretation of inter-city differences among male immigrants. But one discrepancy remains: why do the Chinese not also benefit from New York's small white population? The difference in the coefficients of Chinese and African-Americans indicates that New York's dominant group employers rank the Chinese above African-Americans, yet New York is no more attractive a locale for Chinese workers than are the other two cities. The explanation lies in Table 5.4, which shows that Chinese occupational attainment is statistically indistinguishable from native white in the mainstream economies of all three locales. In such a situation, the size of the white population does not matter because dominant group employers do not wait until the supply of whites is exhausted before considering Chinese. Instead, the two groups are interchangeable. And because Chinese men already share the head of the labour queue with native whites, New York's small white population offers them no occupational benefits that they do not already reap in all three venues.

The case of the Chinese provides a good example of the gender difference in these analyses; Chinese women are the only female group who benefit from a New York location. Chinese aside, New York is not a particularly desirable location for women. Not unexpectedly, African-Americans again are at the centre of the explanation. The African-American coefficient in Model 2 of Table 5.4 is −5.1171 (0.4005), a value below that of the Chinese, but equivalent to or above that of East Indian, West Indian and black African women. In other words, Chinese women are the only group whose position in the labour queue allows them to benefit from the smaller size of New York's white population. A second part of the explanation for Chinese women's New York advantage is that, unlike their male counterparts, they are not interchangeable with whites. In fact, Chinese immigrant females obtain significantly poorer occupations than native whites in the mainstream economies of all three cities. To be sure, most of the other groups of immigrant women suffer a similar fate. And since these others all rank lower in the eyes of New York's employers than African-Americans, these others have quite similar outcomes in the three cities.

One curious result in Table 5.5 is that West Indian women do better in Toronto than in New York or London. As mentioned earlier, a related finding is that West Indian women rank above East Indians in Toronto but are equal to East Indians in New York and London. Recall that in no city do West Indian men rank above East Indian men. Census data is of little help in unearthing the reasons for this gender interaction in the middle rungs of the 'hierarchy of discrimination'. As will be described below, field work in the USA indicates considerable differences in the reception employers accord African-American males and females; possibly a similar process operates among West Indians in Canada but not in Britain or the USA. More research is needed before the processes responsible for these results are understood. At this point, all that can be concluded is that, as far as Britain is concerned, the analysis detects no differences in the outcomes of East Indians and West Indians, despite speculation to the contrary.

The analysis can be summarized in three generalizations. First, across all three cities and on all three outcomes, similarities are the rule. The groups most likely to have outcomes comparable to native whites are foreign-born whites, African Indians and Chinese. This pattern, however, holds primarily for men. As part of the tendency for immigrant women to incur larger penalties than men, foreign-born women very rarely have outcomes comparable to native white women. Still, both sexes' 'hierarchy of discrimination' is roughly similar in the three cities. The above mentioned three groups rank highest, East and West Indians hold the middle, and Africans, Pakistanis and Bangladeshis register the largest deficits. Second, the main difference in the hierarchy of discrimination within cities involves East and West Indians. In most instances, the outcomes of the two groups are statistically indistinguishable. But in New York, East Indian men do better than West Indian men and in Toronto, West Indian women do better than East Indian women. Third, the similarity in the rank order of groups does not mean that each background experiences an identical outcome in each city. The main reason for discrepancies is the presence of African-Americans in the New York labour market. Three male immigrant groups, East Indians, West Indians and black Africans, fare significantly better in New York than in the other two cities because they stand higher in the labour queue than African-American men. But only one female group, Chinese women, is 'upgraded' in this fashion because African-American women hold a relatively better position in the labour queue than African-American men.

Discussion

These results complement a previous comparison of London and New York in which African-Americans also appeared to upgrade the occupations of several non-white groups in New York (Model 1997). This chapter extends that earlier study in several ways. First, the earlier analysis utilized the British Census (SARs) and, therefore, was unable to control for years since migration or for detailed educational attainment. Second, the earlier analysis did not explore unemployment or Goldthorpe class location. Third, the earlier analysis paid scant attention to intra-city differences. Finally, the earlier analysis did not include Toronto. Nonetheless, on those questions that the two studies share, their answers are identical. This correspondence somewhat mitigates the concerns expressed at the outset about the quality of the data. Better data did not alter the results. In the main, both analyses supported the expectations of queuing theory. Yet, some of the findings in this chapter challenge those expectations. The reminder of this section is devoted to interpreting some of these anomalous findings.

Perhaps the gender disparities were the most unexpected. Two findings deserve scrutiny: foreign-born women registered far larger deficits relative to white native-born women, than did foreign-born men relative to white native men, and fewer women's than men's groups experienced an advantage in New York. The discovery that the foreign–native gap is larger for women than men has been observed before. One of the most compelling explanations is Baker and Benjamin's (1997) 'family investment' model. According to this perspective, soon after arrival, immigrant wives find well-paying but 'dead-end' jobs, the earnings of which are used to underwrite their husbands' investments in additional training. Meanwhile, immigrant husbands start out in rather poor jobs but also attend school or other training forums. Eventually the husbands become sufficiently qualified to trade their poor posts for better occupations. But their wives remain trapped in poor jobs because the opportunities these women initially secured did not prepare them for better positions. The net result of these two strategies is that, at mean years since migration (which is the value that the coefficients in this study represent), the job outcomes of immigrant husbands are far closer to the outcomes of their native-born counterparts than are the job outcomes of immigrant wives. Of course, without offering a formal test of this interpretation, it remains tentative; however, it does fit the results quite well.

Since this formulation applies to women in all three cities, it cannot explain why fewer female than male origin groups registered a New York advantage. The gender distinction responsible for the inter-city difference is, rather, that African-American men hold a lower position in the male New York labour queue than African-American women hold in the female labour queue. Although opinion polls and field experiments have proceeded under the assumption that men and women of the same origin receive similar treatment at the hands of the dominant group, interviews with American employers reveal a greater willingness to hire and promote African-American women than African-American men (Holzer 1996; Kirschenman 1991; Moss and Tilly 1996). The main justification for this preference is that African-American males are 'tough', 'unreliable' and 'hostile', while African-American women have the interpersonal skills required by today's service economy. These qualities, in turn, are attributed both to their gender and to their tendency to raise children alone.

Examining this response in depth, Moss and Tilly (1996) conclude that some young black men are 'scary' and at the same time that some white employers indiscriminately reject black applicants. John Ogbu offers a helpful perspective in explaining the former adaptation. In an argument that parallels Willis' (1977) study of the British working class, Ogbu (1987) finds an oppositional subculture among groups whose race, ethnicity, or caste blocks their chances for upward mobility. This subculture disparages mainstream goals, such as high grades and steady jobs, which are interpreted as selling out to the dominant group, and instead prizes attributes like arrogance, bravery and physical prowess. Most attracted to this lifestyle are young black males who live in impoverished, dilapidated and segregated inner city slums (Anderson 1990). Interestingly, ethnographic studies indicate that black girls accept an adversarial culture less frequently than boys (Waters 1996). Their reluctance may be related to the greater willingness of employers to hire and promote black women than black men.

These remarks serve as a useful corrective to the position that minorities are mere pawns in the hands of malevolent elites. To be sure, the balance of power is firmly in dominant groups' hands; nevertheless, immigrants and minorities have some space in which to manoeuvre. Their cultural legacies, political power and economic opportunities inform their choices. Moreover, even individuals facing similar constraints do not respond identically. Thus, the proportion of prime age African-American males embracing an oppositional subculture is modest; most are full time workers. Nevertheless, a single negative encounter is enough to dissuade some employers from risking a repeat experience. Others are deterred on the basis of stereotypes alone. In this way do both minority culture and majority prejudice contribute to a group's rank in the labour queue.

This observation is useful in understanding another anomaly uncovered in the analysis, the strong showing of African Indians. Recall that British surveys and Canadian field experiments indicate that Caribbean blacks hold higher status than South Asians. Moreover East Indians and African Indians are indistinguishable to the average observer. Furthermore, more than half the African Indians in Toronto are Muslims, a group that currently faces stigma in all three nations. In sum, it is hard to imagine that dominant group employers rank this group highly.

One resolution of the discrepancy is to argue that most African Indians work in their own ethnic economy, where they are protected from the sentiments of the dominant group. This interpretation cannot be ruled out because the procedure used above to distinguish ethnic economy workers from dominant economy workers is only approximate. Another possibility is that the analysis underestimates the group's human capital or more accurately, its cultural capital. The term 'cultural capital' is used here to mean collective resources that the group can mobilize to enhance its well being. African Indians hold a number of advantages over their counterparts from the subcontinent (Robinson 1993). These include having been 'twice migrant', which means that the group has already accumulated some experience with respect to adjusting to a new environment. In addition, African Indians have little intention to return, either to Africa or to India, which means that the group has few financial obligations to relatives at origin and has strong financial incentives to make investments at destination. Perhaps most important, however, African Indians functioned as a middleman minority, that is, as economic mediators between rulers and masses in Uganda, Kenya and other East African countries. Middleman minorities have an exceptional record of upward mobility in industrialized countries (Bonacich and Modell 1980). The many causes of this outcome are beyond the scope of the present chapter. However, the process generally involves an intergenerational transition from business to professional pursuits. In pursuing this strategy, group members strive to maximize their qualifications and credentials, which minimizes their vulnerability to a 'hierarchy of discrimination'.

A noteworthy final observation is that Chinese and South Asian immigrants likewise display high rates of self-employment and a strong propensity to work for co-ethnics. But currently these groups also contain significant numbers of dominant economy workers. These workers have not yet attained such high qualifications and credentials that they are no longer dependent on the good opinion of outsiders. Within a generation, however, some of these immigrant groups will follow in the footsteps of the African Indians. It will be interesting to see whether this development produces any revision in what is now a relatively stable cross-national 'hierarchy of discrimination'.

Appendix Niche economy industries by group and city

London	New York	Toronto
Chinese		
Commission agents	Apparel	Finance, insurance and
Restaurants	Eating and drinking	real estate
	places	Food and beverages
East Indian		
Electrical engineering	Miscellaneous retail	Manufacturing
	stores	
Leather and clothing	Health services	
Manufacture		
Commission agents		
Postal services		
African Indian		
Electrical engineering		Finance, insurance and
Rubber and plastic		real estate
Manufacture		
Wholesale		
Retail, automobile retail		
West Indian		
Metal manufacture	Hotels	
	Local government	
Black African		
Sanitary services	Wood products	
	Buses and taxis	
	Miscellaneous retail stores	
	Hotels	
Pakistani		
Leather and clothing	Buses and taxis	
Manufacture	Transport services	
	Food stores	
	Clothing stores	
	Appliance stores	
	Miscellaneous retail stores	
	Automotive services	

Appendix Continued

London	New York	Toronto
Bangladeshi		
Leather and clothing	Buses and taxis	
Manufacture	Variety stores	
Restaurants	Food stores	
Hotels	Miscellaneous retail stores	
	Hotels	

Notes

1. The author thanks Gene Fisher, Eric Maurin and Colin Mills for methodological advice and Michael Hout, Derek Leslie, Robert Kloosterman and Robert Moore for comments on an earlier version. David Ladipo's efforts to merge and comparably code seven waves of the Labour Force Survey are gratefully acknowledged. Despite the many helpful suggestions received, the author accepts sole responsibility for any errors in the data analysis or in the interpretation of results.
2. The work of Jeffrey Reitz constitutes an important exception. See, for example, his book *Warmth of the Welcome: The Social Causes of Economic Success for Immigrants in Different Nations and Cities*, Boulder: Westview Press, 1998.
3. Henry and Ginzberg found that, to obtain ten job interviews, white Canadians had to make 11 or 12 phone calls, white immigrants 13 to 14 calls, black West Indians 15 to 16 calls, and 'Indo Pakistanis' 19 to 20 calls. However, the difference between East and West Indians was not statistically significant.
4. The three cities also differ in the proportion of their white labour force that is foreign born. This figure is 29 per cent in Toronto, 14 per cent in London and 11 per cent in New York. However, the literature review indicates that no non-white group will rank higher than any white immigrant group. Thus, from a queuing perspective, the proportion of the labour force that is white, irrespective of nativity, is the appropriate dimension on which to compare the three cities.
5. In New York, the benchmark is non-Hispanic whites. Taken as a whole, Hispanics comprise 13 per cent of New York's labour force. In the main, Hispanics rank below whites in the labour queue, but to evaluate their position with accuracy would require that they be disaggregated by ethnicity.
6. The LFS has recently added an earnings question, but the number of cases available for analysis is still small. For an initial study, see Leslie *et al.* 1997. Moreover, queuing theory is a less appropriate theoretical framework for explaining earnings than for explaining unemployment, Goldthorpe class, or occupational status. This is because the theory addresses distinct outcomes that are 'zero sum', rather than elastic outcomes that may be shared among contending groups in a variety of ways.
7. Goldthorpe (1995) emphasized that employers and the self-employed experience different employment relations than employees and that these three

groups should not be analysed together. In addition, when studied, employers are assigned to Class I, while small employers and the self-employed belong in the petty bourgeoisie (Class IV). The Canadian and US censuses do not distinguish large employers from small employers and/or the self-employed, making accurate coding of these class positions impossible. As a result, in the analysis below, when Goldthorpe class location is the dependent variable, the sample is *always* restricted to employees.

8. T-tests for within-city differences between East versus West Indians yielded the following results: for New York males t = 2.86, Toronto males t = 1.73, London males t = 1.94; New York females t = 0.08, Toronto females t = −2.96, and London females t = 1.15. A value of 1.96 or greater is required for statistical significance within a confidence interval of 95 per cent.

6
Globalization, Urban Restructuring and Employment Prospects: the case of Germany

Jürgen Friedrichs

Urban regeneration programmes were a delayed response to what initially was perceived as a temporary economic crisis, but then turned out to be a fundamental structural change: de-industrialization, and later, globalization. By the end of the 20th century, this process is not at an end, as the German case shows: more plants are closed, the future of mining is at stake. Production has in part or entirely transferred to countries of lower wages, jobs are created by German-based companies in the Czech Republic, Korea, or China.

Regeneration or revitalization efforts started – depending on the time a city was hit by these changes – in the 1980s. But in the midst of their efforts to adopt their economic base to the trajectory, from goods production to services and information processing, cities were caught by the national recession in the early 1990s. Although there were indications of a recession, and moreover, of fiscal problems in almost all German cities, the short-term boom 1990–92 induced by the German unification, concealed the recession the economies of other European countries surrounding Germany exhibited. By 1993, it became clear that Germany had just postponed the recession; the impact of globalization hit the German economy presumably harder than would have been the case in an earlier period.

Globalization may be defined as an increasing and world-wide process of economic relations. As several authors posit, it negatively influenced the national economy and the cities (for example, Altvater and Mahnkopf 1996; Feagin and Smith 1987; Sassen 1994; Soja 1989, Thrift 1987, 1994), most severely the cities of the old industrial regions. Although the consequences are manifold, for the purpose of

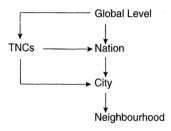

Figure 6.1   A multi-level representation of assumed globalization effects

this chapter it suffices to specify the impact in a general model with four spatial levels. A crucial role is attributed to transnational corporations (TNCs). They are assumed to influence the globalization process by their location decisions and their internal structure (or restructuring), further to influence national bodies such as governments, for instance by exerting pressures towards deregulation, and finally the city by again exerting pressure on urban governments and in addition via their production strategies that affect the local employment market. This reasoning is formally stated in Figure 6.1 and further elaborated below.

The chapter addresses the impact of globalization on the German economy and the consequences of globalization and the national economy on the cities and their employment structure. I will first turn to changes in the national economic conditions, then discuss the impact of TNCs and, thereafter, analyze urban economic and fiscal conditions. In the following section, employment changes in the 1980–94 period are assessed. Six German cities will serve as examples of different trajectories under the conditions of de-industrialization and globalization. The conclusions drawn from the study are presented in the final section.

Impacts of the national economy on cities

The national economic conditions in Germany changed dramatically after 1990. The recession that hit European countries in the late 1980s had only minor repercussions in Germany and was followed by a short period of upswing in the years 1990 to 1992, due to German reunification. According to estimates of the Deutsche Bank Research, the German economy grew in the years 1990 to 1992 by 4.0 per cent annually, whereas other European countries only had growth rates of 1.25 per cent. Furthermore, unification created 1.8 million jobs. West German enterprises

Table 6.1   Investment from and to Germany, 1989 and 1992–94, in DM million

Year	German foreign investment	Foreign investment in Germany
1989	206.555	172.313
1992	287.863	193.624
1993	321.410	200.482
1994	348.257	213.457
% change 1989–94	+68.8	+23.9

Sources: Deutsche Bundesbank 1991: 4, 25; 1996: 10.

were the major winners of this new market. In 1993, it became obvious that growth and not recession was a temporary phenomenon. In monetary terms, the national debt increased between 1990 and 1996 by DM1206 billion – by more than in the entire postwar period until 1989 (DM929 billion). The quotient national debt/GNP rose from 42 per cent at the end of the 1980s to 60.3 per cent in 1996, while this percentage was only 56 per cent in France and the UK in 1996 (Hartwich 1997).

The national budget was constrained by a number of factors. First, there were the costs of the German unification, split into several 'side-budgets' added to the national budget. Estimated costs were DM850 million, *de facto* the net transfer payments from West to East Germany from 1990 to 1996 amounted to DM879 billion. Second, the costs for transferring the capital from Bonn to Berlin, including huge programmes of new construction in Berlin; costs which, according to the 'Transfer Act', are fixed not to exceed DM20 billion up to the year 2000. Third, there were the rising costs for unemployment, that is the subsidies given to the Federal Agency of Labour in charge of transfer payments to the unemployed and, finally, there were the efforts to reduce new debts in order to meet the Maastricht criteria. In fact, Germany's economic position has weakened, perhaps due to delayed reforms of the labour regulations. One indicator, favoured by Sassen (1988, 1994) is foreign investment. In 1995, foreign investment in Germany decreased and even German companies exhibited a negative ratio of foreign to domestic investment. This discrepancy is shown in Table 6.1.

The role of transnational corporations

As suggested by several scholars of the impact of globalization, the international competition leads TNCs to put pressure on national governments (Dicken 1992). To improve their competitiveness, two strategies are used, often by the same company. First, there is the application for subsidies or protective measures for their industry. This obviously is, and was, the case in the mining and steel industry. Thus, German coal production is protected by two treaties: the 'Jahrhundertvertrag' (century contract) obliging steel companies to buy German coal, although the price of German coal at DM210 per ton, by far exceeds the price of imported coal at DM90; the second being the 'Kohlepfenning' (coal penny) obliging households to pay, along with their electricity consumption, an additional amount to subsidize the coal industry. In 1996, subsidies given to the mining industry amounted to almost DM10 billion (DM8.91 billion from the Federal government and 1.0 billion from the Land Northrhine-Westphalia).[1]

The second strategy is to argue for deregulation of trade barriers and work contracts. Although the latter is in Germany not the business of government, but an area for bargaining between trade unions and the employers' associations, the government can interfere. This was the case in the autumn of 1996, when a law was passed (via the Department of Social Affairs) allowing employers to cut wage payments in the case of illness of the employee ('Lohnfortzahlung'). The trade union's reaction to this interference in the autonomy of the 'tariff partners' were strikes in automobile companies attempting to apply this law. The subject is still discussed.

More generally the second strategy aims at reducing welfare state provisions. This is documented in a brochure published in autumn 1994 by the Federal Association of Employers 'Sozialstaat vor dem Umbau' ('Welfare State at the Wake of Restructuring') (Bundesvereinigung 1994). It starts by documenting the expansion of the social security budget to then suggest a series of reforms necessary to adjust the welfare state to the world economic conditions and to secure the competitiveness of the German manufacturing. More specifically, their reasoning is based on two arguments. First, wages in manufacturing are higher in Germany than in all other countries, including Sweden and Switzerland. In 1993, the average wage per hour was DM42.67 in Germany, as opposed to DM37.10 in Japan, DM33.02 in Denmark, DM27.94 in the USA, DM22.15 in Great Britain, DM20.72 in Spain and DM7.80 in Portugal (Bundesvereinigung 1994: 62). This is less the result of difference in direct wages and more the product of the high cost of additional payments for rent, health care and unemployment insurance, which amounted to 80.7 per cent to be added to direct wages in 1996. Second, wage increases in the 1990s exceeded productivity gains.

The association's demands following from these data pertain to a reduction of these additional wage cost elements to increase the competitiveness of the 'Standort Deutschland' (Location Germany), that is German companies. Among others, the association requested a reduction in welfare payments in order to increase the gap between wages and transfer payments as an incentive to seek employment; reduce healthcare benefits and raise individual healthcare payments and insurances; reduce wage payments made in case of illness; reduce rent and pension payments by lowering taxes for individual life insurance contracts (Bundesvereinigung 1994: 17, 19, 26, 39).

This brochure was heavily criticized, dismissed as unrealistic and said to contradict welfare state tenets. However, even at the risk of overstating the case: a reader of this catalogue of demands would in mid 1997 gain the impression that, since the publication was issued, the ruling Christian Democratic Party (in a coalition with the Liberals) is somehow executing these demands and gradually dismantling welfare state provisions and principles which had dominated German policy since the Adenauer era, such as a reduction in eligibility for unemployment aid, reduction in rents and pension levels, higher individual contributions to healthcare, taxation of all sorts of incomes (including rents) and a reduction in the number of state and urban employees.

A further impact was the globalization of manufacturing which led to plant closure, transfer of production and services to lower wage countries and furthermore, establishing new branches in such countries. As the economic advisors concludes: 'The competitiveness of German companies is more and more directed towards investment in foreign countries than export from Germany' (Bericht der Sachverständigenkommision 1997: 68).

An illuminating example is the Siemens company. The company had 379 000 employees, 176 000 of these are based outside Germany in more than 50 countries, total turnover was DM94.2 (61 per cent) in foreign countries (data for 1995/96). The company announced in February 1997 plans to expand their workforce in China from the level of 5000 to 20 000 by the year 2000, and in the same week announced plans to reduce the number employed in Germany in the coming years by 6000 to 8000, especially in the Nürnberg region.

Urban demographic and fiscal conditions

The city's fate is embedded into the national economy. Given the conditions outlined above, urban budgets became increasingly constrained.

By 1996 the total debt of all communes amounted to DM164 billion; the authors of the 'Urban Fiscal Report' state, 'communal finances are in a dead end' (Karrenberg and Münstermann 1996). If cities truly were enterprises, as some claim to be, most of them would have gone bankrupt. To illustrate the dilemma, Tables 6.2 and 6.3 supply data for several basic socio-demographic and fiscal indicators to document the social and fiscal situation in selected cities. The six cities were selected to represent a wide range of economic conditions: München stands for continuous economic growth, Frankfurt and Hamburg for phases of up and downswings, Bremen and Duisburg are examples of decline, while Dortmund is an example of a presumably successful revitalization after a period of decline.

München, Frankfurt/M. and Hamburg have experienced population growth and have comparatively low unemployment rates, although the situation in Hamburg was further aggravated in 1994. In contrast, Bremen, Dortmund and especially Duisburg, lost population and show higher unemployment rates. Judged by these indicators, the above mentioned ranking is validated. With respect to public assistance, the picture is mixed: München retains its outstanding position with low percentages of persons claiming public assistance and low expenditures per inhabitant. However, Frankfurt already had high rates in 1980 and this remains the case in 1995. It is, like Hamburg, an example of growth coupled with distressed conditions for a share of the population. Furthermore, high numbers of foreign-born population will result in higher public assistance rates, since foreign-born and work migrants are affected disproportionally by unemployment (due to their lower qualifications) and, thus, represent a higher share of those receiving transfer payments. The same holds true for Duisburg and Dortmund.[2]

With respect to the fiscal situation, all cities had a nominal increase of tax revenues, but there is a great variation in the percentage of tax revenues coming from the city itself; this ratio can be interpreted as an indicator of a city's tax autonomy (cf. Häussermann, Petrowsky and Pohlan 1995). It shows how independent cities are from external resources, be they transfer payments from richer to poorer cities, federal allotments or money borrowed on the financial market. Evidently, this ratio decreased in all six cities, but had reached a remarkably low level in Duisburg and Dortmund. One reason for the dwindling tax base is related to the changes in the industry composition and economic success or failure of companies: the lower revenues from business tax.

Cities thus became more and more dependent on external sources of revenues, but allotments from the federal budget decrease due to the

125

Table 6.2 Selected German cities: socio-economic indicators, 1980, 1990, 1995

Indicator	Year	München	Frankfurt/M.	Hamburg	Bremen	Duisburg	Dortmund
Population	80	1 298 941	629 375	1 645 095	555 118	558 089	608 297
	90	1 229 026	644 865	1 652 363	551 219	535 447	599 055
	95	1 324 208	653 241	1 707 901	549 357	535 250	598 840
% foreign-born	80	16.4	20.6	9.0	6.4	12.2	8.5
	90	22.3	23.9	12.1	10.4	14.9	10.2
	95	21.6	28.8	14.9	13.6	16.3	12.4
% unemployed	85	2.4	3.0	3.3	5.2	6.6	6.1
	90	3.9	5.8	9.7	12.3	11.8	12.1
	95	6.4	9.7	10.8	13.0	15.7	15.1
% on public assistance	80	2.0	3.9	3.4	5.6	3.6	3.0
	90	2.4	6.7	9.1	8.6	6.3	7.8
	95	2.0	6.8	7.7	8.1	6.6[1]	8.8[1]
Expenditures for public assistance	80	48	177	95	148	119	112
	90	*	*	372	*	266	288
DM per inhabitant)	95	168	442	373	423	352[1]	425[1]

Notes: * No data available.
1. Data refer to 1993.

Sources: Statistisches Jahrbuch Deutscher Gemeinden, diverse vols.; Statistical Reports respective cities; own calculations.

Table 6.3 Selected German cities: economic and fiscal indicators, 1980, 1990, 1994

Indicator	Year	München	Frankfurt/M.	Hamburg	Bremen	Duisburg	Dortmund
Debt per inhabitant	80	850	2719	5582	*	2312	1890
(in DM)	90	2192	7272	11677	*	3193	2099
	94	2100	9810	23226	*	3691	2516
Gross value added	80	77687	82735	82842	72760	64591	63417
(DM per employed)	90	130226	144447	124632	104561	105832	98430
	92	149334	169024	141350	116446	107962	113055
Tax power[1]	80	960	1307	1054	820	697	639
(DM per inhabitant)	90	1532	1866	1340	1001	835	844
	93	1622	1856	1505	1181	876	953
Tax Revenues	80	1888911	1326988	2214274	665378	519559	505508
(in 1000 DM)	90	2774193	2040035	3072515	826064	606910	696367
	94	3041343	2119295	3748418	1011324	627608	825280
Fiscal autonomy	80	55.9	63.2	*	*	43.5	39.8
(in %)[2]	90	50.7	53.9	*	*	33.9	33.7
	94	48.3	43.9	*	*	28.2	30.2

Notes: * No data available.
1. Steuerkraft-Meßzahl.
2. Tax revenues as per cent of total revenues.

Sources: Statistisches Jahrbuch Deutscher Gemeinden, diverse vols ; Statistical Reports respective cities; own calculations.

national fiscal problems described above. At any rate, dependence on external sources constrains urban policies: not only do cities lack the financial means for investment, they also become dependent upon the decisions of regional bodies or the *Land*, hence, their decision autonomy is reduced. Local government becomes urban governance, to use a differentiation introduced by Harding (1994: 367–8). In his terminology, local government refers to a restricted set of urban institutions, such as urban parliament and administration, while urban governance refers to local government plus external actors, like regional and state bodies, and their interventions.

A further aspect of the tax revenues is directly related to globalization; major German companies, such as Siemens, do not pay corporate income tax in Germany, instead these transnational companies choose the country with the lowest revenue tax for their tax declaration. In 1995 Siemens total sales amounted to DM88.7 billion, the gross profit was DM2.6 billion, but the DM518 million corporate income tax was not paid in Germany, although 30 per cent of the gross profit came from taxable turnover in Germany (Blüthmann 1996). While this pattern is economically plausible, since every individual taxpayer behaves in much the same way – trying to pay as little tax as possible – this rational behaviour, however, creates dramatic tax losses for the national state, Germany in this case.

Urban debts have increased over time, most remarkably in Frankfurt/M. and in Hamburg,[3] but Frankfurt/M. has experienced the highest increase in gross added value and received the highest tax revenues per inhabitant. Thus, the situation is less critical than that in Dortmund and, again, Duisburg. Munich stands out as being in the best position if the city-state Hamburg is not taken into account. Nonetheless, most cities in Germany have accumulated debts forcing them to spend 10 to 15 per cent of their budget on interest payments.

A major reason for the increasing debt is expenditure on public assistance. (In contrast, unemployment payments come from the Federal Agency of Labour.) The data document the dramatic increase in this type of transfer payment. The increase is due to three processes: a growing percentage of households/persons no longer receiving unemployment aid and instead receiving public assistance; a growing percentage of single-headed households, of which one in three depends on public assistance; a growing number of households comprising repatriated people, or persons seeking political asylum; and finally among households/persons receiving public assistance, a growing percentage receiving continuous public assistance as opposed to one-off assistance.

The combination of a dwindling local tax base, increasing transfer payments and rising shares of the urban budget devoted to interest rates, strangles urban (regeneration) policies. Cities had to cut expenditures in many domains traditionally expected to be funded by urban governments, such as theatre subsidies, social facilities like youth hostels, educational facilities ranging from adult education to universities. Further, public swimming pools were closed, and some cities even cut the water supply for fountains in parks, other cities started to sell (privatize) public enterprises and to privatize public services. To embark on new projects public–private partnerships and external subsidies for such projects were seen as the solution (Heinz and Scholz 1996).

Employment change and unemployment

Obviously, the qualification–employment mismatch, as documented in the mid 1980s for German cities (Friedrichs 1985; Kasarda and Friedrichs 1985) has increased. The available evidence comes from a recent study (Multhaupt 1996) and data on the increase of long-term unemployed (twelve months and more) since 1993. An even more dramatic indication of this trend is the very fact that unemployment rates even in cities experiencing either revitalization, such as Dortmund, renewed growth, such as Frankfurt/Main, or relatively steady growth, such as München, all exhibit rising poverty rates. In the early 1980s, nobody would have assumed the first city to publish an official 'Poverty Report' to be the city of the most continuous economic and demographic growth – München (Stadt München 1991) – followed by reports from Hamburg, Essen and Bremen.

The main conclusion to be drawn from these data is that urban economic revitalization is only loosely coupled to a reduction in unemployment and poverty rates. Thus, we find a rising number of persons designated as 'structurally unemployed'. This in turn, has two negative effects. The first is to constantly increase the transfer payments of the Federal government to the Federal Agency of Labour, which is in charge of unemployment payments. The second is to increase the public assistance payments made by urban governments, which in turn, reduce the fiscal means for investment into attracting new industries into the area. An illustrative example is the 1997 budget the City of Köln. Of the total household budget of DM6.54 billion 28 per cent is spent on debt and interest payments, while a further 23.4 per cent goes on social transfer payments (*Kölner Stadt-Anzeiger*, 12 March 1997). The impact on the urban condition is now analyzed in greater detail.

The impact of de-industrialization and the even stronger impact of a globalized economy had severe repercussions on the German cities. The industrial structure or, more precisely, the diversity of the structure determined to a large extent their propensity for decline. This has been demonstrated by the internal differentiation and change, even of cities in the same old industrialized region – the eleven Ruhr cities (Friedrichs 1996). The data for the six selected cities in Table 6.4 indicate different degrees of diversity in 1980, with Munich and Hamburg occupying the best positions, followed by Frankfurt/M. which stands out for its high share of the banking and insurance sector. All other cities, in particular Duisburg, had high shares of employment in manufacturing – shipbuilding in the case of Bremen – mining and steel, in the cases of Duisburg and Dortmund. They have lower shares in commerce, banking and insurance and to a lesser extent, services sector industries.

By 1994, the differentiation had increased (see Table 6.5). Bremen and Duisburg still have higher shares in manufacturing (and construction) sectors than the other cities, while Munich and Hamburg have expanded the share in services and in banking and insurance. The latter industrial category, again, has the highest share in Frankfurt/Main. Dortmund has achieved an improvement in its employment diversity, compared to Bremen. The changes are summarized in Table 6.6. It

Table 6.4 Selected German cities: employment by industry category, 1980 (per cent)*

Industry category	München	Frankfurt/M.	Hamburg	Bremen	Duisburg	Dortmund
Agriculture	0.3	0. 2	0.5	0.4	0.4	0.3
Mining	0.9	7.6	1.3	1.5	9.9	11.0
Manufacturing	30.9	27.2	23.0	30.7	43.9	29.4
Construction	7.1	6.3	6.3	6.5	6.0	8.7
Commerce	15.8	16.0	20.0	18.1	12.1	16.5
Transport	6.2	11.8	13.2	13.4	8.7	5.1
Insurance, Banking	7.7	10.2	6.8	4.1	2.0	4.4
Services	23.1	19.2	22.2	18.7	12.7	18.5
Non-Profit organizations	2.9	2.7	1.7	1.6	1.2	1.7
Public administration	5.0	5.6	5.4	5.0	3.0	4.3

Note: * Percentages do not add up to 100 due to rounding errors in data.

Sources: Statistisches Jahrbuch Deutscher Gemeinden, diverse volumes; Statistical Reports respective cities, own calculations.

Table 6.5   Selected German cities: employment by industry category, 1994 (per cent)*

Industry category	München	Frankfurt/M.	Hamburg	Bremen	Duisburg	Dortmund
Agriculture	0.4	0.2	0.4	0.3	0.4	0.5
Mining	1.2	7.6	1.2	1.6	4.6	8.2
Manufacturing	21.9	18.8	18.4	27.7	33.5	20.6
Construction	4.9	4.7	5.1	1.2	6.1	6.6
Commerce	14.2	13.6	17.7	16.3	14.0	16.1
Transport	5.7	13.4	11.1	11.3	9.1	6.0
Insurance, Banking	9.6	14.4	7.1	4.3	2.5	5.8
Services	33.1	25.1	30.5	25.1	21.8	28.2
Non-Profit organizations	4.2	4.0	2.8	3.5	2.9	2.9
Public administration	4.9	5.0	5.8	4.6	5.0	5.0

Note: *Percentages do not add up to 100 due to rounding errors in data.

Sources: Statistisches Jahrbuch Deutscher Gemeinden, diverse volumes, Statistical Reports respective cities, own calculations.

shows the dramatic losses cities have experienced in manufacturing jobs and their capacity to compensate for them with new jobs in the service sector. Duisburg lost almost half of its jobs in manufacturing, and Dortmund one third. However, Dortmund fared better in attracting new jobs in the service sector, although the total employment balance is negative. Obviously, München and Frankfurt were the most successful cities in this trajectory.

Conclusions

The analysis allows for several conclusions pertaining to the impact of globalization on the urban condition and the employment structure. First, the industrial structure in 1980 strongly influenced the cities' economic trajectory and their adaptive capacity. To escape the spiral of decline, as suggested in several models (Friedrichs 1993; Richardson 1978) the city had to attract new industries, supply land for development and co-operate at an early stage with the local universities in technology transfer activities. Dortmund managed this earlier than other cities and was quite successful in implementing a revitalization process.

Second, the transformation of cities is accompanied by rising unemployment and rising poverty rates. However, as the sample of the six cities indicates, cities with low diversity in employment opportunities

Table 6.6 Selected German cities: employment change, 1980–94

Indicator	Year	München	Frankfurt/M.	Hamburg	Bremen	Duisburg	Dortmund
Secondary sector	80	256.459	157.571	234.624	97.286	133.079	111.330
	94	187.100	115.000	190.530	85.900	75.500	73.600
% change 1980–94		−27.0	−27.0	−18.8	−11.7	−43.9	−33.9
Tertiary sector	80	401.768	301.126	529.124	153.253	88.270	114.612
	94	480.000	358.000	577.400	161.700	94.300	132.600
% change 1980–94		+19.5	+18.9	+9.1	+5.5	+6.8	+15.7
Total employed	80	660.404	459.538	767.367	251.471	222.167	226.723
	94	669.100	474.000	771.100	248.400	170.600	207.300
% change 1980–94		+1.3	+3.2	+0.5	−1.2	−23.2	−8.6

Sources: Statistisches Jahrbuch Deutscher Gemeinden, diverse volumes, Statistical reports respective cities, own calculations.

are in a much weaker position to 'afford' these problems, since it constrains their budget to a greater extent than is the case for the more successful cities. We, nonetheless, find poverty in all cities to be increasing and to be spatially concentrated in a few urban areas, predominantly those having a high share of social housing dwellings.

Third, traditional and large companies, such as Krupp, Thyssen or Mannesmann, have expanded further their international businesses and transformed their range of products offering a much greater diversity of products and services, for example telecommunications. The subsidies given to their original industrial production offered them the chance, the time and, indirectly, the capital to expand both by buying companies and by establishing new ones. The effects are positive for the company: the greater stability of a now more diverse company (TNC), but not to the region, because the new jobs created were in other cities or regions and not in the old industrialized ones. (This process remains to be documented more precisely.)

Fourth, TNCs have via the Employers' Association strongly influenced national policy towards more deregulation of labour tariffs. This impact has led to a reduction of welfare provisions, and these in turn have aggravated the problems of employed and unemployed, particularly in cities with less favourable conditions, for example by further reducing tax revenues both from companies and from households, due to their reduced spending power.

The data thus support the propositions set forth in the introductory section. In particular, the three-fold impact of TNCs seems to be a fruitful way to specify the relation between globalization and the lower aggregate levels of 'nation' and 'city'. Finally, we may conclude from the data that the industrial diversity of a city at the beginning of the de-industrialization process strongly influences the city's economic and demographic trajectory. Globalization seems to reinforce the tendencies formerly observed for de-industrialization.

Notes

1. Due to a decision of the Federal Court in 1996 this subsidy no longer has to be paid by households, it therefore comes from the federal budget.
2. It should be noted that Hamburg and Bremen are city-states, hence public assistance expenditures are not fully comparable to those of the other cities.
3. See note 2.

7

A Comparative Perspective on Large-Scale Migration and Social Exclusion in US Entry-Point Cities

William A.V. Clark

Introduction

Mass migration, or more simply the large-scale shifts of population from less developed to more developed regions of the world, and especially to Europe and the United States, is a renewed phenomenon of the late 20th century. Such large-scale flows occurred at earlier points in US history and created the complex and richly textured structure of US society. At the turn of the century, immigrants from Britain and northern and southern Europe, and later Russia, slowly created a mixed and polyglot society. Whether or not one subscribes to the ideas of an assimilationist and integrated society, there is no doubt that the flows of such different ethnic groups slowly created a new and more 'mixed' society than had previously existed in a nation state. The nature of this mixed society, its composition and variation, are well established (Gordon 1964). The recent change from a society largely composed of European migrants, to a society with increasing numbers of Hispanic migrants from Central and South America, and Asian migrants from a dozen different countries, is equally well known (Edmonston and Passel 1994). At the same time, the local variations and the local outcomes of the recent changes in migration are less well established. It is these local variations which are central to the discussions in the present chapter. Even though the national level effects are strenuously debated, do immigrants pay more in taxes than they cost in services? Do migrants affect the wages of the native-born low skilled population? These debates miss the geography of variation in immigrant outcomes and indeed, ignore the affects in just those entry-point cities which may well have the most lasting effects of recent immigration.

Context and theoretical background

There are two strongly held views of recent large-scale immigration in the USA. On the one hand, Kennedy (1996) and Simon (1989) see the recent flows as ultimately beneficial for the migrants, for the USA and for the countries of origin. On the other hand, Borjas (1995) and Bouvier (1991) see recent large-scale immigration as a serious national problem. There is an extensive continuum between Simon (1989) at one extreme, and Bouvier (1991) at the other. Of course the positions on the role of immigration also vary by ethnic group, by ideological position and by economic interest. Despite the intensity of the national debate, or perhaps because of the intensity of the national debate, almost all the studies neglect what is an equally important part of the discussion about immigration. What are the local outcomes? What are the effects of fundamental changes in the scale and composition of immigration on local communities, and especially on the entry-point cities? While the focus in this chapter is on a set of US entry-point cities, the theoretical issues are similar to those in Europe, and now to those in Australia, Canada and New Zealand as well.

The state of the art issues for this presentation revolve around the competing views outlined above and the role of spatial segregation and concentration as the factors which may exacerbate the negative effects of low skills and low incomes. There is increasing evidence that spatial concentrations of long-term unemployed can severely limit knowledge about jobs and opportunities (Wilson 1996). A lack of contacts leads in turn to lack of information about jobs. In the extreme, the concentration and segregation of new immigrants, leads to segregation in other forms of urban life, and in the end to a divided society (Huttman, Saltman and Blauw 1991; Sassen 1994).

Theories about skills and skill acquisition

The concern about local effects of recent immigration is related to a complex interaction of (a) the correlation of the skills of immigrants and the skills of their American born children, (b) the relationship of poverty and success levels and (c) the extent of social exclusion.

It appears that the skill levels of the citizen children of recent immigrants are closely related to the skill levels of their immigrant parents

(Borjas 1994). The explanation for the high correlation between the skills and earnings of ethnic groups over time draws on the notions of Coleman (1988) who argues that parental background and the quality of the ethnic environment influence the rate of intergenerational mobility between parents and children. Borjas (1994: 1713) tested the relative importance of parental inputs and ethnic 'spillovers' on the intergenerational process and confirmed that there is a great deal of persistence in ethnic skill differentials over time.

Success levels are also influenced by language acquisition and use (Chiswick and Miller 1995, 1996). As they note, language skills are an important form of human capital, perhaps even the most important initial form of human capital, and are clearly related to the acquisition of training and skills in general. The empirical tests of the value of English language acquisition show that individuals who speak only English at home, or who speak English well or very well, are likely to have higher earnings than individuals who have difficulties with the English language (Chiswick and Miller 1996: 29). They estimate that the payoff for language fluency is in the order of 16 to 18 per cent over an individual's working life, if the investment in language skills takes a year, and as much as 35 per cent if the acquisition can be accomplished in six months. An important additional finding is that only 55 per cent of the Spanish foreign-born language group are fluent in English compared to around 80 per cent for other language groups (Chiswick and Miller 1996: 13). This further decreases the potential success levels for the largest group of recent migrants to the USA. The finding is consistent with the research which suggests that those groups which are larger, which are more likely to inter-marry, and where the networks in general are stronger, are also likely to be less skilled in the host country's language (Evans 1986). That it is this group which may be disadvantaged will be an important part of understanding the potential for lower success levels and exclusion.

Incomes and poverty

While skills and language are an important part of the trajectories of immigrant success, that trajectory of success is also affected by family income and poverty levels. Of course these factors are not independent of skill levels and indeed greater income is likely to mean higher education levels and a greater impetus to emphasize education as a means to higher earnings. In general the research shows that there are powerful and long lasting effects of growing up in poverty. The work by

Duncan and others (1994) and by Haveman and Wolfe (1995) shows that low income children do not recover from the disadvantages of low parental income, and have one to two years less schooling by the time of young adulthood, and consequently lower earnings. The impact of low income for young children is greater of course for those children who are likely also to have lower language skills.

The third force which is likely to influence the success levels of recent immigrants and their long-term integration into the host society is the level of poverty which is, of course, in turn the outcome of low family income and poor language skills. This is not to argue that individual migrants will not be successful in transcending deprived family backgrounds, but the aggregate affects are such that larger numbers of new immigrants will be more likely to end up in poverty, and potentially in social exclusion. In this analysis the emphasis is on documenting the extent to which the intersection of low skill levels, low earnings and increasing poverty are creating the potential for social exclusion. The levels of social exclusion are measured by the extent of linguistic isolation. The study shows that over time the levels of skills are declining, the earnings decreasing and poverty rates increasing. If the immigration flows remain unchanged, it is likely that very large skill differences among new immigrants will exacerbate the differences between native-born whites, those immigrant groups with high skill levels, and recent unskilled immigrants, who will continue to languish at the margins of society.

It is the intersection of the three dimensions just discussed which is at the heart of social exclusion. Spatial concentration is the outcome of both internal ethnic preferences and the inability to escape inner city low income, poor quality housing. It is in this sense that the low skills, and consequent low earnings, and high levels of poverty generate concentrated areas of new immigrants. If the immigrants reaching such areas have increasingly poor preparation for a post-industrial world, and if the safety net of the welfare state is also reduced, then the possibility for long-term poverty and increasing economic and social polarization (Rhein 1996), or at the very least the marginalization of such groups is a very real possibility (Cross 1992a; Musterd 1994).

Previous findings and research strategy

The nine entry-point cities, which will be used in the analysis in this study, represent the nine states with about 70 per cent of the recent flows to the USA as measured in the 1990 census. In the last decade

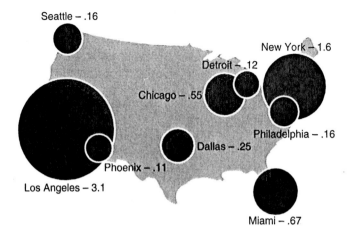

Figure 7.1 Immigration flow (in millions) 1980–94

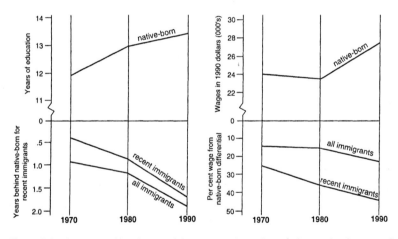

Figure 7.2 Average education and income trajectories of the native-born and immigration groups for nine metropolitan areas

and a half of intense migration about 13.7 million new migrants have been added to the US population. The flows to the nine entry-point metropolitan regions themselves between 1980 and 1994 are approximately 50 per cent of all flows to the USA in that period. The flows vary from almost 3.2 million to the Los Angeles County region to only 0.1 of a million to Seattle. Previous research on the nine entry-point

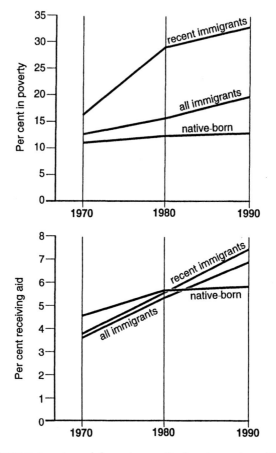

Figure 7.3 Average poverty and dependency ratio for nine metropolitan areas

cities has shown that over time successive waves of immigrants are
doing less well than previous groups (Clark 1998). That research can be
summarized in two diagrams which show the *average* changes of the
nine cities in skill, income, poverty and dependency levels over time.

The average of the trajectories of years of education for the nine
immigrant destinations has been increasing for the native-born population and decreasing for both recent and all immigrants as a group.
Native-born populations have gained almost a year and half of education in the past two decades. While the native-born population has
been improving their general skill levels, the immigrant population has

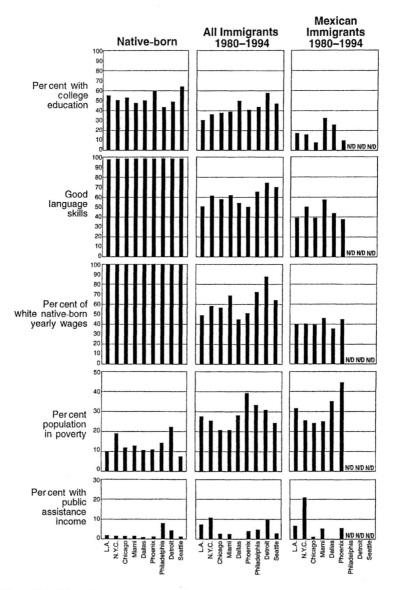

Figure 7.4 Education, income and dependency levels for nine metropolitan areas

Source: Current Population Survey (*poverty and language data from PUMS, 1980–90)

been falling further behind the native-born population. While new immigrants were only about a half year behind in 1970, by 1990 they were almost two years behind, and were almost coincident with immigrants as a whole. Thus, even though new immigrants in 1990 had more years of education than immigrants in 1970, they were not increasing their skills sufficient to keep pace with the native-born population. Not surprisingly the wage differentials were also increasing.

The averages for the nine cities for the native-born showed a slight decrease in constant dollars between 1970 and 1980 but a reasonable increase between 1980 and 1990, though still less than two per cent per year. Wages for all immigrants had decreased from 14 per cent less than the native-born, to almost 24 per cent less, and immigrants who had arrived in the past five years earned 46 per cent less than the native-born in 1990. These rates are substantially 'worse' than those for the USA as a whole and greater than for the individual states of which these entry-point cities are a part. Poverty rates and welfare use parallel the trajectories of skills and wage levels. Although recent immigrants were more likely to be in poverty in 1970, the difference between the native-born and new immigrants was only six per cent. By 1990 the difference was 20 per cent.

The paths of poverty for the native-born, all immigrants and recent immigrants are also quite different. The native-born population in poverty has increased only two per cent over the past 20 years, but the recent immigrant population in poverty has increased from 17 per cent to 33 per cent. The increases in the proportion in poverty are paralleled with increases in the dependent population. The average proportion of the native-born population receiving assistance increased about one per cent over the past 20 years. The change for the immigrant groups was much greater. Overall the proportion receiving assistance doubled in the same 20 year period.

The focus in the present analysis is on the migrants in the last decade and a half and uses data from the Current Population Survey for 1994 or the 1990 Public Use Micro Data samples. Both data sets are individual level data which can be used to examine the skill levels, as measured by the percentage of the population with a college education and levels of language proficiency (the proportion of the population who speak English well or very well), wages, and levels of poverty and dependency. The analysis of social exclusion uses the census tract level data from STF 3 tapes for the nine entry-point cities to calculate levels of concentration of the recent foreign-born population and their levels of linguistic isolation.

Analysis and observations

To reiterate, the analysis in this study expands on the structure of recent flows into the nine entry-point cities, and with that data as a background examines in greater detail the patterns of the foreign-born and recent immigrants in neighbourhoods in Los Angeles County.

Changing levels of skills, earnings and implications for poverty

When we examine the nine entry-point cities in detail there are both striking similarities and important differences. Naturally, there is variation across these entry-point cities. The data on skills, earnings, and measures of poverty and dependency across the cities for the last wave of immigrants (those who arrived between 1980 and 1994) reveal strong contrasts between west coast and southern entry points on the one hand, and the rest of the immigrant cities on the other.

There is, as expected, a contrast between the ratios of the native-born population with a college education and ratios of college educated for all immigrants who arrived in this past decade and a half. The native-born population with a college education varies around 50 per cent. For the immigrant population the variation is between 30 and 40 per cent, although Dallas and Detroit are over 50 per cent, and there is not a great deal of variation between the native-born and immigrants in Detroit and Philadelphia. Of course to some extent this reflects the lower college education rates of the large black populations in those cities, which depresses the average levels of the native born population. Los Angeles and New York show up as having the lowest education levels, as measured by college education. Language skills parallel the patterns of college education.

There is much greater variation in immigrant wages, as measured by the per cent of the native-born white wage levels. Immigrant wage levels in Detroit, Philadelphia and Seattle approach 70 per cent of white native-born wages, but Los Angeles, Dallas and Phoenix barely reach 50 per cent. And, the immigrant poverty population in those latter cities is also high. At the same time it is also high in Philadelphia and Detroit. Public assistance is used by a relatively small proportion of all immigrants which is related to legal eligibility requirements but there are instances of relatively high uses of public assistance.

The results provide support for an argument about bifurcation in immigrant groups and across cities. Immigrants in Los Angeles, Dallas and Phoenix are doing much worse than those in Seattle, Philadelphia and even Detroit, and this may be true independent of variations in composition. Clearly, some immigrants are doing well enough to create an immigrant population with college rates of 40 per cent, and incomes almost 70 per cent of the white native-born. The results provide additional support for the Waldinger and Bozorgmehr (1996) arguments which emphasize the importance of decomposing immigrant groups. The data for Mexican immigrants provide a window on this issue. For this group of immigrants the education rates are low, the wages less than 40 per cent of the white native-born population and the poverty rates in the case of Phoenix, are over 40 per cent. A simple logit model which examines the probability of immigrants having a college education illustrates the complex interrelationship of age, sex, period of entry and country of origin.

The data are for immigrants in the workforce and over 25 years of age. The variables and models are significant for all cities. The levels of explanation, as measured by correct predictions and rho square, indicate that the models fit very well to reasonably well, except for New York and Miami. There is considerable detail in Table 7.1, but the essential point for this study is the relative impact of country of origin on the likelihood of having a college education. Clearly age plays a role, and for half of the cities older immigrants do not have college experience, but for Miami, Dallas, Detroit and Seattle, older immigrants do have college experience. Again, the results testify to the impact of the type of immigrant entering particular cities. But, for our analysis it is significant that for every city the coefficient for Mexican/Central American origin or Southeast Asian origin, is one of the most important standardized predictors of the likelihood of college experience. The importance of this finding is twofold. First, it is a quantitative assessment of the earlier visual presentation about the proportions of new migrants with college experience. Second, the results reiterate the potential problems of bifurcation of immigrant experience. In the past waves of immigration, neither immigrants nor the native-born had significant educational experience. Now the issue is increasingly the role of education in success in the labour market. The data for a sub-set of the immigrant entry-point cities emphasize the problems of large numbers of labour market participants who do not have, nor are likely to acquire, adequate educational training to compete in a post-industrial society.

There are two obvious conclusions from the analysis to this point. First, there are quite large-scale local effects and that these effects vary across cities. The findings in this chapter extend those from an earlier

Table 7.1 Logistic coefficients for college/no college as a function of age and background

	Los Angeles	New York	Chicago	Miami	Dallas	Phoenix	Philadelphia	Detroit	Seattle
Age	-.077 **2**	-.112 **2**	-.146 **1**	.039 **3**	.230 **2**	-.632 **1**	-.355 **1**	.122 **2**	.446 **4**
Age Sq.	.001 **3**	.001 **3**	.001 **3**	-.001 **1**	-.003 **1**	.007 **2**	.003 **2**	-.002 **1**	-.006 **3**
Nat. citizen	.700 **4**	.635 **4**	.848 **4**	1.332 **2**	-.055	-1.364 **4**	2.011 **3**	-.812 **3**	.657
Mex. Origin	-2.650 **1**	-1.042	-2.301 **2**	-.122	-2.777 **3**	-4.543 **3**	-1.661 **4**	-1.065 **4**	26.40
S. Asian origin	-1.537	-26.10 **1**	–	–	-2.332 **4**	–	.351	-.813	-27.85 **2**
Since 1986	.297	-.368	.156	.634 **4**	1.355	1.353	-.650	.390	26.72 **1**
Male	.083	.205	.707	.089	-.301	.628	-.271	-.299	-.881
Intercept	2.920	2.496	3.196	.836	-2.912	15.84	8.611	-.426	-8.150
Rho sq.	.67	.23	.55	.33	.63	.82	.56	.40	.49
Correct pred.	83%	61%	77%	66%	81%	91%	78%	69%	73%

Note: bold numerals indicate the relative size of the standardized coefficients.

Source: US Bureau of the Census, Current Population Survey, 1994.

investigation (Clark 1998), of the temporal changes in immigrant skill wage and poverty levels. The second conclusion which can be drawn from this analysis is that there is evidence that even though skill levels may have declined over time there is still a substantial proportion of immigrants who are matching, or will match, native-born skills and salaries. The data from the logit analysis demonstrate clearly that Mexican origin, or refugee immigrants, pose the greatest likelihood for social exclusion, poverty and dependency.

What is the evidence that these lower skills and poorer earnings may be translated into greater concentrations of poverty, dependency and social exclusion? The study now turns to measuring the extent of that isolation and exclusion and the nature of that concentration in Los Angeles as a case study.

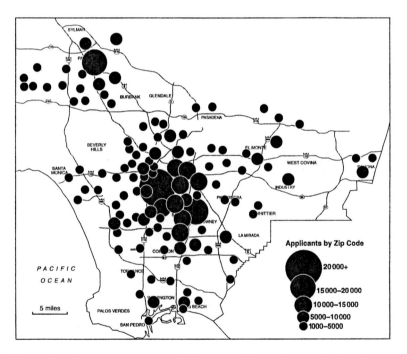

Figure 7.5 The concentration of Mexican origin applicants for legalization under IRCA

Source: Michael Hoefer, The Legalization Program in California. Los Angeles, Fourth Annual Demographic Workshop, 1991.

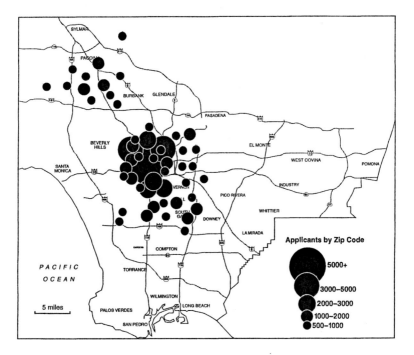

Figure 7.6 The concentration of Central American applicants for legalization under IRCA

Source: Michael Hoefer, The Legalization Program in California. Los Angeles, Fourth Annual Demographic Workshop, 1991.

Measuring spatial concentration and social exclusion

Los Angeles with the largest single influx of recent immigrants is an appropriate case study for analyzing the nature and extent of immigrant concentration and associated social exclusion. To gain a visual impact of immigrant concentration I use the 1990 requests for amnesty under the Immigration and Reform Control Act (IRCA) of 1986. That act was designed to convert illegal to documented residents, and applied to migrants who had been resident prior to 1982, but it also allowed Special Agricultural Workers to request documentation with as little as three months residency. These requests for legalized status have been plotted by zip codes (postal codes) for Mexican and Central American immigrants. The Mexican and Central American applicants were almost totally concentrated within a seven mile radius of the

Central Business district. The concentration of Central American migrants in neighbourhoods close to the downtown is especially intense. But even the much larger Mexican migrant population is notable for the concentration in inner city neighbourhoods and reiterates the well established tendency of new immigrants to cluster in central locations. It is this spatially concentrated area which is the basis of the specific study of immigrant concentration.

Spatial concentration

While overall numbers and proportions are one part of the story of a potential underclass population, the extent to which the poverty population is concentrated, is an additional important element of the future trajectory of immigrant dependent populations. The literature provides considerable evidence that distressed neighbourhoods with large numbers of poor can decrease the chances of success of those who locate in such neighbourhoods (Abramson and Tobin 1995; Kasarda 1993). If

Table 7.2 Distribution and concentration of the foreign born, recent migrants and linguistically isolated in Los Angeles County

	Tract Concentration		
	Number of tracts (%)		
Cumulative % of variable	Foreign born	Recent migrants 1985-90	Linguistically isolated
20	107 (6.3%)	78 (4.7%)	77 (4.7%)
50	371 (22.5%)	298 (18.1%)	355 (21.6%)
80	844 (51.2%)	727 (44.1%)	628 (38.2%)

Distribution
of tracts:

	Foreign born	Recent migrants 1985-90	Linguistically isolated
90th Percentile	10,126		
3rd Quartile			5949
Median			
1st Quartile			
10th Percentile	2328	2965	
	1355	521	1139
	740	260	450
		117	165

these persons are foreign-born, recently arrived and linguistically isolated, we identify an at risk population of poverty and dependency. Again, the argument is not that all recent Hispanic immigrants are poor, nor that all of the new immigrants will fall into poverty. Rather the argument is about the concentration of a poor and isolated population with consequent effects on their long-term trajectory within the host society.

What are the levels of concentration? The foreign-born population is almost 31 per cent of the total population and 20 per cent are in 6.1 per cent of the census tracts in Los Angeles County. If we think of the tracts as neighbourhoods, then the level of concentration is very high. Fifty per cent of the foreign-born are in a little over a fifth of all tracts. Recent migrants (those who arrived between 1985 and 1990) make up about 7 per cent of the total Los Angeles County population but 20 per cent of them are concentrated in only 6.5 per cent of the tracts. Fifty per cent of the recent immigrants are in less than one fifth of the neighbourhoods. The most telling statistic which speaks directly to social isolation from mainstream society is the concentration of the linguistically isolated, the population which speaks only a non-English language, or does not speak English well. Twenty per cent of these people are located in only 4.7 per cent of the neighbourhoods and 50 per cent are again in about one fifth of all tracts.

A graphical portrayal of the spread of these measures of concentration shows that some neighbourhoods have very large numbers of foreign-born. At least one large tract has more than ten thousand foreign-born persons (see Table 7.2). But, perhaps even more notable, a quarter of all tracts had at least 2300 foreign-born persons. The number of recent migrants (those who arrived between 1985–90) is lower but again a quarter of all of the tracts had at least 500 recent immigrants. It is in these neighbourhoods that the linguistically isolated are heavily concentrated. A quarter of all tracts had a minimum of 1139 linguistically isolated persons and the most intense concentrations were in tracts with over 5000 persons.

The spatial analysis focuses on census tracts with majority Hispanic populations and on the concentrated areas of applicants for amnesty shown in Figures 7.5 and 7.6. The larger Hispanic majority population is a sprawling region from the eastern valley communities of Sylmar and Pacoima to suburban-like communities in Southgate,. Downey, Pico Rivera and El Monte. There is considerable diversity across this larger region but within it there is a sub-set of tracts with high levels of recent immigration, linguistic isolation and associated poverty and

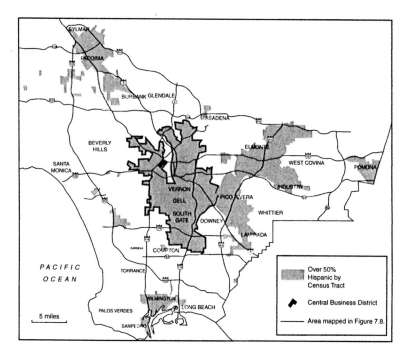

Figure 7.7   Tracts with 50 per cent or more Hispanic population

crowding. The core set of 240 tracts portrayed in Figure 7.8 has high
levels of all characteristics. Nearly half the tracts have more than 30 per
cent of the population in poverty, and half the tracts have high levels
of room crowding (more than 1.50 persons per room). The core region
has nearly 42 per cent of the Los Angeles County Hispanic poverty
population and 42 per cent of the Hispanic population classified as linguistically isolated. If we place these results in the theoretical context
of limited outcomes of limited access to education, and the impacts of
low incomes on children's success levels, then the impact of these concentrations takes on significance beyond the debates about immigrants
at the national level. The data here suggest a very constrained potential
for immigrants, or their children, to escape the low end jobs, the associated poverty and the round of continuing restricted opportunities.
The data are yet another confirmation of the Ortiz (1996) aggregate
findings that Hispanics in Los Angeles are unlikely to follow positive
immigrant trajectories.

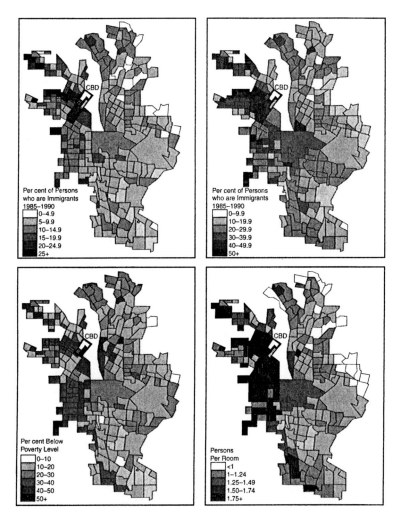

Figure 7.8 Concentrations of the proportion of recent immigrants linguistic isolation, poverty, and crowding in 1990 by census tract. See Figure 7.7 for location within metropolitan Los Angeles

Conclusion

The issue is the future of the concentrated populations we have been examining and brings us back to the dual conceptions of recent mass migration. One view emphasizes such inner city communities as way stations to the larger (integrated) society. A second less sanguine view asks whether the process of the past will/can occur in the late 20th century. The increasing evidence of poorer adaptation, lower wages and increasing dependency suggests that the old *laissez faire* approach to immigration has potential problems.

Within Los Angeles there appears to be an emerging spatial concentration which is similar to inner city concentrations of black poverty. Immigration is creating and sustaining a 'balkanization' of society in which ethnic groups are competing for inner city housing space. The demographic trends of white flight, and now black middle class flight also, to distant suburbs and the large-scale immigration of a low skill and often poorly educated population appear to be trapping these new arrivals in poverty and isolation in overcrowded inner city neighbourhoods.

The data in this study are yet another piece of evidence that documents the increasing problem for new Hispanic migrants for whom the traditional ethnic saga of hard work is unlikely to lead to upward and outward mobility. In fact the evidence from this study provides specific evidence, albeit ecological, of the effects of low education levels and linguistic isolation on increasing poverty in inner city neighbourhoods. If this data is placed along side the anecdotal data on high drop-out rates, street gangs and inner city crime, the outcomes for these new migrants are likely, without significant social intervention, to be a long downward spiral into poverty and hopelessness.

These conclusions can also be set within the recent changes in public assistance. The Personal Responsibility and Work Reconciliation Act (welfare reform) removes many of the support services which were available to recent but legal immigrants (Clark and Schultz 1997b). While the estimates vary considerably, there is evidence that several hundred thousand immigrants will be ineligible for basic support services or will have the already modest benefits further reduced. It is this context that concentrations of 'at risk' populations may become the new underclass.

8
Globalization Effects on Employment in Southern California, 1970–90

Ivan Light, Rebecca Kim and Connie Hum

In the broadest sense, globalization refers to all processes that incorporate the peoples of the world into a single world society (Nederveen Pieterse 1994: 161). These processes are economic, cultural and political. However, in the narrower economic sense used here, globalization means movement toward a globally integrated market for labour and capital, especially the latter. *Global restructuring* is economic globalization in process. Global restructuring theory accounts for a multiplicity of linked changes around the world in terms of the resurgent power of financial capital in a world with ever fewer barriers to trade. At the core, restructuring theory calls attention to local economic changes produced by resource shifts in the globalized market. In that global market, capital flows freely across international boundaries in response to profit incentives and labour, more inhibited, flows more freely than before (McLean Petras 1983: 48–9; Zolberg 1991). One could dub this scenario the production of the local by the global.

Global restructuring theory proclaims the supremacy of big capital. The agents of global restructuring are transnational corporations and money-centre banks that, spanning continents, reallocate jobs and work among them in response to profit incentives and indifferent to political or cultural loyalties or boundaries (Bornschier and Stamm 1990). These transnational corporations and banks are the dominant actors in the globalized economy. Additionally, restructuring theory claims that profit incentives have created an international urban hierarchy centred upon three world cities and a number of supporting major cities. From these supreme organizing nodes, London, Tokyo and New York in Sassen's influential account, transnational business corporations reach out to control the regional economies they penetrate.[1] As a result, local and regional economies operate more than previously as players in an international script written by distant financiers.[2]

From this core claim, restructuring theory extracts three key propositions. First, restructuring theory proposes that in the new, globalized world, multinational and transnational corporations strip middle-level production jobs away from high-priced workers in developed countries, assigning their tasks instead to newly opened factories in cheap-labour countries of the Third World.[3] Second, as jobs exportation unravels, transnational corporations centre financial control, producer services and advanced technology in Japan, Western Europe and the United States (Savitch 1990: 151; Scott and Storper 1993: 3–4, 11). Third, both these changes alter the income structure of these developed countries (Sassen 1988: 22–3, 136). That is, the expansion of these highly paid sectors increases the number and share of the most affluent in these countries while the ex-production workers increase the number and share of the poor.[4] The middle class dwindles in size while the numbers of the wealthy and of the poor increase.

Globalization, migration and informalization

Moore and Pinderhughes declare that, 'The growth of an informal economy is part and parcel of late twentieth-century economic restructuring' (Moore and Pinderhughes 1993: xxvii). This judgement epitomizes restructuring theory, which explains the growth of informal economies in the developed countries as a by-product of newly polarized income distributions arising from global restructuring (Sassen 1988: 484–5; Sassen-Koob 1989: 70; see also Sassen-Koob 1985: 255).[5] Continuing, restructuring theorists explain immigration in terms of growing effective demand for the products of cheap, immigrant labour.[6] At the top of the income distribution, newly rich, dual earner households need servants, gardeners and nannies (Wrigley 1997, chapter 9). Immigrants from poor countries will take these low-wage jobs; unemployed native workers will not.[7] These immigrant workers receive no social security benefits, no employer-paid health care, their wages are not reported to tax officials and their job tenure is casual. Therefore, underpaid employees of rich households cannot afford mainstream products and services that require a mainstream income. Like the newly impoverished natives of the ex-middle class, dismissed from their production jobs, they look for discounted goods produced and sold in the informal sector. Like the rich, the immigrant poor buy

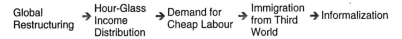

Figure 8.1 Globalization, immigration and informalization

clothing manufactured in the informal sector. Unlike the rich, who buy them in fancy boutiques, the workers of the informal sector and the distressed ex-middle class natives buy cheap garments manufactured in the informal sector from informal sector vendors.

Figure 8.1 shows how globalization theorists explain immigration and informalization. Their explanation is linear (Frey 1996–97: 26). First, global restructuring changes the income structure of the advanced countries, increasing the number and share of the wealthy in total income while diminishing the income share of the poor but increasing their number. The hour-glass income distribution creates demand for low-priced goods the poor can afford as well as for personal services the rich wish to buy. Responding to the new demand for personal servants as well as for informal production workers, immigrants from poor countries swarm into the great cities of the developed world where they produce both. Much of this production is informal. Whether they work for wealthy households or for industrial sweatshops, the immigrant poor receive substandard pay and benefits, often paid in cash. However, in this view, globalization-induced changes in demand completely explain immigration and informalization.[8]

Critique of restructuring theory

Restructuring theory parsimoniously links economic processes in the advanced and developing countries, thus crafting a coherent vision of a master process of which immigration and informalization are incidental by-products. No wonder restructuring theory has enjoyed wide popularity. However, as arguments have matured, globalization theory has attracted criticism of basically three sorts. One criticism addresses globalization's overemphasis upon global structure at the expense of local agency as well as its economism and linear determinism.[9] Here economism means overemphasis upon market forces to the neglect of cultural, social and political responses (see Fernandez-Kelly and Garcia 1989: 250; and Fligstein 1997). Determinism means the utter elimination of political choice and of immigrant agency.[10] Thus, Logan and Swanstrom observe that the global restructuring literature represents markets as natural forces separable from and superior to national and local states.[11] Instead, they insist that 'a great deal more [political] discretion exists to shape economic and urban restructuring than is commonly believed' (Logan and Swanstrom 1990: 5–6). Kloosterman declares that interregional differences prove that restructuring does not determine urban outcomes (Kloosterman 1996b: 468). Marxist critics have taken a similar tack. Gottdiener and Komninos wish to escape 'one-dimensional, deterministic explanations' in order to forge 'approaches that consider political and cultural as well as economic dimensions' (Gottdiener and Komninos 1989: 8).

A second critical direction, upon which this chapter builds, claims that restructuring wrongly seeks to explain immigration that is actually produced by related but distinct causes. This argument exposes the unwarranted extension of restructuring theory's reach beyond its grasp. One case in evidence here is migration networks whose effects have been wrongly attributed to global restructuring. Migration networks build strength as migrations mature and the mature networks assume responsibility for migrations, eclipsing the global forces that initially caused them (G. Simon 1995: 220; see also Light 1999). Therefore, globalization no more explains immigration than eating explains digestion. A complete explanation of immigration requires attention to the independent role of migration networks just as a complete explanation of digestion requires attention to the independent role of stomach acids and enzymes.

A related case already in evidence is the immigrant economy in the immigration-receiving countries. Immigrant economy is the employment sector that arises when immigrant employers hire other immigrants. The immigrant economy has only been studied in the garment industries of Amsterdam and Los Angeles, but its presence in other industries is undeniable (Light, Bernard and Kim 1999). Cornelius has produced the only measure of the immigrant economy's total size. In his labour market study of San Diego, Cornelius found that immigrant employers hired one-third of all immigrant workers in the city.[12] Naturally, these hires expanded the immigrants' job base beyond what the American economy would have provided, thus expanding the carrying capacity of San Diego. When they hire other immigrants, immigrant entrepreneurs utilize their human capital, social capital and cultural capital. All these resources originate outside the destination economy, in the lands of their origin and none owes its existence to the demand of the metropolitan economy for cheap labour. Therefore, to the extent that immigrant economies swell the employment of immigrant workers above and beyond what native employers would offer, it is incorrect to claim that migration from the Third World is a product of globally restructured demand in the labour importing countries.

Finally, globalization need not exclude other explanations of immigration-linked economic changes in the developed countries. As Massey and his colleagues (1993: 448) have observed, '... the conditions that initiate international movement' need not 'perpetuate it across time and space.' Just as, to continue the metaphor, eating precedes and induces but does not complete digestion so globalization may initiate migration-linked economic changes that, once underway, owe their continuation and expansion to causes that did not engender them. In this case, path dependent causalities offer more satisfactory explanatory models than simple ones. Pursuing this approach, Light has proposed the concept of 'spill-over migration' to accommodate migrations whose motor changes from globalization-induced demand to migration networks in midstream (Light 1999). In this case, as Hamnett has explained, declining incomes at the bottom end result from labour markets saturated by network-driven migration rather than from independent dynamics of the host economy.[13]

What is demand-driven migration?

To illustrate and amplify these criticisms, developed already elsewhere, we review below the extensive globalization research on Los Angeles, seeking to understand what economic effects global restructuring theory can and cannot explain. Our point of departure in this endeavour is dual. One is a theoretical explication of what a demand-driven migration would entail; another is a close empirical look at whether Los Angeles really experienced a demand-driven migration from the Third World between 1970 and 1990. The Los Angeles case does not, we submit, represent the demand-driven migration that global restructuring theory requires. Rather, the evidence suggests, migration to Los Angeles quickly changed motors from the demand side to the supply side as migration networks took control. In this metropolitan case, an important one for global restructuring theory, evidence points to the need for more complex models of migration and informalization than global restructuring theory delivers.[14]

What, after all, does demand-driven migration require? Global restructuring theorists have not even raised this question, much less answered it. However, so long as they remain demand-driven, demand-driven migrations are insatiable consumers of migrant labour. Insatiability arises because, as the receiving economy grows, partially because of immigrant labour, the demand for additional immigrants grows apace. The more immigrants enter the demand-driven economy, the more the economy grows; and the more the economy grows, the more immigrants the economy demands. A key indicator of unsatisfied demand for immigrant labour is high and rising real wages and relative wages that keep up with or surpass the real wages of native-born workers. Another is an unemployment rate among immigrants that does not increase during the demand-driven phase of the migration. In the past, when the demand-driven phase of an immigration has ended, declining real wages of immigrant workers have developed because earlier cohorts of immigrant workers partially or fully saturated labour demand for immigrant labour. As labour markets approach saturation, the real and relative wages of immigrants fall. In fully saturated labour markets, the real wages of immigrants are zero and immigrant unemployment reaches 100 per cent. Declining real and relative wages of immigrants are a sign that immigrant labour niches are deteriorating. Therefore, whatever else may drive them, immigrations that continue in the face of declining real wages are *not* demand-driven.

Two historic examples help to frame this issue independent of Los Angeles, the case in evidence here. During the Great Migration of European whites to the USA, between 1880 and 1914, real wages of the native whites declined about 10 per cent. Although the wages of European immigrants, male and female alike, were consistently higher than or as high as those of the native whites, their real wages declined too (Blau 1980: 37; Fraundorf 1978: 219; Shergold 1976: 459–60). This decline suggests that European immigrants continued to arrive in the USA in great number after their real wages had begun to decline. Evidently, even the robust economy of the USA could not absorb all the immigrant labour that arrived without wage declines. However, precisely that absorption defines demand-driven immigration. Therefore, in a strict sense, the Great Migration of European whites was not demand-driven in its second phase even if it was demand-driven in the first phase. After the demand-driven phase ended, and real wages began to decline, something other than demand continued the Great Migration.

A second example tells a comparable story. During the interwar migration of five million native blacks from the American south to northern, central (Harrison 1991: vii) and western cities – a major transformation of American society in the 20th century – the earliest black migrants received real wages as strong as those paid later black migrants until 1929. In that depression year demand for urban labour collapsed. The real wages of black migrants naturally dropped, remaining low until 1942 when war production began. Black migration from the south declined drastically at the beginning of the Great Depression in apparent response to declining real wages. The co-ordinated decline of real wages and of inter-state black migration signalled a demand-driven migration because when the demand slackened, the migration slackened. War production hugely increased the real wages of southern blacks, raising them well past the real wages blacks had received before the Great Depression. War production also reinvigorated a black migration that had slowed during the Great Depression but had not stopped (Groh 1972: 60; Trotter and Lewis 1996: 251). When the war ended in 1945, and war production ended too, demand for black production workers slowed, and the real wages of migrant black workers declined through to 1970 (Groh 1972: 113; Henri 1975). *Nonetheless*, the black migration continued unabated until 1970 despite the decline in real wages, prompting Sydney Walton to declare the continuing migration economically irrational (Walton 1994: 38).

This second historical example shows that postwar black inter-state migration rolled on for 15 years after real wages of inter-state migrants dropped in 1946. It also shows that abrupt declines in labour demand (caused first by depression and later by peace) reduced real wages for black migrants from the south. Therefore, judging by its decline after 1929 and recrudescence in 1942, the internal migration of blacks from Dixie was only demand-driven up to the Second World War. The inter-state migration then switched motors in 1946 and continued until 1960, despite declining real wages. Noting the discrepancy, Groh attri-butes the postwar continuation of inter-state black migration to technological change in agriculture.[15] In any case, like the migration of the European whites, which had preceded it, the inter-state migration of southern blacks passed through a demand-driven phase into a second phase when the motor of migration changed. Neither of these historical migrations remained demand-driven throughout their entire duration; their demand-driven phase ended, and real wages declined, but migration continued anyway. These examples suggest that current migrations may also continue after their demand-driven phase has ended.

Los Angeles restructures

Los Angeles had undergone 25 years of well-documented restructuring by 1990 (Light 1988: 69–74; Soja 1987). Indeed, this global restructuring created the Pacific Rim trading area of which Los Angeles became the second-ranking city behind only Tokyo. As is already well understood, in this quarter century of painful transition, heavy manufacturing industry left southern California for the Pacific Rim, leaving behind high technology, aerospace, defence and immigrant-staffed sweatshops (Allen and Turner 1997: 185). The real wages of manufacturing workers stagnated and declined in the protracted, industrial egress (Soja *et al.* 1983; see also Soja 1989). New jobs in service industries employed many persons displaced from manufacturing but usually at much lower wages (Scott 1988, chapters 6–9). As elsewhere, ostentatious, newly rich millionaires became more prominent on the high end and desperately poor, unskilled immigrants at the low end of the income distribution.[16]

In this southern California region, where feverish globalization has been underway for 25 years, we wish to ascertain whether migration was actually demand-driven throughout the period. The two largest groups of immigrants were Latinos and Asians. These two groups accounted for 83 per cent of international migrants in the Los Angeles region in 1990 (Sabagh and Bozorgmehr 1996: table 3.2). Between 1970 and 1990, the foreign born increased from 11 per cent to 32 per cent of the population of Los Angeles County (Sabagh and Bozorgmehr 1996: 85). Except for non-Hispanic whites, whose immigration peaked early and then declined, all the immigrant groups in southern California have continued to field very large immigration cohorts in every five year period. In the specific case of Mexicans, the largest immigrant group, the immigration cohorts grew consistently in size between 1950 and 1989, reaching their maximum in 1989. Yet, as we shall show, all this immigration has continued in the face of declining real incomes for immigrants. In this respect, of course, southern California was not unique, for, as Borjas has shown, age-adjusted immigrant cohorts in the entire USA received successively lower wages relative to natives in every decade since 1950 (Borjas 1989).

Comparing four ethno-racial groups in southern California, Light and Roach found that the wages of whites in the private sector increased 3.92-fold in the 20-year period; wages of blacks increased more than those of whites; wages of Asians increased as much as those of whites; but the wages of Hispanics increased only 72 per cent as much as did the wages of whites, falling seriously behind the pack (Light and Roach 1996). This result indicates falling real wages for Hispanics, but not for Asians. However, research directed specifically at immigrant Latinos and immigrant Asians finds that both Asian immigrants and Latino immigrants experienced declining real incomes and increased unemployment over the 20-year period in Los Angeles and its region.[17] Cheng and Yang undertook a cohort analysis of Asian immigrants who arrived in southern California in the 1960s, the 1970s, and the 1980s. Summarizing their results, they declare the evidence indicates 'erosion' of the Asian immigrants' economic welfare in this period:

> Compared with subsequent cohorts at comparable periods of time, the 1960s cohort seems to have done somewhat better in the first decade of residence. ... Moreover, the 1980s cohort seems to be doing worse than the 1970s cohort at the end of the first decade of residence – as one might have expected given the tremendous expansion in immigrant numbers and the immigrant convergence on a limited number of occupations and industries.
>
> (Cheng and Yang 1996: 323)

Lopez, Popkin and Telles undertook a similar, cohort analysis of the earnings of Salvadoran, Guatemalan and Mexican immigrants in Los Angeles, comparing real earnings in three successive periods (Lopez *et al.* 1996: 299). Their evidence compares mean earnings of immigrant men aged 25–64 in 1975–79, 1980–84, and 1985–89 for Salvadorans, Guatemalans and Mexicans. All three Latino groups show continuous decline in 1989 dollar earnings over each successive period. Overall declines were between 30 per cent and 40 per cent of initial real wages. Ong and Blumenberg find that real hourly compensation in the private sector of Los Angeles increased only 14.5 per cent between 1969 and 1989 compared to an increase of 98 per cent between 1948 and 1969. However, among immigrants, they find, real wages actually declined 13 per cent between 1970 and 1980 (Ong and Blumenberg 1996; Schimek 1989). Studying three cohorts of Mexican immigrants to Los Angeles, Ortiz also finds evidence of declining real wages between 1970 and 1990. She writes, Mexican immigrants of the 1960s cohort, '... saw their real earnings advance steadily from the beginning to the end of the period. ... More disturbing is the fate of subsequent cohorts, who not only slipped further behind native whites with each decade but failed to recapture the very modest earnings of their predecessors' (Ortiz 1996: 257). According to Ortiz, the real wages of Mexican women immigrants declined even more than those of Mexican men.[18]

Restructuring self-employment

Self-employment offers another and more complex test of globalization's economic impact on Los Angeles and southern California. Under a regime of global restructuring, job-exporting regions increase self-employment for two reasons. First, self-employment increases because the exportation of production jobs strips native-born workers of secure, high-wage production jobs, encouraging them to undertake self-employment as a survival strategy. We call this jobs-export self-employment.[19] It is a defensive form of self-employment that protects living standards of displaced workers. However, a second, equally genuine increase in globalization-induced self-employment is positive, not defensive. This positive increase arises from expansion of incorporated self-employment, the highest income sector of the entire labour market, in reflection of the enhanced demand for high-income professional/technical workers that restructuring notoriously brings (Allen and Turner 1997: 188).

However, we must distinguish these two globalization-driven increases in self-employment from network-driven increases in self-employment that occur among immigrants. Network-driven increase in self-employment is neither positive nor attributable to globalization. Network-driven increases occur when network-driven immigrants, having saturated labour markets in the destination economy, turn in desperation to low income self-employment, especially in the informal sector. When this process occurs, heavy immigrant influx overwhelms demand for immigrant entrepreneurs, driving down the average economic returns of entrepreneurship. This result is similar to the increase among displaced native production workers, whose jobs were exported; however, the increase of self-employment among immigrants is network driven.

Rates of incorporated and unincorporated self-employment did increase in southern California between 1970 and 1990, a period of intense global restructuring. Combining all four major ethno-racial categories, Light and Roach reported that aggregate self-employment increased 2.29-fold in the 20 years whereas the general labour market increased only 1.80-fold (Light and Roach 1996: 196). Incorporated self-employment and unincorporated self-employment both increased. The increase in incorporated self-employment occurred among all ethno-racial categories, and promoted the absolute and proportional growth of the highest income stratum in each, thus contributing to income polarization. Increases in unincorporated self-employment were less universal. Among the native born, increases in self-employment outstripped increases in waged employment among whites and Hispanics. Rates increased faster among women than among men (see Table 8.1). Among the foreign-born, increases in self-employment

Table 8.1 Wage employment and self-employment in 1990 by ethno-racial category, nativity and gender

	Number, 1990		Index, 1970–90	
	Employees	Self-employed	Employees	Self-employed
Native Whites				
Men	1 374 026	261 693	108	150
Women	1 150 660	123 124	151	280
Total	2 524 686	384 817		
%Women	45.6	40.0		
Foreign Whites				
Men	125 983	42 955	124	210
Women	102 924	4 366	145	197
Total	228 907	57 321		
%Women	44.9	25.1		
Native Blacks				
Men	185 518	14 103	153	150
Women	200 050	7 336	201	179
Total	385 568	21 439		
%Women	51.2	34.2		
Native Asians				
Men	50 231	6 819	209	105
Women	45 190	2 941	264	226
Total	95 421	9 760		
%Women	47.3	30.1		
Foreign Asians				
Men	204 690	44 605	984	1 438
Women	185 950	23 213	1 074	n.a.
Total	390 640	67 818		
%Women	47.6	34.2		
Native Hispanics				
Men	265 110	21 797	191	245
Women	223 708	10 028	271	627
Total	488 818	31 825		
%Women	45.7	31.5		
Foreign Hispanics				
Men	631 527	50 624	659	817
Women	381 434	23 309	746	1 793
Total	1 012 961	73 933		
%Women	37.6	31.5		

Source: US Census of 1990, 5% Public Use Sample.

outstripped increases in wage employment among white, Asian men and Hispanics.

The financial return of incorporated self-employment kept pace with the wages of private-sector workers among whites and blacks, but not among Asians and Hispanics. Among Hispanics, the income of the incorporated self-employed increased only 73 per cent as much as did Hispanic wage income in the private sector. However, the income gains of the unincorporated self-employed were appreciably better than the income gains of the unincorporated self-employed. Among all four ethno-racial categories, the earnings of the unincorporated self-employed failed to keep pace with earnings of coethnic wage earners in the private sector (Light and Roach 1996: 201). The discrepant earnings trajectories of the incorporated and the unincorporated self-employed suggest that growth in high-end demand permitted the incorporated sector to absorb newcomers without declining incomes. In contrast, the uniformly declining incomes of the unincorporated self-employed suggest supply-driven increases that overwhelmed demand for marginal entrepreneurs, driving down average incomes. The two groups whose unincorporated self-employment increased the most in number (whites, Hispanics) increased their self-employment earnings less than the two groups (Asians, blacks) whose numbers increased least. Light and Roach attribute the increased supply of white entrepreneurs to jobs export, and the increased supply of Hispanic entrepreneurs to network-driven saturation of labour markets.

Human capital

Immigrant earnings might decline because later immigrant cohorts had lower average educational levels than earlier cohorts. Because income increases with education, declining educational levels should produce declining incomes. In this case, changes in average educational levels (rather than the saturation of labour markets) might account for declining real incomes of immigrants. In point of fact, the mean educational levels of Asian immigrants in Los Angeles and in the USA did decrease between 1970 and 1990, but the mean educational levels of Hispanic immigrants were stable or increased slightly (Borjas 1990: 231–2). One might suppose that the Asian case repels explanation in terms of market saturation whereas the Hispanic case supports it.

However, the interpretation of declining educational levels is not simple.[20] After all, if successive immigrant cohorts display lower educational levels, we must invoke progressive saturation to field a demand-driven explanation. *Progressive saturation* arises when the first immigrant cohort saturates the highest-level demand in the destination economy, then gives way to a second cohort, lower in educational level, which saturates a lower level demand. In turn, that second cohort gives way to a third cohort, still less skilled, which saturates a still lower-level demand. In this way, a host economy could successively attract immigrants ever lower in human capital, paying each cohort less than its better-educated predecessor. However, although progressive saturation is a plausible explanation of declining educational levels among immigrants, progressive saturation does not fit global restructuring theory. According to restructuring theory, globalization increases opportunities at the top and at the bottom of the reception economy without saturating either the top or the bottom. If progressive saturation occurs, with erosion spreading down the ladder, and educational levels decline, global restructuring cannot explain it.[21]

Moreover, as Massey and his colleagues have explained, declining cohort quality can result from network migration (Massey *et al.* 1993: 453). Indeed, network migration is the prevailing explanation of declining cohort quality. Networks produce declining cohort quality when initially high-level cohorts, who responded directly to demand, later promote the subsequent entry of less-qualified kin. Indeed, by prioritizing family reunification, the US immigration law encourages precisely this outcome. That is, when initial immigrants qualify for admission because of needed occupational skills, the immigrant cohort that arises has high educational levels. When this skilled cohort later applies for family reunification, the people they sponsor have lower educational levels than their sponsors. In this way, migration networks, amplified by the US immigration code, drive down the average educational level of successive migration cohorts. Migration network theory can explain declining cohort quality whereas global restructuring theory cannot.

Turning now to the Hispanic immigrants, whose average educational level in southern California was low but stable, we find that global restructuring cannot explain this outcome either. First, Allen and Turner conclude that 'employment restructuring did not precede immigration' in southern California. On the contrary, 'the presence and prospects of low-wage immigrant labor encouraged job growth' that took advantage of the labour supply.[22] Second, if Hispanic real incomes are declining and Hispanic educational levels are stable, we cannot escape the deterioration of the Hispanic immigrants' economic status. Deteriorating economic status implies saturation of market demand whereas global restructuring requires strong and insatiable demand.

Even if global restructuring once opened new demands to immigrants, low level as well as high level, saturation of those new demands would signal the end of demand-driven immigration. When demand is saturated, a demand-driven immigration ends unless it substitutes another motor. If immigration accelerated or even continued at the same level in the face of declining real wages, then something other than demand now drives the immigration. That something could plausibly be a network-driven migration that continued when demand was saturated.

Conclusion

Global restructuring explains many features of southern California's economic trajectory between 1970 and 1990. Declining wages in manufacturing industries, the egress of more than one million native-born whites from the region, increased self-employment by whites, and especially by white women, and across-the-board increases in incorporated self-employment – global restructuring easily explains all these phenomena. However, global restructuring does not explain the acceleration of immigration in the face of declining real wages and self-employment incomes for employed immigrants. Even when we take account of cohort quality, whether declining or stable, global restructuring cannot provide an explanation that does justice to the southern California evidence. On the other hand, we know that network migration organized all the immigrants to southern California in every year of this period. For example, Cornelius reported that 70 per cent of immigrant workers in San Diego had found their current job '... through social networks – relatives or friends employed at the same firm where they now work' (Cornelius 1997: 14). Migration networks are compatible with strong immigrant influx in the face of declining real incomes, but global restructuring theory is not.

Without wishing to dismiss globalization, whether as theory or process, we do propose that globalization theorists have extended their reach beyond their grasp. In southern California, immigration rather quickly outstripped globalizing demand and its motor switched to the migration network. At least in southern California and, we suspect, much more broadly in the developed countries, migration is now and has long been a network-driven process. This theoretical point has policy implications because, if left to itself, network-driven migrations may potentially continue even beyond the point at which economic conditions in metropoles are *worse* than those in the originating villages. This possibility arises because migration networks can make it easier to migrate in search of a job in New York or Los Angeles than to find a job in one's homeland neighbourhood. Therefore, until conditions are appreciably *worse* in the destination than in the homeland, migrants will continue to prefer the easy path of the migration network to the difficult path of finding a job in their home neighbourhood.

Notes

1. 'The foreign investment that drives economic globalization is managed from a small number of global cities, whose structural characteristics create a strong demand for immigrant labor' (Massey *et al.* 1993: 446).
2. 'Global forces and transnational flows are becoming more and more dominant at the national and local levels' (Knight 1989: 25).
3. 'The single largest factor locally is the precipitous loss of over 42 000 manufacturing jobs (19 per cent of the manufacturing job base) in the metropolitan area between 1979–1989, jobs which, on average, paid $28 218 per worker in 1989. In contrast, the industries which contributed the most net growth in employment over the 1979–1989 decade, retail trade and services, had average earnings per worker of $10 504 and $19 171 in 1989, markedly below those in manufacturing. Furthermore, because a large number (over 72 000) of the new jobs in these industries came from new establishments over this period, it must be noted that new establishments in retail and services had even lower average earnings per worker than existing retail and service establishments ($8779 for retail and $11 849 for services)' (White and McMahon 1995: 50).
4. 'The world economy is managed from a relatively small number of urban centers in which banking, financing, administration, professional services, and high-tech production tend to be concentrated…. Poorly educated natives resist taking low-paying jobs at the bottom of the occupational hierarchy, creating a strong demand for immigrants…. Native workers with modest educations cling to jobs in the declining middle, migrate out of global cities, or rely on social insurance programs for support' (Massey *et al.* 1993: 447).
5. For a critical evaluation of the polarization thesis, see Hamnett 1994b.
6. '…The expansion of the high-income work force, in conjunction with the emergence of new cultural forms in everyday living, has led to a process of high-income gentrification, which rests, in the last analysis, on the availability of a vast supply of low-wage workers' (Sassen 1991: 279, see also pp. 281, 282).
7. Waldinger points out that the emergent demand for low-wage labour in American cities did *not* require impoverished immigrants as globalization theory maintains. After all, unlike European cities, American cities already had an existing labour reserve of impoverished, unemployed and underemployed native-born blacks. These blacks were available to take the low-wage service and manufacturing jobs that globalization created. Instead the

Latino, Caribbean, and Asian immigrants got these jobs, monopolizing the entire informal sector, and the native-born blacks remained impoverished and unemployed. The causes of this perplexing outcome, Waldinger declares, must be sought first in the folklore of American labour markets that disparage the desirability of black American employees. This is a cultural issue. Second, in Waldinger's view, the social networks of the immigrants allowed them to outcompete native blacks for initial access to the growing informal sector, and then to exclude native blacks from their newly acquired industrial niches (Waldinger 1996).

8. 'The presence of large immigrant communities then can be seen as mediating in the process of informalization rather than directly generating it: the demand side of the process of informalization rather than directly generating it: the demand side of the process of informalization is therewith brought to the fore.' (Sassen 1991: 282).

9. '... Larger translocal economic forces have far more weight than local policies in shaping urban economies.' (Sassen 1990: 237); 'Global forces and transnational flows are becoming more and more dominant at the national and local levels' (Knight 1989: 25).

10. 'There is an explanatory tension, particularly evident in the social sciences, which is usually termed the "structure–agency" dichotomy. Some explanations operate at the higher "structural" level, offering a highly generalized explanation. Other explanations operate at the more specific level of "human agency" and focus upon individual actions. For example, at the "human agency" level international production would be regarded as the result of individual decisions by business enterprises to invest in particular locations outside the firm's home country. In one sense, all such decisions are unique. They are made by individuals on the basis of their perception of their firm's needs, and on the extent to which different locations meet such needs. But although at one level – that of the internal decisions of the business enterprise–international investment and location decisions are, indeed, unique, they are also part of a more general structure: the capitalist market system' (Dicken 1992: 121).

11. For someone who says exactly this, see Peterson 1981.

12. '... immigrants are not just employees but owners of the businesses where they work. Among firms we studied in San Diego last year, more than one-third (34.0 per cent) were immigrant-owned.' (Cornelius 1997: 9).

13. '... The polarisation thesis, as it effects growth at the bottom end of the occupational and income distributions, may be contingent on the existence of large-scale ethnic immigration and a cheap labour supply' (Hamnett 1994: 408).

14. 'The tendency towards polarization should manifest itself more clearly in larger cities than in nations as a whole. Polarization should be especially articulated in these larger cities, not only because de-industrialization has hit urban areas hardest, but also because both types of services are spatially concentrated there.' (Kloosterman 1996b: 469).

15. 'By the mid-1950s the war booms had run their course but the new migration had not; it was holding at near-record levels of some 150 000 people a year. A new element was involved. Technology was forcing out those who still remained on the farm ...' (Groh 1972: 60).

16. '... The new industrial complex has contributed to a transformation in the social structure of major cities where it is concentrated. This transformation assumes the form of increased social and economic polarization' (Sassen 1991: 329).
17. 'The wage gap for Mexican immigrants increased in California as well as in Los Angeles, but the gap increased less in the state than in Los Angeles. Mexican immigrant mens' wages declined from 67% of white mens' wages in 1960 to 60% in 1980' (Vernez 1993: 150).
18. '... a significant number of immigrants in California and the United States currently have very low wages, and the evidence suggests that their wages will not improve substantially throughout their working lives. This evidence, combined with the fact that more-recent immigrants have had lower (age-adjusted) wages relative to earlier immigrants, has substantial ramifications for public-service usage and tax revenues into the future' (Schoeni *et al.* 1996: 67).
19. On the other hand, job-importing regions present already self-employed workers with attractive, new jobs that reduce their incentive to self-employment.
20. For a summary of the cohort quality debate see Borjas 1996.
21. Reyneri observes that migration chains notoriously exaggerate opportunities in the destination economy, promoting more immigration than the destination economy can actually absorb. As a result, immigrants anticipate a rosier job supply than actually exists in their destination. However, in this case, demand does not drive the migration. Rather, the illusion of demand drives the migration. That illusion is a product of the migration network so the migration network (not the reception economy) is actually driving demand in this situation. One cannot salvage demand-led immigration by phantom demand. See Reyneri 1997.
22. See Allen and Turner 1997: 186. The authors add (on p. 197), 'The effect of this labor surplus has been to depress wages, not only for immigrants themselves but also for those born in the United States.'

9

Social Polarization in London: the Income Evidence, 1979–93

Chris Hamnett

Introduction

The last few years have seen a major debate on the existence, form, extent and causes of social polarization in modern Western societies. The definition of polarization has varied considerably, however, and as Pinch (1993) has pointed out, two different conceptions of polarization seem to have taken root on different sides of the Atlantic. On the one hand, the theories put forward by Harrison and Bluestone (1988) and Sassen (1991) are concerned with the changing social and spatial division of labour, and with the implications of a shift from manufacturing to services for the changing structure of occupation and earnings. In this version of polarization, the structure of occupations and earnings are becoming increasingly bifurcated into highly skilled and highly paid professional and managerial jobs on the one hand, and low skilled and lowly paid jobs on the other. America, it is feared, has turned into a society where the middle classes have shrunk in number, and there has been relative growth at both the top and the bottom ends of the occupational and earnings spectrum. Hence, the concern about the so-called 'shrinking middle' or what is termed the shrinking middle class (Kuttner 1983; Lawrence 1984; Levy 1987).

On the other side of the Atlantic, Pahl (1988) has focused on the changing organization of work, and has pointed to the tendency for employment and incomes to bifurcate between households with no earners and households with multiple earners. Looking at household income units, Pahl suggested that, contrary to the American model, polarization in Britain might be taking place between a comfortable 'middle mass' of households, often with two or more earners, and a

168

residualized group with no earners. This perspective has recently been echoed by Williams and Windebank (1995) who are strongly critical of the 'individual in the workplace' approach to social polarization. This chapter examines the evidence for the existence of social polarization and inequality using data from the General Household Survey (GHS) on household incomes and number of earners in both London and Great Britain between 1979 and 1993. It shows that, at the household income level, there is little evidence for polarization in Britain along American lines, although there is a marked increase in inequality.

The social polarization debate

Pinch (1993) has suggested that the form and extent of social polarization in the structure of cities in the advanced economies is 'one of the most complex and controversial issues in the social sciences' (p. 779). But, as I have argued elsewhere (Hamnett 1994a, 1994b, 1996), there is an unfortunate tendency to use the term polarization in a loose, catch-all way to refer to growing social divisions and inequality in contemporary cities. In addition, its existence is frequently taken for granted rather than empirically examined, and the theory put forward by Sassen regarding the nature and generative mechanisms of social polarization in American cities, is too often uncritically accepted as having equal applicability in Europe.

Sassen-Koob (1984, 1985) says that changes in the social and spatial division of labour have led to a dramatic shift in the structure of economic activity in global cities. This is particularly associated with the growth of financial and business services and with the decline of manufacturing industry. She argues that the service sector has a much more polarized occupational and earnings distribution than manufacturing industry, with a combination of both highly skilled and highly paid jobs and low skilled and low paid jobs which has:

> brought about changes in the organization of work, reflected in a shift in the job supply and polarisation in the income distribution and occupational distribution of workers .... The occupational structure of major growth industries ... in global cities in combination with the polarised occupational structure of these sectors has created and contributed to a growth of a high income stratum and a low income stratum of workers
>
> (Sassen 1991: 9)

We need to be very clear about what this thesis is claiming. First, it argues that there should be an increase in the proportion of well paid and low paid jobs at the expense of medium paid jobs. It is a thesis about the changing structure of the paid labour force and about earnings. It is not about income distribution as a whole, although Harrison and Bluestone (1988) do examine this, nor does it have much to say about the growth of unemployment or the distribution of work among different types of household.

This is where Pahl's research on the distribution of work and income within and between households in contemporary society is of interest. He argued that changes are taking place in the distribution of paid employment between households such that: 'certain households are becoming increasingly more fortunate, whereas others are becoming increasingly more deprived' (p. 250). Pahl argued that there is a growing division between 'work rich' households, where two or more members are in paid employment, and 'work poor' households, where nobody is working. Pahl suggested that:

> This emphasis on the household as the salient social and economic unit, rather than the individual, has important implications for contemporary social structure. Whilst the occupational structure based on individual jobs typically produces a hierarchically structured pyramid of advantage, these new tendencies allows a sizable proportion of households incorporating low or modest incomes to have a higher position in the hierarchy as a result of their collective work practices
>
> (1988: 252)

Pahl went on to point out that the 1981 census revealed that 34 per cent of households had two earners, and a further 12 per cent had three or more earners. Taking out those households with no economically active members, 57 per cent of households were multiple income earners. He argued that working-class households are no less likely than middle-class households to have multiple earners and suggests the cumulation of advantage and disadvantage may have major implications for social stratification. Williams and Windebank (1995) have also argued that the appropriate focus for polarization should be the household rather than individuals. More generally, Pahl has observed that the term 'social polarization' can clearly be used in different ways, and he pointed out that:

> ... in the enthusiasm for detecting new divisions in western capitalist society, there is a danger that those proposing new models may run

ahead of the evidence. General statements of apparent clarity and simplicity are made which cover great complexities and confusions.
(1988: 257)

Similarly, Fainstein *et al.* (1992: 13) note that: 'If the concept of a polarizing city is of any real utility, it can only serve as a hypothesis, the prelude to empirical analysis, rather than as a conclusion which takes the existence of confirmatory evidence for granted'.

Pahl suggested a number of possibilities in terms of the changing structure of social polarization. Looking at household income units, he outlined three possible alternatives. First, the social structure could be changing from the traditional pyramid to an onion shape, where: 'the middle is fattening out as a comfortable middle mass emerges based on homeownership and the household work practices organized around multiple earners and the cumulation of informal work'. Second, it is possible that the middle of the onion is getting fatter but the top and bottom can be seen as sliced off and moving up and down respectively away from the middle. Third, Pahl suggested that the image of the pyramid may be giving way to a dumbbell model with more rich and more poor and fewer in the middle. This is how Sassen (1991) and Harrison and Bluestone (1988) view polarization and it is different from the onion shape envisaged by Pahl.

There is strong evidence that American household incomes have been moving in this direction since the early 1970s (Harrison and Bluestone 1988), but how has the distribution of household incomes changed in Britain since the late 1970s and how do these changes relate to the changes in London? Some of Pahl's propositions have been tested by Dale and Bamford (1989) using data from the General Household Survey for the period 1973–82. They analysed trends in paid work and found that, as expected, there had been:

a steady increase in the proportion of households with no-one in paid work, from 25 per cent in 1973 to 34 per cent in 1982, with some evidence that the greatest rate of change was between 1980 and 1982. Conversely, there is a steady decline in the percentage of households with at least one earner
(1989: 484)

They found no evidence, however, of an increase in the proportion of two-earner households and they concluded that if a process of polarization was operating in British society, it was more clear at the no-earner pole than at the multi-earner pole. They also examined the evidence for Pahl's view that multi-earner household incomes would be expected to increase more rapidly than other household incomes. They found, however, that although the level of income for multi-earner households was considerably higher than for other household types, and the size of the gap increased over the period, there was no evidence that rates of increase were higher than other groups.

Dale and Bamford's work was valuable, but it only examined the situation for 1973–82, and the period from 1979–82 found Britain in the depths of a major recession. It is, therefore, important to attempt to update some of their analyses with 1990s data. This is done below using GHS data from 1979 and 1993. In taking 1979 as a starting date, one object was to see to what extent income polarization and inequality has increased both in Britain, and London, during the Thatcher years, as is often argued. If polarization between households in terms of incomes and earners is taking place in London, is it taking place along American lines or what Pahl sees as British ones?

The structure of the chapter is as follows. The first section looks at the definition and measurement of inequality and polarization of income and earnings and the characteristics of the GHS data source. The third section looks at household income trends, the fourth section at changes in income by number of earners and the fifth section at links between household incomes, socioeconomic groups, economic activity, status and ethnicity. In all cases, data for London is compared to Great Britain, to try to determine the extent to which changes in income polarization or inequality may be greater in London.

Income polarization and inequality

Unfortunately, debate on the polarization thesis has often been marked by a failure to specify what is meant by the term polarization and how it can be operationalized and measured. First, it is necessary to distinguish between earnings and income. Earnings data relate to earnings from employment, and are usually available only for individual earners and, by definition, exclude the unemployed. Income data includes income from a variety of sources including unemployment pay and other transfer payments such as pensions, and it has the advantage of enabling us to look at overall household income. This is important, as questions of income inequality and income polarization are particularly salient at the household level (Williams and Windebank 1995).

Second, as Pahl points out, 'there is an important distinction between images based on numbers of households or numbers of people and images based on the amount of wealth held by people at different levels. The thesis of the shrinking middle is less concerned with numbers in the category but more with the amount of wealth the category receives' (p. 260). We think Pahl is wrong in this, in that the shrinking middle thesis is more concerned with the size of the various groups than with the amount of income they receive. But the distinction Pahl makes is very important. To put it crudely, the question is whether the rich are getting richer, and the poor (relatively) poorer, or whether there are absolutely or relatively more rich and more poor people? Unfortunately, this is rarely distinguished in the polarization literature.

Kloosterman (1996b), following the OECD, distinguishes between inequality and polarization. In this usage, income or earnings inequality refers to extent of dispersion between levels of income/earnings, whereas polarization relates to changes in the absolute and relative size of the groups in different income groups over time. Are the top and bottom ends of the distribution growing at the expense of the middle? These differences are frequently confused and greater income inequality is often taken as an indication of polarization. But, although greater inequality and polarization may be related in practice, they are analytically distinct, and it is possible for one to occur without the other. Inequality is usually measured by calculating ratios to see how various parts of the distribution have changed relative to the median or the mean and how their shares have changed. But, as polarization relates to the size of various income groups, changes in such ratios will not capture the relevant trends. In these cases it is necessary to measure changes in the size of the top, bottom and middle of the income distribution to see whether they have got bigger or smaller over time after adjusting for inflation (see Esteban and Ray 1994).

Kloosterman (1996b) devised a specific method to calculate polarization. For a chosen base year, the earnings distribution is divided into a low (first 25 per cent), a middle (next 50 per cent) and a high segment (top 25 per cent). The two cut-off points, expressed in money terms (whether earnings or household income) are then transferred (correcting for the rate of inflation) to another year. Subsequently the shifts between the three wage segments can be calculated in terms of the numbers of wage earners. A rise in the proportion of earners/incomes in the top and bottom groups and a fall in the middle group over time is construed as evidence of polarization. Where earnings/incomes are growing faster than the general rate of inflation, there will be a tendency for the size of the upper income groups to grow at the expense of the lower ones whereas, as in the USA, where the earnings of many groups are rising below the general rate of inflation, the size of the lower groups may increase. A more common method used by Harrison and Bluestone (1988) compares the changing proportions of three groups in relation to the median – those with earnings/incomes more than twice the median, those with under half the median and the remainder. This has the advantage of taking the changing median into account but it is also partly a measure of changes in inequality.

A note on the General Household Survey: the GHS, which began in 1971, is 'an annual, cross-sectional, nationally representative survey carried out for government' (Dale and Bamford 1989). It is a multipurpose survey based on an achieved sample of about 10 000 private, non-institutional, households each year. The Great Britain sample size in 1979 was 11 500 households and 9850 in 1993–94. The sample size for London in 1979 was 1200 and 1050 in 1993 which is adequate for most analyses. Dale and Bamford make three important methodological points about the GHS. First, the sampling unit in the GHS is the household. Second, because the data are cross-sectional, a different sample of households is taken each year. Third, most variables refer to a fixed point in time, usually the week before the survey. Thus, data on unemployment, for example, relates to the period at the time of the survey. We would add that as the GHS is a sample survey, it is subject to sampling error. We have not included any statistics on likely sampling error in this chapter, but we have generally excluded categories where the sample size is less than 30. In most cases it is far larger. GHS data include all earners, full and part-time, and those below the tax threshold. It is thus a more inclusive data source on earners than the only competing source, the New Earnings Survey.

Earnings polarization, 1979–93

Although the chapter focuses on household income, it is useful to look first at the GHS data on individual earnings, not least because this enables us to shed light on some of the issues raised by Sassen regarding earnings polarization.

The GHS earnings data for London are remarkable. Using Kloosterman's method they reveal a marked upward shift in earnings between 1979 and 1993. Table 9.1 shows that when the 1979 earnings thresholds are adjusted to 1993 prices, the proportion of earners in the bottom 25 per cent of earnings in 1993 fell by nearly 4 percentage

Table 9.1 Polarization of real earnings in London and Great Britain, 1979–93

	Greater London			Great Britain		
	1979	1993	ppc	1979	1993	ppc
Bottom 25 per cent of earnings	25.0	21.1	−3.9	25.0	25.0	0
Middle 50 per cent of earnings	50.0	28.8	−21.2	50.0	36.1	−13.9
Top 25 per cent of earnings	25.0	50.1	+25.1	25.0	38.9	+13.9

Source: GHS, 1993 prices.

points in London and the proportion of earners in the middle 50 per cent of earnings fell by 21 points, while the proportion of earners in the top 25 per cent in 1979 had risen to 50 per cent by 1993. The upwards shift in earnings is far more marked in London than it was in Great Britain as a whole where there was a redistribution of 13.9 points from the middle 50 per cent to the top 25 per cent of earners. This reflects the fact that real incomes rose more rapidly in London than in Britain as a whole over this period. These findings are in sharp contrast to those of Harrison and Bluestone (1988) and Clarke and McNicholas (1996) and indicate that, despite the rapidly growing earnings inequality (Hamnett and Cross 1998) in both London and as Great Britain as a whole, that on a quartile basis, the overall trend was strongly upwards.

This shift is even more marked at the decile level (see Table 9.2).With the exception of the bottom decile, which grew by 1.6 points, the proportion in every other decile up to the eighth fell substantially. There was a small increase in the size of the ninth group and a large increase (+22.4 per cent) in the proportion of earners in the 1979 top decile earnings band adjusted to 1993 prices. If this is taken as evidence of polarization, in the sense that there are relatively more rich and more poor, it is an extremely skewed polarization, with an increase at the top end 15 times greater than at the bottom in proportionate terms.

It is, therefore, clear that, using Retail Price Index (RPI) adjusted data, neither London nor Great Britain as a whole have witnessed an increase in earnings polarization such has been found in the USA where there has been a substantial increase at both the top and the bottom ends. On the contrary, what we have witnessed in Britain is an upwards shift in earnings although, as will be shown later, this has been combined with a massive increase in earnings inequality.

Table 9.2 Decile-based measure of change in total gross weekly earnings for 1979 and 1993

Great London

Decile point (%)	Gross weekly individual earnings at that point in 1979 (£s)	Decile	Size of group in 1979 (%)	Size of group in 1993 (%)	Percentage point change in size of group 1979–93	Percentage point change in size of group 1979–93
10	61.40	1. 0–10	10	11.6	+1.6	+1.6
20	103.51	2. 10–20	10	5.5	−4.5	
30	141.85	3. 20–30	10	6.6	−3.4	
40	170.21	4. 30–40	10	5.2	−4.8	
50	195.16	5. 40–50	10	5.0	−5.0	
60	219.81	6. 50–60	10	4.5 } 44.0	−5.5	−24.0
70	250.35	7. 60–70	10	7.4	−2.6	
80	286.77	8. 70–80	10	6.9	−3.1	
90	355.25	9. 80–90	10	14.9	4.9	
		10. 90–100	10	32.4	+22.4	+22.4
		Total: 100%	100%	100%	Nil	Nil

Great Britain

Decile point (%)	Gross weekly individual earnings at that point in 1979 (£s)	Decile	Size of group in 1979 (%)	Size of group in 1993 (%)	Percentage point change in size of group 1979–93	Percentage point change in size of group 1979–93
10	44.39	1. 0–10	10	11.1	+1.1	+1.1
20	79.55	2. 10–20	10	9.8	−0.2	
30	115.30	3. 20–30	10	7.8	−2.2	
40	145.95	4. 30–40	10	7.1	−2.9	
50	172.91	5. 40–50	10	6.8	−3.2	
60	200.33	6. 50–60	10	6.7 } 63.9	−3.3	−16.1
70	230.50	7. 60–70	10	7.7	−2.3	
80	267.31	8. 70–80	10	8.4	−1.6	
90	325.74	9. 80–90	10	9.6	−0.4	
		10. 90–100	10	25.0	+15.0	+15.0
		Total: 100%	100%	100%	Nil	Nil

Note: Earnings adjusted to April 1995 prices.

Source: Tables 9.2–9.19 General Household Surveys 1979 and 1993 (OPCS via ESRC Data Archive and MIDAS).

It could be argued that RPI is not the most appropriate measure and that it is better to adjust the earnings categories using median earning change for Great Britain. This is shown in Table 9.3. The results are less marked but the overall pattern is broadly similar. The proportion of earners in London with earnings in the lowest decile in 1979 has risen by 2.9 percentage points by 1993. The proportion with earnings in the middle 70 per cent fell by almost 20 points, while the top two deciles increased by 3.8 and 13 percentage points respectively. If this is taken as evidence of earnings polarization, it is polarization of a very asymmetric kind where by far the greatest proportionate growth has been at the top end of the distribution. At the decile level, it appears that there has been a very large rise in the proportion of earners who, in 1993 had earnings which, at 1979 levels would have comprised the top decile of earners. This shift was most marked in London which suggests that earnings, particularly those at the top end of the distribution, rose much more rapidly than in Britain as a whole. In Great Britain there was clearer evidence of polarization with the lowest decile growing by 3.5 points and the top decile by 7.9 points.

Household income polarization, 1979–93

The major question we wish to address in this section is the extent to which households in London and in Great Britain have become more polarized in the sense that, adjusting 1979 incomes for inflation, and comparing the adjusted levels to 1993 incomes there are more households at the top and bottom ends of the household income distribution in 1993 than in 1979. We also wish to see to what extent, there has been an increase in income inequality in terms of both dispersion and shares of total income.

Looking first at the Kloosterman polarization measures, we see from Table 9.4 that changes in the proportion of households in different income categories broadly parallels that of earnings, although the shift from the middle to the top quartile is less marked than for earnings. In addition, the growing share of households in the bottom quartile of incomes is more marked than it is for earnings. Thus, although polarization is still very positively skewed, there is nonetheless a significant increase in London in the proportion of households in the bottom 25 per cent of incomes. This is not manifest in Great Britain as a whole where growth was entirely in the top 25 per cent (+9.8), with losses in both the middle 50 per cent and the lowest 25 per cent. This supports Buck's (1994) finding that polarization is more marked for household

Table 9.3 Decile-based measure of change in total gross weekly earnings for 1979 and 1993

Decile point (%)	Gross weekly individual earnings at that point in 1979 (£s)	Decile		Size of group in 1979 (%)	Size of group in 1993 (%)	Percentage point change in size of group 1979–93
Great London						
10	66.41	1.	0–10	10	12.9	+2.9
20	116.50	2.	10–20	10	7.7	−2.3
30	159.11	3.	20–30	10	7.7	−2.3
40	188.65	4.	30–40	10	5.8	−4.2
50	216.93	5.	40–50	10	6.4	−3.6
60	243.08	6.	50–60	10	6.9	−3.1
70	280.04	7.	60–70	10	7.2	−2.8
80	320.38	8.	70–80	10	8.6	−1.4
90	397.39	9.	80–90	10	13.8	−3.8
		10.	90–100	10	23.0	+13.0
			Total: 100%	100%	100%	Nil
Great Britain						
10	49.51	1.	0–10	10	13.5	+3.5
20	87.38	2.	10–20	10	10.2	+0.2
30	128.15	3.	20–30	10	9.3	−0.7
40	161.30	4.	30–40	10	8.9	−1.1
50	192.23	5.	40–50	10	8.1	−1.9
60	222.64	6.	50–60	10	8.0	−2.0
70	255.64	7.	60–70	10	7.7	−2.3
80	296.70	8.	70–80	10	7.0	−3.0
90	364.10	9.	80–90	10	9.4	−0.6
		10.	90–100	10	17.9	+7.9
			Total: 100%	100%	100%	Nil

Great London grouped sizes: 1979: 10 / 80 / 10; 1993: 12.9 / 64.1 / 23.0; change: +2.9 / −15.9 / +13.0 / Nil.

Great Britain grouped sizes: 1979: 10 / 80 / 10; 1993: 13.5 / 68.6 / 17.9; change: +3.5 / −11.4 / +7.9 / Nil.

Note: Earnings revalued by median earnings to April 1995 values.

Table 9.4   Gross household incomes, London and Great Britain, 1979–93

	Greater London			Great Britain		
	1979	1993	ppc	1979	1993	ppc
Bottom 25% of incomes	25.0	27.2	+2.2	25.0	22.5	−2.5
Middle 50% of incomes	50.0	37.5	−12.5	50.0	42.7	−7.3
Top 25% of incomes	25.0	35.3	+10.3	25.0	34.8	+9.8

Table 9.5   Changes in gross weekly household income by decile, 1979–93

	Greater London			Great Britain		
	1979	1993	ppc	1979	1993	ppc
10	10	10.6	+0.6	10	9.6	−0.4
20	10	9.1	−0.9	10	8.0	−2.0
30	10	12.4	+2.4	10	10.7	+0.7
40	10	11.2	+1.2	10	11.5	+1.5
50	10	5.9	−4.1	10	9.1	−0.9
60	10	6.5	−3.5	10	6.1	−3.9
70	10	6.3	−3.7	10	6.9	−3.1
80	10	6.7	−3.3	10	7.3	−2.7
90	10	7.7	−2.3	10	9.2	−0.8
100	10	23.6	+13.6	10	21.6	+11.6

incomes than earnings in London because of the rapid growth of unemployment during the 1980s and early 1990s. Overall, the pattern is one of asymmetric relative polarization. This is confirmed by the decile data which show that there was a growth in the proportion of households with incomes in the first, third and fourth deciles and a large growth of households with incomes in the top decile (+13.6) (see Table 9.5).

The 1979 distribution of annual household income is bi-modal with twin peaks around £3–5000 pa (the retired) and £12–20 000. In 1993 the higher of these two peaks had disappeared, and a much larger proportion of households had incomes, in 1993, in the £25–50 000 range than in 1979. There was no indication of a higher proportion of households with lower incomes. The overall pattern does not appear to be that of a shrinking middle and growth at both ends of the distribution, but rather a shrinking middle and a sharp increase at the top end.

The figures in Table 9.5 were adjusted for retail price inflation. But if incomes rise more rapidly than inflation across the board, as has clearly happened, then the result will be an upwards shift, which will be particularly marked if incomes in the top quartile or top decile have risen much faster than other incomes. Arguably, this will overstate the magnitude of the upwards shift. In these circumstances, it may be appropriate to adjust 1979 incomes to 1993 levels using the Great Britain median income change. This is done in Table 9.6 but it produces a very similar set of figures to those produced using the retail price deflator. In Great Britain the proportion of household incomes in the bottom decile increased by 1.3 points, while the middle eight deciles collectively declined by 10.9 points and the top decile increased by 9.6 points: over seven times the bottom decile. In London, the proportion of households in the bottom decile of incomes grew by 2.5 points, the middle eight deciles shrank 14.1 points and the top decile grew by 11.6 points, 4.6 times the growth in the bottom decile. Thus, even on this basis, income polarization in London, while more marked than in Great Britain was still highly asymmetric with far greater growth at the top.

It is possible to use another measure to examine the extent of polarization in Britain. This looks at changes in the number and proportion of households who had incomes less than half or more than double

Table 9.6   Changes in gross weekly household income by decile, 1979–93

	Greater London			Great Britain		
	1979	1993	ppc	1979	1993	ppc
10	10	12.5	+2.5	10	11.3	+1.3
20	10	8.9	−1.1	10	7.4	−2.6
•30	10	12.1	+2.1	10	11.1	+1.1
40	10	10.3	+0.3	10	11.4	+1.4
50	10	6.1	−3.9	10	8.8	−1.2
60	10	7.4	−2.6	10	7.0	−3.0
70	10	5.4	−4.6	10	6.8	−3.2
80	10	7.1	−2.9	10	7.5	−2.5
90	10	8.6	−1.4	10	9.1	−0.9
100	10	21.6	+11.6	10	19.6	+9.6

Note: figures adjusted by change in Great Britain median income.

Table 9.7 Proportion of households with incomes of less than half or more than double median household income, 1979 and 1993

	Great Britain			Greater London		
	1979	1993	ppc	1979	1993	ppc
% households half<median income	28.9	27.9	−1.0	31.8	32.3	+0.5
% households>2x median income	11.3	21.4	+10.1	7.6	23.9	+16.3

the median income in 1979 and 1993. This is the method used by Harrison and Bluestone (1988). Using this method we find that proportion of 'poor' households with incomes of less than half the median, fell very slightly in Britain from 28.9 per cent in 1979 to 27.9 per cent in 1993. Conversely, the proportion of 'rich' households with incomes more than twice the median doubled from 11.3 per cent to 21.4 per cent. In London, the changes were more marked. The proportion of 'poor' households rose by 0.5 per cent from 31.8 to 32.3 per cent (a rather higher proportion than in Britain as a whole), while the proportion of rich households more than tripled from 7.6 per cent to 23.9 per cent (see Table 9.7). Again, this is a very asymmetric form of polarization.

In terms of Pahl's (1988) attempt to visualize alternative forms of polarization it would seem that, where household income is concerned, Britain is moving away from a christmas-tree shaped pyramidal distribution, with a very broad base and a bulge in the middle, towards a somewhat steeper pyramid, rather than towards the American hourglass or to an onion shaped distribution. It seems a substantial group of households have moved up into higher income levels, particularly in London where high income growth has been marked.

Changes in household income inequality: 1979–93

Although the Harrison and Bluestone polarization measure suggests growth of what we have termed asymmetric income polarization in both London and in Britain as a whole, with most of the growth at the top end of the income distribution, there has also been a massive increase in income inequality in London, and in Great Britain as a whole, over the period 1979–93. This can be shown in a variety of ways. First, the coefficient of variation (the standard deviation divided by the mean) a measure of the spread of incomes, rose substantially both in London (from 0.82 in 1979 to 1.07) in 1993 and in Great Britain (from 0.74 to 1.22). This is indicative of rising income inequality. The inter-quartile and inter-decile ratios also increased significantly, particularly in London where inter-quartile ratio rose from 3.66 to 5.11 and the inter-decile ratio from 8.09 to 12.27. In Great Britain the inter-quartile ratio rose from 3.49 to 4.08 and the inter-decile ratio from 7.4 to 10.1. The greater increases in London suggest that distinctive processes were operative there, possibly connected with the rapid growth of high incomes during the 1980s and early 1990s.

Tables 9.9a and 9.9b consider the distribution of household incomes in more detail using decile groups. Part A of the table shows the percentage share of aggregate income received by households in each decile group. For Great Britain as a whole, the top decile received 25 per cent of total household income in 1979. This rose to 31 per cent in 1993: an increase of 5.75 percentage points. In London the proportion was very similar in 1979 at 26 per cent but this had risen to 33 per cent in 1993: an increase of 7.22 percentage points. It can be seen that the second highest decile also had a slightly higher share of total household income in 1993 than in 1979, but nowhere near as much as the top decile. In Great Britain it rose by 0.9 points and in London it rose 1.5 points. Shares of all other deciles fell, particularly in the middle of the distribution. Income inequality has, therefore, greatly increased in Great Britain and in particular in London. Overall, the top two deciles saw their share of total income increase by 6.64 points in Great Britain and by 8.72 points in London, while every other group saw a decrease. In London, the share of the lowest two deciles fell from 4.5 per cent to 3.2 per cent, the shares of the lowest three deciles from 8.35 per cent to 6 per cent and the shares of the lowest four deciles from 14.1 per cent to 10 per cent.

Part B of the table shows the mean household income within each of the ten decile groups in 1979 and 1993 and both absolute and percentage changes over the period. It shows a number of points. First, the existence of marked income inequality in 1979, and second the marked intensification of income inequalities in the period 1979–93, with a sharp increase in the inter-decile ratio and major income increases in the top four–five deciles, particularly marked at the top end. For the top decile, mean household income rose by 66 per cent in London and 55 per cent in the UK. But, whereas real incomes rose in every category in Britain, and in the rest of the south east, although by very small percentages for the lowest five deciles, in London the lowest five income groups experienced real reductions in mean income from

Table 9.8 Changing household income distribution, 1979–93: summary statistics

Statistic All Households	Units or Derivation	Great Britain			Greater London			Rest of the South East		
		1979	1993	Change 1979–93	1979	1993	Change 1979–93	1979	1993	Change 1979–93
Median	(£s at April 1995 prices)	248.91	257.97	4%	269.4	279.78	4%	278.88	320.82	15%
Mean	(£s at April 1995 prices)	274.92	347.48	26%	301.71	392.37	30%	311.77	409.27	31%
Standard Deviation	(£s at April 1995 prices)	202.09	425.18		246.97	418.71		227.79	419.22	
Coefficient of Variation	(Standard Deviation/Mean)*100%	74	122	48ppc	82	107	25ppc	73	102	29ppc
Inter-Quartile Ratio	(Upper Quartile/Lower Quartile)	3.49	4.08	0.59	3.66	5.11	1.45	3.36	4.21	0.85
Inter-Decile Ratio	(Upper Decile/Lower Decile)	7.40	10.10	2.7	8.09	12.27	4.18	8.01	10.97	2.96

Table 9.9a Changing household income distribution, 1979–93

Decile Income Groups	Great Britain Percentage Share of Aggregate Income			Greater London Percentage Share of Aggregate Income			Rest of the South East Percentage Share of Aggregate Income		
	1979	1993	Percentage Point Change	1979	1993	Percentage Point Change	1979	1993	Percentage Point Change
1	1.94	1.56	-0.38	1.79	1.22	-0.57	1.75	1.35	-0.40
2	2.90	2.40	-0.50	2.71	2.03	-0.68	2.81	2.30	-0.51
3	3.98	3.38	-0.60	3.85	2.78	-1.07	4.09	3.37	-0.72
4	5.83	4.71	-1.12	5.72	3.99	-1.73	6.08	4.85	-1.23
5	8.03	6.45	-1.58	7.91	5.85	-2.06	8.05	6.79	-1.26
6	9.91	8.52	-1.39	9.77	8.21	-1.56	9.79	8.86	-0.93
7	11.75	10.87	-0.88	11.67	10.69	-0.98	11.63	11.51	-0.12
8	13.85	13.66	-0.19	14.02	13.93	-0.09	13.71	14.15	0.44
9	16.80	17.69	0.89	16.80	18.30	1.50	16.79	17.57	0.78
10	25.01	30.76	5.75	25.78	33.00	7.22	25.30	29.25	3.95
Sample (N)	9722	8814		1209	1046		1724	1699	

Table 9.9b Changing household income distribution, 1979–93

Decile Income Groups	Great Britain				Greater London				Rest of the South East			
	Mean weekly income (£s)		Change 1979–93		Mean weekly income (£s)		Change 1979–93		Mean weekly income (£s)		Change 1979–93	
	1979	1993	(%)	(N)	1979	1993	(%)	(N)	1979	1993	(%)	(N)
1	53.31	54.34	1.9	1.03	53.90	47.61	−11.7	−6.29	54.68	55.13	0.8	0.45
2	79.63	83.41	4.7	3.78	81.83	80.01	−2.2	−1.82	87.21	94.06	7.9	6.85
3	109.41	117.48	7.4	8.07	115.48	108.61	−5.9	−6.87	127.80	137.70	7.7	9.90
4	160.42	163.50	1.9	3.08	172.58	157.81	−8.6	−14.77	188.76	198.31	5.1	9.55
5	220.94	224.30	1.5	3.36	238.52	228.65	−4.1	−9.87	251.55	277.88	10.5	26.33
6	272.51	296.08	8.6	23.57	297.06	320.76	8.0	23.70	305.84	364.59	19.2	58.75
7	323.01	377.30	16.8	54.29	351.72	421.75	19.9	70.03	361.32	470.78	30.3	109.46
8	380.34	474.90	24.9	94.56	422.63	544.68	28.9	122.05	428.34	578.75	35.1	150.41
9	462.04	614.18	32.9	152.14	506.51	722.00	42.5	215.49	521.67	718.73	37.8	197.06
10	687.70	1069.47	55.5	381.77	776.83	1290.06	66.1	513.23	791.02	1196.49	51.3	405.47
Sample (N)	9722	8814			1209	1046			1724	1699		

1979 to 1993. The increase in household income inequality has thus been far more marked in London than in Great Britain as a whole.

It is clear, notwithstanding the lack of any strong polarization trend using Kloosterman's measure, and the general upwards shift in incomes relative to inflation, that income inequality has increased dramatically in London and in Britain as a whole. Overall, what appears to have happened, is that the size of the 'rich' group, whether measured in terms of the top quartile or decile of incomes, or in terms of the proportion of incomes more than double median income, has grown substantially in Great Britain and, to an even greater extent, in London, while the size of the 'poor' group, measured in terms of the lowest decile or the proportion of households with incomes less than half median income, has risen only marginally. But because of the discrepancy in the rate of income growth at the top and bottom, income inequality both in Great Britain and particularly in London has increased very substantially. Thus, there seem to be more 'rich' and a stable proportion of 'poor', but the richer have become much richer, while the incomes of the poorest 50 per cent have fallen in real terms. The proportion of the 'poor' group increased slightly, although the poor have become poorer, relative to the 'rich', particularly the top decile who have seen their incomes increase substantially. We would stress that although income polarization has grown asymmetrically, in the sense that the size of the rich groups has grown, there has been a major increase in inequality, particularly in London where the gulf between rich and poor has widened alarmingly.

Changes in numbers of household earners and implications for inequality

Pahl considered shift in the numbers of household earners per household to be of considerable significance for household income and in this section, we examine the changes from 1979 to 1993 paying particular attention to both dual earners and households with no earners. Table 9.10 and 9.11 show this. Table 9.10 shows that the proportion of no earner households rose dramatically in both Great Britain and London over the period – from 31.2 to 41.1 per cent in Great Britain and from 30 to 41.4 per cent in London: percentage point changes of 10 and 11.4 respectively. In Great Britain the proportion of one, two and three + earner households fell sharply. In London, the proportion of one earner households rose very slightly and the proportion of two earner households fell sharply (-7.8 percentage points). This is partly the result of the rapid growth of unemployment in London during the

Table 9.10 The changing distribution of households by number of earners in household, Great Britain and Greater London, 1979–93

	London % ppc			Great Britain % ppc		
	1979	1993	change	1979	1993	change
No earner households	30.0	41.4	11.4	31.2	41.1	10.0
One earner households	34.0	34.4	0.4	31.0	28.4	−2.7
Two earner households	28.4	20.6	−7.8	30.2	26.2	−4.0
Three + earner households	7.6	3.6	−4.0	7.6	4.3	−3.3
All households	100	100	–	100	100	–

Table 9.11 Absolute and per cent change in median gross weekly household income by number of household earners, Greater London and Great Britain, 1979–93

£'s 1995	Greater London			Great Britain		
	Median 1979	Income 1993	% change 1979–93	Median 1979	Income 1993	% change 1979–93
No earner households	84	105	+25.3	83	111	+33.0
One earner households	258	355	+37.6	242	302	+24.8
Two earner households	409	657	+60.5	368	487	+32.4
Three + earner households	608	856	+40.9	538	651	+21.1
All households	269	280	+3.9	249	258	+3.6

1980s but it also reflects the rise in single living which is of considerable importance in London in particular. The Great Britain figures indicate a continuation of the trends picked up by Pahl and Dale and Bamford. If we exclude households with no earners from the data, the proportion of one earner households in Great Britain rose from 45.1 per cent to 48.1 per cent, and the proportion of two earner households rose very slightly from 43.8 per cent to 44.5 per cent, while the proportion of three + earners fell from 11.1 per cent to 7.3 per cent. This reflects a trend towards smaller, single person households in Britain. In terms of the changing distribution of household types, the evidence does not support Pahl. Dual earner households are not becoming proportionately more important either in London or in Britain.

Looking at change in median household incomes in London over the period, we see that no earner households had an average increase of 25 per cent, one earner households of 38 per cent, three earners of 41 per cent and two earner households of no less than 60.5 per cent. This compares to increases of 33 per cent, 25 per cent, 21 per cent and 32 per cent respectively in Great Britain (see Table 9.11). It is clear that, after Pahl, there has been a shift in the distribution of work and rewards, and that two earner households in London fared far better than any other group. It should be noted here that the intuitively surprising increase of only 4 per cent in overall median household incomes – far below each of the groups – is a product of the changes in both the median income of each group and the changing relative importance of each group. Because of the large increase in the proportion of households with no earner (whose incomes are lower than all other groups) and the fall in the proportion of households with one, two or three earners, this depresses overall median household income change. The important point, however, is that two earner households in London have increased their median incomes far more than any other group, and by more than double that of no earner households. This should be compared to the lack of differences for Great Britain and it points to the importance of dual managerial and professional households in London (Butler and Hamnett 1994). These groups have seen the highest increases in earnings and dual earner professional and managerial households have done very well during the 1980s and early 1990s. In absolute terms, the differences are even more marked. Median income for no earner households in London rose by £21 compared to a rise of £248 for two and three earner households: a differential of almost 12 times. In terms of household income, rather than numbers of households, Pahl is correct in regarding the major division as being between no earner households and dual earner households.

The pattern is similar for mean income shown in Table 9.12. Although all household types saw their mean real incomes rise, the increase was greatest (+77 per cent) for two earner households and lowest for one earner households (+37 per cent). No earner households saw their incomes rise by 51 per cent, though this was from a relatively low base. Once again, it is clear that two earner households in London have seen much greater increases in real income than any other group, though the increase in real income for no earner households was surprisingly high at 51 per cent, and no earner households saw the greatest

Table 9.12 Absolute and per cent change in mean gross weekly household income by number of earners in household, Greater London, 1979–93

£'s 1995	Greater London			Great Britain		
	Median 1979	Income 1993	% change 1979–93	Median 1979	Income 1993	% change 1979–93
No earner households	97	147	+50.7	97	155	+60.4
One earner households	298	407	+36.8	266	359	+34.7
Two earner households	432	766	+77.5	392	574	+46.4
Three+ earner households	641	933	+45.6	574	732	+27.4
All households	302	392	+30.0	275	347	+26.4

percentage increase in income of any households in Great Britain. This may reflect the impact of occupational pension schemes rather than any increase in state pensions and other benefits such as unemployment benefit. Indeed, state pensions levels are now indexed linked to inflation rather than to the increase in earnings. Their value is thus likely to fall over time relative to earned income. It should also be stressed that the absolute increase in mean income of no earner households in London was, at £49 per week, far smaller than the increase for two earner households – £335 per week. It can be seen that the differences in incomes for no earner households are relatively small, running from £40 per week in the case of the lowest 5 per cent to £200 per week in the case of the 80th percentile. The highest no earner household (95th percentile) received £400 per week. This is a reflection of the fact that many of these households are dependent on social security. The variation for other household types is much greater, particularly for two and three earner households who received much higher incomes than the one-earner households. At the 75 per cent point one earner households received about £430 per week, but this amount is surpassed by two earner households at the 45 per cent point of the distribution. At the 75 per cent point, two earner households, income totalled almost £700 per week. Whereas in Greater London the income distribution of no earner households is remarkably similar to that for Great Britain, as is that for one earner and all households, the incomes of two and three+ earners are consistently higher. This suggests that Pahl's thesis regarding the growing gap between no earner and multiple earner households is even more applicable in London than it is in Britain as a whole. Multiple earner households in London are relatively very affluent.

Why should mean and median household incomes have risen by much more in London than elsewhere, and why should two earner households in London have experienced the highest increases of any household type? The answer may lie with the socioeconomic composition of different households, and the greater relative importance of professional and managerial occupations in London, especially in financial and business services, may have helped drive these increases.

Changes in household income by socioeconomic group of the principal earner

Its a key element of Sassen's (1991) polarization thesis that income change is linked to changes in occupational composition. The growth of the professional and managerial groups at the top, particularly in business and financial services, is associated with the growth of high incomes, while the growth of the less skilled in personal services at the bottom end is linked to the growth of low incomes. The census shows no evidence of a growth at the low end of the occupational distribution, and this is confirmed by the GHS. Table 9.13 shows that the proportion of professional earners in Britain rose from 4.3 to 6 per cent while the proportion of managers rose from 9.8 to 16.6 per cent, an increase of 6.8 points. In London, professionals increased from 5.4 to 8 per cent and managers from 10.5 to 21.3 per cent. The 'other non-manual' group increased by 4.3 points in Britain, while the skilled manual and semi-skilled decreased by 5.3–6.3 points each, and the unskilled contracted slightly. The pattern of change in London was similar. Both the census and the GHS point to an upward shift in occupational composition, rather than to polarization.

But what of income change by occupational group? Table 9.14 shows median and mean household incomes by socioeconomic group of principal earners. It shows that income change is strongly occupation related. Professional and managerial median household income rose 29 per cent in Great Britain 1979–93, while other non-manual incomes rose by 13 per cent. Median incomes in households with a skilled manual principal earner fell by 14 per cent, and semi-skilled and unskilled incomes fell by between 2 and 3 per cent. The changes in London were even more dramatic. Professional incomes rose by a remarkable +63 per cent and managerial incomes by a more modest 33 per cent. Other non-manual incomes grew by 20 per cent. Professionals in London,

Table 9.13 Socioeconomic group of individual earners, 1979 and 1993

Group	SEG of Principal Earner SEG	Group name	Frequency in sample 1979	Frequency in sample 1993	Percentage of valid cases 1979	Percentage of valid cases 1993	Percentage point change 1979-93
			All earners (male and female)				
			Great Britain				
1	3,4	Professional	534	544	4.3	6.0	1.8
2	1,2,13	Managerial	1227	1496	9.8	16.6	6.8
3	5,6	Other non-manual	4041	3291	32.3	36.6	4.3
4	8,9,12,14	Skilled manual	3255	1854	26.0	20.6	-5.4
5	7,10,15	Semi-skilled	2624	1318	20.9	14.6	-6.3
6	11	Unskilled	816	466	6.5	5.2	-1.3
7	16,17, gov	Other	32	31	0.3	0.3	0.1
Missing			43	6			0.0
Total		All households	12572	9006	100.0	100.0	0.0
			Greater London				
1	3,4	Professional	87	80	5.4	8.0	2.6
2	1,2,13	Managerial	170	214	10.5	21.3	10.8
3	5,6	Other non-manual	670	419	41.5	41.8	0.2
4	8,9,12,14	Skilled manual	334	144	20.7	14.4	-6.3
5	7,10,15	Semi-skilled	263	110	16.3	11.0	-5.3
6	11	Unskilled	86	36	5.3	3.6	-1.7
7	16,17, gov	Other	3	0	0.2	0.0	0.2
Missing			2	2			
Total		All households	1615	1005	100.0	100.0	0.0

Table 9.14 Changing household incomes by socioeconomic group of principal earner, 1979–93

April 1995 prices	Median household income				Mean household income			
	£s 1979	£s 1993	1979–93 (%)	Change (N)	£s 1979	£s 1993	1979–93 (%)	Change (N)
Great Britain								
Professional	433.23	560.71	29.4	127.48	468.42	648.69	38.5	180.27
Managerial	338.86	438.77	29.5	99.91	368.73	529.82	43.7	161.09
Other non-manual	237.92	268.19	12.7	30.27	262.28	340.27	29.7	77.99
Skilled manual	283.15	243.79	−13.9	−39.36	296.28	299.55	1.2	3.45
Semi-skilled	154.95	152.47	−1.6	−2.48	201.93	215.57	6.8	13.64
Unskilled	114.40	110.44	−3.5	−3.96	160.95	160.77	−0.1	−0.18
Other	384.46	428.71	11.5	44.25	388.24	451.05	16.2	62.81
All households	248.91	257.97	3.6	9.06	274.92	347.48	26.4	72.56
Greater London								
Professional	407.70	664.01	62.9	256.31	453.83	826.80	82.2	372.97
Managerial	391.61	522.94	33.5	131.33	441.27	606.36	37.4	165.09
Other non-manual	255.62	308.06	20.5	52.44	281.40	369.70	31.4	88.30
Skilled manual	317.22	203.06	−35.9	−113.78	322.91	288.39	−10.7	−34.52
Semi-skilled	139.32	153.30	10.0	13.98	206.71	240.27	16.2	33.56
Unskilled	128.67	97.39	−24.3	−31.28	175.78	138.62	−21.1	−37.16
Other	497.89	NA	NA	NA	497.89	NA	NA	NA
All households	269.40	279.78	3.9	10.38	301.71	392.62	30.0	90.66
Rest of South East								
Professional	488.23	595.64	22.0	107.41	521.65	753.25	44.4	231.60
Managerial	393.15	499.62	27.1	106.47	423.27	557.10	31.6	133.83
Other non-manual	253.24	309.90	22.4	56.66	280.70	381.00	25.7	100.30
Skilled manual	284.43	313.01	10.0	28.58	305.16	358.38	17.4	53.22
Semi-skilled	156.06	159.61	2.3	3.55	203.81	231.42	13.5	27.61
Unskilled	131.07	117.75	−10.2	−13.32	171.57	151.44	−11.7	−20.13
Other	417.96	382.06	−8.6	−35.9	429.45	506.42	17.9	76.97
All households	278.88	320.82	15.0	41.94	311.77	409.27	31.3	97.50

Note: *479.89* Caution! Based on less than 30 cases.

many of whom are employed in business, financial, legal and related services, have had the biggest rises in household incomes.

By contrast, median incomes of skilled manual households in London fell by a remarkable 36 per cent, while those of the unskilled fell by 24 per cent. This suggests the increase in income inequality in London was driven by growth at the top end as well as by decline in skilled manual incomes. The changes in mean income were even more remarkable at the top end with mean professional household incomes rising by 82 per cent in London, managerial incomes by 37 per cent and other non-manual incomes by 31 per cent. These increases were generally paralleled in Great Britain in a less marked form, though managerial household income rose 44 per cent.

The mean household income of skilled workers in Britain rose by 1.2 per cent but fell by almost 11 per cent in London and the incomes of unskilled households fell by 21 per cent. It is clear, therefore, that the shift in occupational composition and the growth of professional and managerial incomes has played a major part in the growth of household incomes at the top end, particularly in London.

Dual earner professional and managerial households

If Pahl's thesis regarding the advantaged position of dual income professional and managerial households is correct, we would expect to find that these households have particularly high incomes. The GHS evidence confirms this. It shows first that the proportion of households in Great Britain with one professional or managerial earner increased by 5.7 percentage points between 1979 and 1993 from 18.4 to 24.1 per cent and the proportion with two or more such earners doubled from 2.1 to 4.2 per cent. This is particularly impressive when set against the context of a decline in the overall proportion of households with two or more earners. The trend is even more apparent in London. Households with one professional or managerial earner rose by 6.1 per cent points from 21.1 to 27.2 per cent, and the proportion with two or more professional earners trebled from 1.5 per cent to 4.8 per cent.

What is most remarkable, however, is the rate of increase in incomes of dual professional and managerial households. The Great Britain median increased by nearly 70 per cent between 1979 and 1993, far more than the two earner median (+ 32.4 per cent). The result of these increases is that the national dual professional/managerial (DPM) median in 1993 was £805, nearly £550 above the national median of £258. The astonishing rates of increase in national DPM incomes are not quite matched in London, but the absolute levels of DPM incomes in London were significantly higher at the start of the period. Nonetheless, median gross DPM income in London in 1993 was nearly £1000 per week, well above the £657 of all two earner households in the capital, and four times the median for all households in London. Although relatively few in number, DPM households constitute the new affluent of London, and of Britain as a whole.

Household income, economic activity status and unemployment

If dual earner professional and managerial households represent one end of the income spectrum, households where two or more members are unemployed may represent the other. These households are the locus of multiple employment disadvantage. There has been a major change in the proportion of these groups in Great Britain since the late 1970s, primarily as a result of the two recessions. The GHS indicates that in 1979 the proportion of economically active household heads in Great Britain was 65.5 per cent, of whom 62.7 per cent were employed compared to just 2.8 per cent unemployed. By 1993 the proportion of economically active heads had fallen to 59.7 per cent and the proportion of employed had fallen 10 points to 52.7 per cent while the proportion unemployed had risen to 7 per cent. In London the fall in the proportion of the economically active in employment was much more dramatic – from 64.5 per cent to 51.8 per cent and unemployment rose from 2.2 to 9 per cent. There has thus been a major change in the economic activity status of household heads. Looking at the number of unemployed persons in households, the proportion of households with one person unemployed in Great Britain doubled from 4.9 to 9.6 per cent and the proportion with two persons unemployed rose fourfold from 0.3 to 1.2 per cent. In London, the figures were 3.9 to 11.9 per cent (a fourfold increase) and 0.3 to 2.3 per cent (an eightfold increase) (see Table 9.15).[1]

Table 9.15 Numbers and per cent of unemployed persons by household, 1979–93

Number of unemployed	1979				1993			
	GB	%	GL	%	GB	%	GL	%
0	9213	94.8	1158	95.8	7850	89.1	897	85.8
1	477	4.9	47	3.9	850	9.6	124	11.9
2	32	0.3	4	0.3	108	1.2	24	2.3
3+	–	–	–	–	6	0	1	0
Total	9722	100	1209	100	8814	100	1046	100

Table 9.16 Median and mean household income by number of unemployed persons in household (£'s p.w. 1993)

Number of unemployed	Great Britain		Greater London	
	Median	Mean	Median	Mean
0	276	361	305	415
1	161	247	163	261
2	114	180	124	237

Table 9.17 Changes in median real household income 1979–93 for employed and unemployed heads

Median household income	Great Britain	Greater London
Employed heads	+29.2	+38.4
Unemployed heads	–17.0	–3.7

The household income figures for households with different numbers of unemployed people (Table 9.16) show that, the median income for households with no unemployed person in Great Britain, 1993 was £277 per week. For households with one person unemployed it was £160, and for households with two persons unemployed it was £114. In London, the corresponding figures were similar at £305, £163 and £124 respectively.

Using a different measure, and looking at the changes in median household income by the employment status of the head of household (Table 9.17) in Great Britain, the median income of households where the head was employed rose by +29.2 per cent 1979–93, whereas the median income of households where the head was unemployed fell by −17 per cent. In London the changes were +38.4 per cent and −4 per cent respectively. This suggests that households with an unemployed head tend to fare rather better in London than in Britain as whole, possibly because there are better opportunities for other household members to get a job in London.

Changing household incomes and full- and part-time earners

It is well known that earnings for part-time workers are lower than those for full-time workers and one of the key elements in Pahl's thesis, and in much subsequent work on employment change, concerns the impact of part-time work versus full-time work on the household. The

GHS shows that median household incomes for household heads in full-time work were higher than for those in part-time work and that the gap increased over time. In Great Britain the median household income where the head was in full-time work in 1979 was £343 compared to £271 where the head was in part-time work. By 1993, the figures were £450 and £321: increases of 31 per cent and 18.5 per cent respectively. In London, the increases were 49 per cent and 27.5 per cent respectively. The size of the gap between full-time and part-time workers has thus increased considerably.

Household income, gender and ethnicity

Thus far, the discussion and analyses have been presented for all households disaggregated only by number of earners, number of unemployed persons, economic activity status and socioeconomic group of principal earner. There has been no mention of variations in household income by gender or ethnic composition. This is very important and some key findings are given below.

The term 'head of household' is well known to be gender biased, taking a male husband or partner as 'head' if one is present. It is, therefore, sensible to look instead at the gender breakdown of principal earners. The GHS reveals significant changes here, with the proportion of female principal earners for all households in Great Britain increasing by 8 points from 28.8 per cent in 1979 to 36.9 per cent in 1993. In Greater London, the increase for all households was 10 points from 33.2 per cent to 44 per cent. The increase for one person households was a remarkable 16.7 points in Great Britain, from 28.8 per cent to 45.5 per cent. In London, the increase was less marked: from 35.5 to 46.9 per cent. Females now comprise almost half of all single person households in both Great Britain and in London.

Households with female principal earners have incomes far below those of their male counterparts in both Great Britain and London, but the gap has narrowed (Table 9.18). In 1979 households with a female

Table 9.18 Gross total weekly household income by sex of principal earner

Great Britain	1979 Median	1993 Median	Abs change	% change
All households	248.91	257.98	+9.07	+3.6
Male principal earner	300.51	327.33	+26.82	+8.9
Female principal earner	92.86	146.15	+53.33	+57.4

Table 9.19 Total gross weekly household income by ethnic group of household head, Great Britain and Greater London, 1993

	Mean Income			Median		Median GL		Mean GL	
	GB	% of W	N =	GB	% of W	GL	% of W	GL	% of W
White	350	100.0	8367	259	100.0	294	100.0	415	100.0
Asian	339	96.8	182	292	112.7	334	113.6	377	90.8
Black	238	68.0	136	140	54.0	127	43.2	232	55.9
Other	299	85.4	107	184	71.0	176	59.9	286	68.9

principal earner had a median income of only £92.86 compared to £300.5 for males, and the respective figures in 1993 were £146.1 and £327.3. The absolute increase for females was double that of males and the percentage increase was 57.4 per cent to 8.9 per cent. The gap is nonetheless still very wide, reflecting the dominance of males as principal earners in two and three earner households.

It is frequently argued that, as a result of their disadvantaged labour market position, earnings and household income are lower for some ethnic minorities particularly those of Caribbean origin or descent, than they are for the white population of Britain. Analysis of the GHS shows that there are considerable differences in mean and median income by ethnicity. In both Great Britain and London the mean of Asian and black households is below that of white households, marginally so in the case of Asian households, about two-thirds in the case of blacks. Where median incomes are concerned, the difference is far greater. Asians have a somewhat higher median income than whites in both Great Britain and London (112 per cent), but black median income is very considerably lower – 54 per cent of whites in Great Britain and 43 per cent of whites in London. This highlights the relative poverty of blacks in London relative to both white and Asian households. This may be a reflection of differences in household structures, with a higher proportion of single parent households in the black community or it may be a reflection of their labour market position (Hamnett and Randolph 1988) in low paid jobs and unemployment (Table 9.19).

Conclusions

We argued in the introduction that the idea of social polarization, particularly the American version, is in danger of becoming a new conventional wisdom and we pointed to the discrepancy which Pahl first identified between the USA and the European experience. We also pointed to the important distinction between polarization, as measured by the absolute or relative size of different income groups, and income inequality. We have shown that although income inequality increased markedly in Britain 1979–93, partly as a result of the rise of unemployment and partly as a result of the rapid growth of professional and managerial incomes, there is no evidence of polarization in the American sense. With the exception of the bottom decile of incomes which showed a small increase, the dominant pattern in London and in Britain as a whole has been an upward shift in its inflation adjusted income distribution, particularly from the top half of the income distribution into the top decile. It should be stressed, however, that this upwards shift (all deciles barring the lowest one have seen an increase in real incomes) has been accompanied by a massive increase in income inequality. The rich have got much richer and there are far more of them, particularly in London, and the income gap between them and the lower deciles has increased dramatically, but this is not a polarized income distribution in the sense used by Harrison and Bluestone or Sassen.

The distribution of household incomes in Britain or London has not shown absolute or relative growth at both the top and the bottom ends which the social polarization thesis predicts. Instead, the transfer seems to have been from the middle to the top end of the household income distribution. It is, however, a far more unequal income distribution than in 1979, and the degree of income inequality was both higher and increased more rapidly in London than in Great Britain, which lends support to Sassen's idea that global cities in general have more unequal incomes than the nation as a whole as a result of the concentration of high income earners in these cities.

We have also shown that Pahl's stress on the number of earners is important and that households with two earners have done very well compared to other groups. This is especially so where dual income professional and managerial households are concerned, particularly in London where they appear to form the most affluent group of households. At the other extreme, the proportion of households with two or more unemployed members have increased very sharply, although the absolute numbers are still small. Household incomes for this group are among the lowest recorded. We also found very sharp differences in median household income between households with a female principal earner and a male principal earner and less sharp, but nonetheless important, differences by ethnicity of head of household. To this extent, we would argue that Pahl's argument about the importance of the distribution of work between households is borne out. In Thatcher's Britain, from 1979 to 1993, dual earners have fared better than any other type of household, and two earner professional/managerial households have done best of all.

To be in the top decile of incomes was bliss, to be in the bottom a grim struggle. But, while this may be said to constitute a polarization of work and rewards in the sense that Pahl suggests, it is far more difficult to argue that there has been polarization in Sassen's use of the term. What we seem to be seeing in Britain is a growing divide between the top and bottom of the labour market in terms of employment combined with growing income inequality.

Note

1. The definition of household head used is the principal earner if one was present, or the adult male in a two or more person household if one was present.

10

The Effects of Immigrants on African-American Earnings: a Jobs-Level Analysis of the New York City Labour Market

David R. Howell and Elizabeth J. Mueller

Introduction

The improvement in the relative economic status of African-American workers in the 1960s and 1970s was reversed in the 1980s, a decade that also featured a collapse in the relative (and real) wages of the least skilled (Blau and Kahn 1992; Bound and Freeman 1992; Levy and Murnane 1992). At the same time, the USA experienced the largest absolute and per capita levels of immigration since the early part of the century. Significantly, these recent immigrants have been far less skilled, at least in terms of educational attainment, than earlier waves of immigrants in the postwar period. Friedberg and Hunt (1995) report that 43 per cent of new immigrants did not possess the equivalent of a high school degree. And according to a recent study by David Jaeger (1995), in the 50 largest metropolitan areas employed male immigrants were about 16 per cent of the civilian workforce with less than a high school degree in 1980; by 1990 this figure was over 30 per cent. For women, this figure rose from 17 per cent to almost 28 per cent.

Not surprisingly, there is a concern that, whatever benefits immigrants bring to communities, they tend to undermine the standing of lower skilled native-born workers in urban labour markets. In the public policy arena, perhaps the greatest concern has been over the employment and wage effects on younger African-Americans. If this growing presence of low skill immigrants represents an increase in the pool of available labour, we should expect (in the absence of compensating demand increases) a bidding down of native-born wages.

Downward wage effects may be present even if the growth in recent immigrants simply reflects rising demands for labour that is unmet by native-born and earlier cohorts of foreign-born workers, or if they are simply replacing these more established workers as they leave the local labour market for unrelated reasons. The reason is that these newcomers may bring lower reservation wages (at least initially) and/or a lower ability to shelter themselves from wage competition, which may in turn lower wage norms for all workers in the relevant jobs.

Although low skill labour markets are presumed to be highly competitive in the sense that they are characterized by substantial wage flexibility, until very recently the consensus in the research community has been that there is little or no evidence of observable downward wage effects of immigrants (see the surveys by Borjas 1994; DeFreitas 1996; and Friedberg and Hunt 1995). Borjas (1994) has termed this failure to find negative wage effects an 'unresolved puzzle'.[1] It seems particularly puzzling since the sharp growth in the supply of low-skill immigrants took place during a decade in which the power of labour market institutions to shelter low-skill workers from intense wage competition was severely eroded (Fortin and Lemieux 1997).

In part, the failure to find earnings effects from sharply rising supplies of low skill foreign-born workers in increasingly deregulated labour markets may reflect the dominant research methodology, which has been to explore these effects with across-metropolitan tests. Since immigrants are overwhelmingly concentrated in a small number of urban labour markets, such as Los Angeles, New York, Houston, San Francisco and Miami, we would expect wage effects to be concentrated in these same cities. In addition, the effects of increasing supplies of low skill workers on wage outcomes are likely to be strongest for workers in *jobs* that are unsheltered by unions, civil service rules, or craft- and firm-specific skill requirements. Indeed, if wage-setting for low skill workers takes place mainly at the job-level (see Thurow 1975),[2] then the effects of a large increase in labour supply should be explored at the level of detailed jobs in specific metropolitan labour markets.

This chapter explores the possible wage effects of immigrants on African-Americans[3] across jobs in the New York metropolitan area in the 1980s. Among men aged 18 to 65 who worked at least 20 weeks in 1980, African-American men had much lower employment rates than foreign-born men or even than foreign-born black men.[4] By 1990, while the employment rate for African-American women had risen, it fell for African-American men, reaching a level below that for foreign-born women.[5] Equally troubling, and in sharp contrast to foreign-born men, African-American men held a smaller share of total male employment (for those working at least 20 weeks) in 1990 than they held in 1980 (see Table 10.1). Unlike their male counterparts, African-American women increased their share of total female employment.[6] Have recent immigrants had a greater downward effect on male than female African-American earnings at the job level?

The growth of the foreign-born share of the NYC labour market, particularly among low skill workers, and the declining relative position of African-American men raises a number of employment-related questions that have not been adequately addressed to date. Do African-American men and women tend to work in the same jobs as foreign-born workers, particularly foreign-born black workers? While we have a good idea about the industries in which African-Americans work, little study has addressed employment trends at the *job* level – detailed occupation–industry cells. Defined as the jobs in which a group is highly concentrated, both in terms of size (numbers of workers) and share (the fraction of all workers employed in the job), what are the key African-American 'job niches' in New York City? Did they increase, maintain, or lose hold on these jobs in the 1980s? Was the share of recent immigrants in African-American job niches statistically associated with differences in African-American wage levels? If so, was this link stronger by 1990, after a period of high low-skill immigration? More precisely, was the *change* in African-American earnings at the job level associated with the *change* in the number of immigrants in these job niches?

In this chapter we address these questions using data grouped into 'jobs', created by aggregating individual-level Census data for the

Table 10.1 Native and foreign-born shares of female and male employment in the New York metro area, 1980 and 1990 (ages 18–65 with 20+ weeks worked in previous year)

	Female		Male	
	1980	1990	1980	1990
Black native-born	15.7	16.3	11.8	11.6
Black foreign-born	6.1	9.4	4.4	7.6
Immigrant within last 15 yrs	13.9	15.8	14.1	19.3
Total foreign-born	22.4	32.1	23.4	36.2
Public sector share	18.6	18.5	17.5	16.6

Source: Tables 10.1–10.6 US census 1980 and 1990.

New York Metropolitan area into detailed occupation–industry cells for 1980 and 1990.[7] This job level focus allows us to concentrate on the particular areas of the labour market where effects are likely to occur. The first section presents an overview of the distribution of employment for native-born blacks and immigrants using a 'job contour' framework developed by Gittleman and Howell (1995) which categorizes jobs into six groups based on job quality (see below). While the distribution of black workers across these contours changed little, the share of immigrants grew substantially in all six job contours. Recent immigrants continue to be heavily concentrated in secondary jobs where wage-based competition among groups is likely to be the strongest.

Native-born black workers are highly concentrated in particular jobs, and strong wage effects would be most likely to occur if recent immigrants were successful in competing for them. The significance of ethnic job niches is well established in the immigration literature (Model 1993; Waldinger 1996), and is usually understood as a job in which a demographic group (defined by race, ethnicity, gender, and foreign/native-born status) is highly concentrated. In the second section we identify the 12 largest native-born black job niches separately for male and female workers and present the change in the foreign-born share of employment for each. We find that while the average foreign-born share in the 12 black female niches was about 16 per cent in 1980, it was over 31 per cent in 1990. Across black male job niches, the foreign-born share increased from just over 20 per cent to about 37 per cent in this decade.

Substantial penetration into black native-born job niches by recent immigrants may signal either crowding or the adoption of low-wage management strategies aimed at reducing labour costs, or both. Low-wage management strategies became increasingly attractive in the 1980s as changes in public policy and social norms undermined the effectiveness of protective labour market institutions. In this setting, the immigrant share of job employment may have negative effects on wage levels, particularly for African-Americans. The third section presents the results of regression tests of this hypothesis for detailed jobs in the New York City area. Our findings confirm that the recent immigrant share of job employment is negatively associated with African-American male earnings (in all jobs) in both 1979 and 1989. In addition, the *change* in the recent immigrant share of job employment show a strong negative association with the *change* in African-American male earnings in this decade. The results for females are more ambiguous. The separate tests for 1979 and 1989 do not produce measurable immigrant wage effects on African-American female workers. But like the results for men, the *change* in recent immigrant share is strongly associated with the 1979–89 change in female African-American average job earnings.

Changes in the New York City job structure

We begin by documenting the distribution of various racial and national origin groups across jobs grouped by various measures of job quality. This allows us to see where immigrants enter the New York City labour market, where they are most concentrated and how their concentration compares to that of African-American workers. Without a strong overlap between the types of jobs held by these two groups, particularly in the more competitive secondary (low-skill, low-wage) sector of the labour market, we would not expect to find that immigration affects the earnings of African-American workers.

A job contour framework

Using standard Census and Current Population data, the best measure of a 'job' is to make use of both industry and occupation level data (Costrell 1990). Why are occupation–industry cells a better level of job analysis than either industries or occupations separately? There are vast differences in the quality of jobs in each industry, no matter how narrowly defined is the industrial sector (orderlies and doctors in the hospital industry, for example). Similarly, occupation groups include very different kinds of jobs depending upon the industry of employment. Compare, for example, the earnings of a legal secretary with a secretary employed in, say, a private university. Or compare the pay of a truck driver for a local furniture store with a driver for the US Postal Service.

One could, therefore, define jobs by both occupation and industry and then group these occupation–industry cells into a small number of categories based on a variety of indicators of job quality. This would offer the advantages of both simplicity (a small number of job groups) and usefulness (job groups that are relatively similar in terms of quality). Using cluster analysis, Gittleman and Howell (1995) grouped 621 jobs (94 per cent of the non-agricultural workforce) on the basis of 17 measures of job quality[8] and found that the structure of jobs could be characterized in three tiers, or 'segments', each with two component 'contours'. Each of these job contours employed between 11 and 21 per cent of total employment in 1979 (see Table 10.2). The segments and

Table 10.2 Job contours

Job contour	Characteristics of jobs in contour	Jobs typical of contour
Primary sector jobs		

1. Independent primary(private sector)	high earnings
	high share with
	  health and
	  pension benefits
		professional
		managerial
		high-wage sales

2. Independent primary (public sector)	high cognitive skills full-time	teachers police, firefighters postal workers managers/ administrators

3. Routine white-collar	moderate wages
	moderate cognitive
	  skills
	low strength/physical
	  demands
	full-time
		nurses
		health technicians
		clerical workers

4. High wage blue-collar	moderate/high wage
	low cognitive skills
	high share with
	  health and pension
	  benefits
	high share unionized
	high strength/
	  physical demands
		truck drivers
		assemblers
		machine operatives

Secondary sector jobs		

5. Low-wage blue-collar	low wages
	few union members
	benefits rare
	low cognitive skills
	high strength/physical
	  demands
		machine operatives
		carpenters and painters
		cooks and misc. food
		  occupations in retail
		  trade

6. Low-wage service	poverty level wages
	benefits rare
	high share of
	  part-time,
	  part-year work
	higher education levels
	  than in contour 5
		cashiers
		sales in retail trade
		child care workers
		household workers

contours conform nicely to the divisions in the labour market
described in segmentation theories (Gordon, Edwards and Reich 1982).
These six contours were defined using national data for 1979 (primarily from the 1980 Census). Nationally, average earnings ranged
from $17 400 in the highest contour (the private independent – primary
contour), where 86 per cent worked full time, to $4700 in the bottom
contour (the low-skill service contour), where only 37 per cent were
full time. Despite educational attainment that was almost a year and a
half greater (12.8 compared to 11.4), the average hourly wage varied
greatly across the two contours of the second segment of the labour
market, the routine white-collar and high-wage blue-collar contours.
The hourly average wage in routine white-collar jobs was just 70 per
cent of the high-wage blue-collar wage ($5.24 compared to $7.44). Not
surprisingly, 75 per cent of routine white-collar job holders were
female, compared to just 15 per cent of high-wage blue-collar employees. Both unionization and health insurance coverage were also highest
in the high-wage blue-collar contour.

The distribution of workers across job contours in New York City

We employed this job contour framework to discover where recent
immigrants were found in the New York City labour market in 1980
and how their distribution across job contours changed during the
1980s. To begin, we checked the consistency of the contour framework
developed with national data to conditions in New York City. Figure
10.1 reports average 1980 wage and salary earnings for all workers with
at least 20 weeks of work in the New York City labour market by job
contour, separately for males and females.[9] The bars show that earnings generally decline from left to right for both men and women,
confirming that the nationally defined job contours (Gittleman and
Howell 1995), which were defined to range in quality from contour 1
(highest) to contour 6 (lowest), reflect the relative quality of jobs (at
least when defined as average earnings) in NYC. A closer look shows
that each pair of contours (1 and 2, 3 and 4, 5 and 6) appears to lie on
a plateau, suggesting that the six contours can also be usefully viewed
to comprise three labour market segments (independent primary, subordinate primary and secondary).

Figure 10.2 presents the distribution of employment across job contours by sex in 1980. Male workers were concentrated in contours 1 and
5 while most female workers held jobs in contours 3 and 6. Table 10.3
reports virtually no change in the distribution of employment across

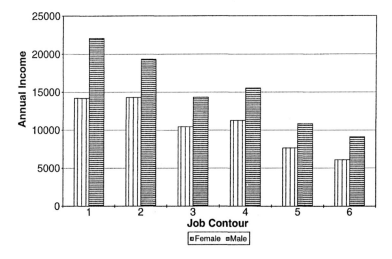

Figure 10.1 Average income by job contour in 1980, by sex

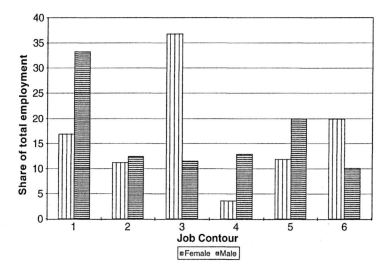

Figure 10.2 Distribution of employment across job contours, by sex, 1980

the contours for men, but a substantial upward shift for women. While 16 per cent of all experienced (20 weeks plus) women held private independent primary jobs in 1980, 22 per cent held these jobs in 1990. There was also a 3 percentage point shift towards public independent

Table 10.3 Distribution of employment across job contours New York metropolitan area, 1980–90

Contour	Female %			Male %		
	1980	1990	Change	1980	1990	Change
1	16	22	6	31	31	0
2	11	14	3	12	13	1
3	35	30	−5	11	11	0
4	4	4	0	12	12	0
5	12	12	0	22	22	0
6	22	19	−3	11	12	1

Table 10.4 Distribution of employment across job contours for native-born black and recent immigrant workers in the New York metropolitan area, 1980–90

Contour	Native-born black %			Immigrant %		
	1980	1990	Change	1980	1990	Change
Female						
1	9.8	14.9	+5.1	9.9	14.3	+4.4
2	12.1	17.1	+5.0	3.4	5.8	+2.4
3	32.3	30.7	−1.6	26.8	23.3	−3.5
4	6.1	5.9	−0.2	3.6	2.9	−0.7
5	17.7	15.2	−2.5	23.6	22.7	−0.9
6	21.9	16.2	−5.7	32.7	31.0	−1.7
Male						
1	15.0	15.9	+.9	23.5	22.8	−.7
2	11.6	14.0	+2.4	4.3	5.2	+.9
3	11.5	12.4	+.9	11.9	10.3	−1.6
4	17.9	17.7	−.2	10.8	10.7	−.1
5	31.6	27.9	−3.7	35.1	35.3	+.2
6	12.3	12.1	−.2	14.3	15.7	+1.4

primary jobs. These increases were made possible by shifts away from routine white-collar (contour 3) and low-wage service (contour 6) jobs.

We look next at how the structure of employment in the metropolitan area has changed for the recent immigrant and native-born black populations. Table 10.4 reports the distributions of native-born black and recent immigrant workers across job contours in 1980 and 1990; each column sums to 100 (per cent). The top panel shows that while the distributions of African-American and immigrant women were broadly similar (both heavily concentrated in contours 3, 5 and 6), African-American women were much more highly represented in the independent primary contours (1 and 2) and less concentrated in the secondary contours (5 and 6) than were recent immigrant women. The lower panel of Table 10.4 shows that with the notable exception of the very best jobs (contour 1), African-American men had a higher quality mix of jobs than recent immigrant men: 11.6 per cent held jobs in contour 1 in 1980, compared to just 4.3 per cent of immigrant men; and while about 34 per cent of African-Americans held secondary jobs (contours 5 and 6), almost half of all employed immigrant men worked at these jobs in 1980.

This table shows that the quality mix of jobs improved most for native-born black women, followed by immigrant women and native-born black men. Only immigrant men experienced a downward shift: their concentration in the secondary contours increased slightly, by about 1.5 percentage points. Based on these data, we should be alert to possible gender differences in the effect of immigration on African-American workers.

Another dimension of employment change that may be relevant for understanding wage trends is the change in recent immigrant share of employment within each contour. A sharp increase in a population known to be least capable of resisting employer efforts to reduce wages may signal either crowding or a downward shift in wage norms. Figures 10.3a and 10.3b show that with one exception (a small decline in contour 4 for females), recent immigrants increased their share of employment in each contour. This growth in the presence of immigrants was most pronounced in the secondary contours, particularly for men, where the increases were in the order of 30–35 per cent (7–8 percentage points).

Unlike immigrant workers, the African-American share of employment in the two secondary sectors declined over the 1980s. This could be viewed as a positive development if this decline reflected a shift to better jobs as a result of skill upgrading or greater access to good jobs. It might, however, simply reflect an abandonment of the secondary labour market by low skill African-Americans, particularly men, in the face of greater competition from foreign-born workers. That the latter accounts at least partially for the observed employment shifts seems plausible given the adverse employment trends for native-born black men outlined at the beginning of this chapter. We examine employment trends in more detail in the next section by focusing on native-born

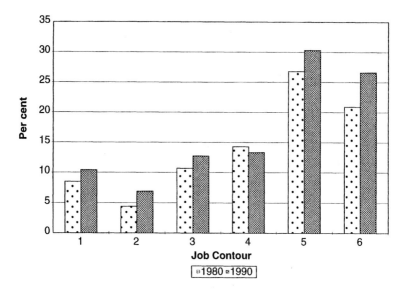

Figure 10.3a   Recent immigrants as a share of employment by job contour, 1980 and 1990: females

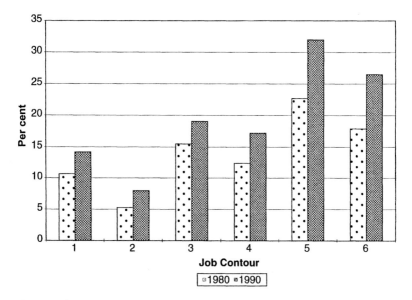

Figure 10.3b   Recent immigrants as a share of employment by job contour, 1980 and 1990: males

black job niches – those jobs in which African-Americans are most highly represented and concentrated.

African-American job niches in 1980

The last section examined employment shifts in NYC with a job contour framework in which each contour is defined as a group of jobs of broadly similar quality. In this section we focus on a small number of jobs in which African-American workers are concentrated in relatively large numbers. We define a 'job niche' for any given demographic group as a job (occupation–industry cell) in which (1) a group's share of job employment is at least 150 per cent of its share of the metropolitan area's employed work force, and (2) there are at least 99 workers of that demographic profile in our sample.[10] For African-American men, this employment share threshold was 18 per cent since this group comprised about 12 per cent of the 1980 New York metropolitan area employed workforce in our sample; for native-born black women, the threshold was 24 per cent. These criteria produced 12 female and 12 male job niches (a threshold of 100 would have resulted in 11 male niches). The smallest job niche comprised just under 1 per cent (0.8 per cent) of employment in both the male and female samples.

Female job niches

Table 10.5 presents the 1980 and 1990 shares of employment in our 12 African-American female job niches held by native-born black, foreign-born black and total foreign-born women. Additionally, the last column presents the public sector share of job employment. The jobs are listed in order of employment size (the largest is listed first). The column labelled 'job niches' defines each niche, giving the occupation on the first line and the industry on the second. General office clerks define three of the 12 job niches. Health service occupations – the focus of much case-study research on West Indian women (Mueller and Howell 1996) – appear in two others. Perhaps most significantly, the second largest niche for native-born black women in New York City was household workers in 1980; over the course of the decade, the African-American share of this job declined from 36 to 15 per cent – by 1990, this job was no longer an African-American job niche.

In 1980, African-American women were heavily concentrated in a small number of industries in New York City. Ten of the 12 job niches were located in just three industries: four were in the welfare

Table 10.5 African-American female job niches in the New York metro area, 1980 and 1990.

Job niches	Black native-born Share of total female employment in job %		Black foreign-born Share of total female employment in job %		Total foreign-born Share of total female employment in job %		Public sector Share of total female employment in job %	
	1980	1990	1980	1990	1980	1990	1980	1990
Occupation/Industry title	(1)	(2)	(3)	(4)	(5)	(6)	(7)	(8)
1 Misc. health service workers: Med. services; Hospitals	32	29	25	33	36	52	25	0.22
2 Household workers: Private households Hs; Pers. Services	36	15	26	24	26	78	0	0
3 Health Technicians: Med. services; Hospitals	29	23	15	16	25	37	24	23
4 Social, Relig, Rec. Wkers: Welfare Services & Educ.	38	34	11	11	21	26	63	53
5 Postal Clerks, Mail Carr's: Transp., Com. & Pub. Util.	60	51	10	5	8	24	100	100

6	Computer Eqt. Operators: Transp., Com. & Pub. Util.	45	47	9	12	15	21	4	11
7	Child Care: Welfare Services & Educ.	31	22	5	14	12	45	75	27
8	Personal Service Workers: Welfare Services & Educ.	40	28	31	16	44	49	46	45
9	Teachers Aides: Welfare Services & Educ.	29	23	2	5	7	25	86	75
10	General Office Clerks: Med. Services & Educ.	37	31	6	12	13	27	40	39
11	General Office Clerks: Public Administration	35	49	4	8	10	21	100	100
12	General Office Clerks: Transp., Com. & Pub. Util.	33	39	7	9	14	22	18	21
	Means	34.4	30.2	10.5	11.0	16.3	31.3	46.4	41.2

services and education industries; three in medical services and hospitals; and three in transportation, communications and public utilities.[11]

While these 12 jobs accounted for 10.6 per cent of all experienced female workers in the metropolitan area in 1980, they employed 23.3 per cent of all African-American female workers. This figure declined to 20 per cent in 1990. Even more striking is the concentration in the first five jobs listed, in which 16.1 per cent of all African-American female workers worked in 1980 and 14.6 per cent worked in 1990. In these largest five female job niches, African-American women accounted for between 29 and 60 per cent of total female employment. These five jobs were also job niches for foreign-born black women; column 5 shows that these workers held between 10 and 26 per cent of the employment in these jobs (the 150 per cent threshold for a foreign-born black female niche is 9 per cent). Interestingly, the black native-born share of these largest niches declined over the 1980s, while the share of black foreign-born workers increased or was stable in four of the five. *Among the full set of 12 job niches, foreign-born black workers experienced a declining share in only two niches, compared to nine niches for native-born black women.*

The results are even more striking for all foreign-born female workers (columns 5 and 6). While foreign-born female workers were not particularly concentrated in African-American job niches in the 1980 (the foreign-born female threshold is 34 per cent), *the foreign share increased sharply from 1980 to 1990 for each of these 12 native-born black female job niches.* For example, the foreign-born share rose from 36 to 52 per cent for health service workers; from 26 to 78 per cent for household workers; and from 12 to 45 per cent for child care workers. The last row shows that the mean share of foreign-born workers in these 12 African-American female job niches almost doubled, from 16.3 per cent in 1980 to 31.3 per cent in 1990.

Finally, with just a few exceptions, these female African-American job niches were characterized by large shares of public sector jobs. Despite the fact that the second largest job niche had no public sector workers, 35.5 per cent of the workers in these 12 job niches held public sector jobs, about twice the rate (18.6 per cent) for the entire sample of female workers. Columns 7 and 8 show that the three job niches showing a substantial decline in the public share of female job employment were in the welfare services and education industries. For all 12 niches, the last row shows that the mean public share fell from 46 to 41 per cent, due in large part to the privatization of child care (row 7).

Male job niches

Table 10.6 lists our 12 native-born black male job niches. These jobs accounted for 9.2 per cent of total male employment but 18.1 per cent of African-American male employment in 1980. The largest three niches in both 1980 and 1990 were located in the transportation, communications, public utilities industry group: bus and taxi drivers, postal clerks/mail carriers and heavy truck drivers. It is worth noting that two of these 12 native-born black male niches, miscellaneous health service workers and social, religious and recreation workers also qualify as African-American female niches.

Two African-American male job niches with large declines in native-born black employment shares were bus and taxi drivers and heavy truck drivers (in transportation, communications and public utilities) and business service workers (in business and repair services and in welfare services and education). Because of their relatively high earnings, perhaps the most serious erosion in the employment share of African-Americans in African-American job niches took place among bus, taxi and truck drivers in the high-wage transportation, communications and public utilities industries (niches 1 and 3). Compared to a mean earnings for all 12 niches of $12 379 in 1979, bus and taxi drivers earned $13 509 and truck drivers earned $14 063.

But the central finding here is that foreign-born men (columns 5–6) as well as foreign-born black men (columns 3–4) sharply increased their share of employment in all 12 African-American male job niches. The last row shows that the mean employment share increased from 7.1 to 12 per cent for foreign-born black workers and from 20.4 per cent to 36.9 per cent for all foreign-born workers. Yet, the mean African-American share of employment in their job niches remained unchanged over the decade at just over 22 per cent. This suggests that recent immigrants are replacing mainly white workers in these African-American job niches. This pattern may be significant for African-American wages if the replacement of older white men by younger immigrants has the effect of bidding down the prevailing wage for the job – particularly the prevailing wage for native-born black men.

Columns 7 and 8 show the public sector share of male job employment in the 12 African-American job niches. While 17.5 per cent of all male jobs in the NYC metropolitan area were in the public sector, 40.4 per cent of the workers in these African-American niches held government jobs (not shown in the table). The last row of Table 10.6 shows that the average public share of employment in these 12 niches was 36.9 per cent in 1980, falling slightly to 34.9 per cent in 1990.

Table 10.6 African-American male job niches in the New York metropolitan area, 1980 and 1990

	Occupation/Industry title	Black native-born share of total male employment in job %		Black foreign-born share of total male employment in job %		Total foreign-born share of total male employment in job %		Public sector share of total male employment in job %	
		1980	1990	1980	1990	1980	1990	1980	1990
		(1)	(2)	(3)	(4)	(5)	(6)	(7)	(8)
1	Bus and Taxi Drivers: Transp., Com. & Pub. Util.	21	18	8	16	28	56	24	18
2	Postal Clerks, Mail Carriers: Transp., Com. & Pub. Util.	22	25	3	6	8	25	100	100
3	Heavy Truck Drivers: Transp., Com. & Pub. Util.	28	21	2	12	10	36	11	13
4	Cooks: Private households; Personal Serv.	20	22	4	8	16	25	43	45
5	Misc. Health Service Workers: Med. Services & Hospitals	30	31	25	25	36	50	37	35

6	Security: Business and Repair Serv.	33	34	10	19	18	34	4	4
7	Building Service Workers: Finance, Ins. & Real Est.	18	19	5	11	34	58	23	15
8	Precision Workers: Transp., Com. & Pub. Util.	26	26	4	11	14	26	55	59
9	Building Services: Business and Repair Serv.	21	15	7	10	40	60	3	5
10	Building Service Workers: Welfare Services & Educ.	22	17	4	10	20	40	55	59
11	Building Services Workers: Med. Services & Hospitals	23	26	16	22	35	60	35	28
12	Soc., Relig. & Rec Workers: Welfare Services & Educ.	29	31	5	10	14	28	66	56
	Means	22.7	22.3	7.1	12.0	20.4	36.9	36.9	34.9

In summary, our analysis of the largest African-American job niches shows that foreign-born workers increased their share of employment in each of the 12 male and 12 female job niches. By 1990 foreign-born workers accounted for over 25 per cent of the workforce with over 20 weeks of work in all 12 male niches. In sharp contrast, in 1980 foreign-born employment reached at least 25 per cent in only four of these African-American job niches. Similarly, among female job niches, at least 20 per cent of employment was foreign-born in each of the 12 niches in 1990; ten years earlier there were only five niches with at least this foreign-born share. Particularly for female job niches, the increases corresponded to declining native-born black employment shares. But in most cases, it appears that most of the foreign-born gain occurred at the expense of white native-born workers, many of whom moved out of the metropolitan area (see Waldinger 1996).

Earnings analysis

The previous section documented the extraordinary success of immigrant workers in carving out for themselves large portions of native-born black job niches in New York during a decade in which the capacity of labour market institutions to shelter low-wage workers from wage competition was significantly undermined. If this success stemmed at least in part from wage competition, and if African-Americans are among the workers in a given job who are (for whatever reason) most vulnerable to this competition, then we should expect to find negative effects on the share of immigrants in total job employment on mean African-American earnings across jobs in the New York metropolitan area. Since immigrants appear to have made the greatest employment gains in the lowest wage female African-American job niches (household and personal service workers), whereas African-American men lost ground relative to foreign-born workers in several relatively high wage job niches (primarily as drivers in the transportation, communications and public utilities industries), we expect that any downward wage effects would be most pronounced for male workers.

We test for effects of immigrants on African-American earnings with jobs-level regressions for 1979 and 1989 and for the change in earnings from 1979 to 1989. Our unit of analysis is the job, defined as a detailed occupation–industry cell. The Gittleman–Howell classification scheme consists of 621 cells and covers about 94 per cent of the national workforce. Our aim was to include as many of these jobs as possible while ensuring that there were enough observations in each cell for statistical reliability. We chose to include the job if there were at least five native-born black females (males) in the cell in our sample. Since it is a 5 per cent sample, this means that in each of the 316 male and 294 female jobs that met this constraint for 1979 there were at least 100 African-American workers employed in the New York metropolitan area. In the 1979–89 wage change tests this threshold was required for both years, producing a sample of 253 male jobs and 240 female jobs. We include those between 18 and 65 years of age who worked at least 20 weeks in 1979 (1989).

The separate tests for 1979 and 1989 attempt to determine whether the immigrant share of employment had a measurable wage effect for those African-Americans strongly attached to the labour market at the beginning and end of the decade. A comparison of the coefficients for each year may also offer some insight about the impact of the surge of immigration in the 1980s on average African-American job earnings: if the *increase* in immigration had an effect, the (presumed) negative coefficient for 1989 should be larger than for 1979.

In these tests for 1979 and 1989, mean log earnings of native-born blacks by job are regressed, separately for men and women, on the new immigrant job share (immigrants arriving within the previous 15 years employed as a per cent of all employees in the job), controlling for (1) mean native-born black (NBB) years of schooling, (2) mean NBB weeks of work, (3) two labour market 'structure' measures (the public sector share of total job employment and a dummy variable for secondary jobs, which are identified on the basis of 17 job quality measures – including wages – at the national level for all workers), and (4) a 'concentration' measure (the NBB share of total job employment). If the recent immigration share has an explanatory role, its coefficient should be negative and significant. If the growth in immigration in the 1980s has an additional effect, the immigrant share coefficient should be larger – and, thereby, explain more earnings variation – in 1989 than in 1979.

As a further test, we regress the 1979–89 *change* in black native-born earnings on the 1980–90 *change* in immigrant share. In addition to mean NBB educational attainment (1980) and change in weeks worked variables (1979–89), we include two 'structural' controls: the share of workers employed in public sector jobs in 1980 (presumably these are relatively sheltered jobs, suggesting a positive wage change effect) and a dummy for secondary jobs (jobs that are relatively unsheltered from wage competition, suggesting a negative wage change effect). To account for differences in labour market demand facing workers in different jobs, we include a measure of the 1980–90 change in total job employment (greater labour demand should, all else being equal, increase the African-American wage, suggesting a positive wage change effect).

We also include the level of black native-born earnings in 1979. Since this measure is highly correlated with mean NBB educational attainment across jobs, we run separate tests for each (shown in columns 1 and 2 of Table 10.7). Reflecting some combination of higher level of job-related skills and bargaining power (labour market shelters), relatively high mean job earnings in 1979 may indicate being well-positioned to take advantage of the more competitive labour markets of the 1980s, suggesting a positive wage change effect. On the other hand, higher African-American wage levels may also measure the incentive employers have to reduce wage levels while remaining competitive for the best low-wage (immigrant) workers, suggesting that we might expect a negative wage change effect.

Finally, we also include two 'concentration' variables, the share held by native-born black in 1980 and the change in that share from 1980–90. The reasoning here is that the greater the concentration of native-born blacks and the greater the increase in this concentration, the lower will be the growth of African-American earnings *if* this concentration and its change over time is a flag for poor quality, dead-end jobs. This suggests a negative wage change effect.

In sum, we can conclude that there is evidence for a negative effect of immigrants on African-American earnings if one or more of the following predictions is confirmed: *first*, the coefficients on the share immigrant variable will be negative and significant with appropriate controls in the 1979 and 1989 tests; *second*, the share immigrant variable will account for more variation in earnings in 1989 than in 1979; and *third*, the 1980–90 change in the immigrant share variable will be negative and significant in the earnings change test, even when controlling for the immigrant share in 1980. The presence of strong immigrant wage effects will be most convincing if all three predictions are confirmed.

Tables 10.8a (males) and 10.8b (females) present the results for the 1979 and 1989 tests. Both unweighted and weighted (by NBB employment) are presented. As expected, the education and weeks worked measures are large and highly significant with the correct (positive) signs for both men and women. For men, the education coefficient indicates a 2–3 per cent increase in NBB earnings with each additional year of schooling in 1979, increasing to 3.7–4.4 per cent in 1989.

The public share of jobs has the expected positive and significant coefficient for male earnings in 1979 but the magnitude of the effect

Table 10.7 Determinants of the 1979–89 change in male and female black native-born earnings at the job level in the New York metropolitan area (standard errors in parentheses)

	Male			Female		
	1	2 (weighted)	3	1	2 (weighted)	3
Black NB	.009			−.017		
educ 80	(.024)			(.025)		
Black NB		−.678	−.428		−.814	−.69
income 79		(.129)	(.102)		(.116)	(.087)
Black NB	2.52	1.99	2.18	1.65	1.46	1.73
weeks 79–89	(.37)	(.36)	(.36)	(.393)	(.358)	(.392)
Share public 80	.0009	.0029	.0018	.001	.0018	.0004
	(.0014)	(.001)	(.0009)	(.001)	(.001)	(.0007)
Secondary	.000	−.193	−.128	.019	−.281	−.271
dummy	(.075)	(.078)	(.058)	(.077)	(.076)	(.053)
Employ	.0037	.003	.002	.0006	.003	.001
growth	(.003)	(.003)	(.002)	(.002)	(.002)	(.002)
Black NB	−.0111	−.0175	−.011	−.0067	−.0068	−.001
share 80	(.0047)	(.0043)	(.003)	(.0039)	(.0032)	(.002)
Black NB	−.518	−.829	−.672	.64	.451	.124
share 80–90	(.558)	(.531)	(.473)	(.426)	(.388)	(.307)
New immig	−1.33	−1.51	−.804	−.627	−1.26	−2.33
share 80–90	(.45)	(.42)	(.343)	(.46)	(.427)	(.327)
Adj R Square	0.193	0.275	0.226	0.098	0.255	0.348
N	253	253	253	240	240	240

Note: Covers individuals ages 18 to 65 with at least 20 weeks worked in 1979 (1989) living in NYC, Westchester and Nassau counties. Includes only jobs with at least 100 native-born black workers in both 1979 and 1989.

Source: 5 per cent Public Use Microdata Sample, US Census.

was small: a 10 percentage point increase in share of public jobs produced a 1–2 per cent increase in mean NBB job earnings. Far more important was the dummy variable for secondary jobs, which, controlling for education, weeks worked and the other three variables, lowered mean job wages for NBB men by 14–16 per cent in 1979 and by 15–19 per cent in 1989. All else being equal, the relative concentration of NBB men in jobs had strongly negative effects for their own earnings: the coefficients indicate that a 10 percentage point higher NBB share was associated with 4–6 per cent lower mean job earnings in 1979, increasing to 8–10 per cent lower earnings in 1989.

The results for our key variable, new immigrant share, show similar strong negative effects. A 10 percentage point higher share of recent immigrants in total male job employment is associated with 4–5 per cent lower NBB male earnings. Across jobs weighted equally this negative wage effect of recent immigrants increased substantially over the decade, from 4.5 to 7.1 per cent. The weighted results, however, show no increase from 1979 to 1989.

Table 10.8b presents the results for African-American women. The results in the first row show a much higher return to education than NBB men received. This appears to be particularly so for NBB women in jobs where they are the largest in number. Across jobs weighted equally, the return was 8.5 per cent, which compares to 2.5 per cent for NBB men; this figure increased to 13.3 per cent in 1989, compared to just 3.7 per cent for men. Weighted by the number of NBB female

Table 10.8a   Determinants of African-American male earnings at the job level for the New York metropolitan area, 1979 and 1989

	Unweighted		Weighted	
	1979	1989	1979	1989
Black NB Education	.025	.037	.022	.044
	(.008)	(.012)	(.008)	(.012)
Black NB Weeks	.045	.036	.055	.048
	(.004)	(.004)	(.005)	(.004)
Share public	.0012	.0012	.0019	.0013
	(.0005)	(.0006)	(.0004)	(.0005)
Secondary dummy	−.156	−.186	−.139	−.152
	(.03)	(.038)	(.027)	(.033)
Black NB job share	−.0058	−.0094	−.0044	−.0083
	(.0016)	(.0019)	(.0014)	(.0015)
New immigrant share	−.0045	−.0071	−.0052	−.0054
	(.0015)	(.0017)	(.0013)	(.0015)
Adj R Square	.561	.508	0.667	0.632
N	316	336	316	336
Mean black NB job earnings	12 280	23 394	12 280	23 394

Notes: 1. Dependent variable is the log of mean native-born black wage and salary income by job (standard errors in parentheses).
2. Covers individuals ages 18 to 65 with at least 20 weeks worked in 1979 (1989) living in NYC, Westchester and Nassau counties. Includes only jobs with at least 100 native-born black workers.
Source: 5 per cent Public Use Microdata Sample, US Census.

workers, the return to years of schooling increased from 12 per cent to 15 per cent over this decade.

Like the results for NBB men, all else being equal, employment in a secondary job produced a strong negative effect on earnings for African-American women, but the share of public employment has little impact. Interestingly, in both the weighted and unweighted tests, the public share variable shows no effect in 1979 and a *negative* effect in 1989. Although public sector jobs are clearly a critically important source of employment for NBB women, these results suggest that by the end of the 1980s they received, if anything, lower pay in public jobs (although we caution that these job level tests are not specifically designed to test this hypothesis).

In sharp contrast to NBB men, mean job earnings for African-American women are *higher* in jobs in which their share of job employment is

Table 10.8b Determinants of African-American female earnings at the job level for the New York metropolitan area, 1979 and 1989

	Unweighted		Weighted	
	1979	1989	1979	1989
Black NB education	.085	.133	.12	.151
	(.012)	(.014)	(.01)	(.012)
Black NB weeks	.03	.035	.06	.047
	(.005)	(.004)	(.005)	(.004)
Share public	−.0005	−.0011	.000	−.0015
	(.0005)	(.0005)	(.000)	(.0004)
Secondary dummy	−.254	−.115	−.172	−.148
	(.037)	(.039)	(.031)	(.033)
Black NB job share	.0048	.0033	.0032	.0059
	(.0016)	(.0014)	(.0012)	(.001)
New immigrant share	.0018	−.0038	.0033	−.0015
	(.0014)	(.0018)	(.0012)	(.0014)
Adj R Square	0.514	0.596	0.722	0.764
N	294	285	294	285
Mean black NB job earnings	10 052	20 889	10 052	20 889

Notes: 1. Dependent variable is the log of mean native-born black wage and salary income by job (standard errors in parentheses).
2. Covers individuals ages 18 to 65 with at least 20 weeks worked in 1979 (1989) living in NYC, Westchester and Nassau counties. Includes only jobs with at least 100 native-born black workers.
Source: 5 per cent Public Use Microdata Sample, US Census.

highest. A ten percentage point' higher NBB female share was associated with 3–5 per cent higher earnings in 1979 and 3–6 per cent higher earnings in 1989. In terms of change over time, African-American women again appear to have benefited most in jobs in which they were most highly represented: the weighted results show an increase from 3.2 per cent to 5.9 per cent over this decade.

On the effects of recent immigrants, the results for NBB women are far weaker than for their male counterparts. In 1979, only the weighted results show much impact, and the effect was *positive*: a ten percentage point higher immigrant share produces 3.3 per cent higher earnings. A decade later, the impact had turned negative and this may be important (see below), but these coefficients are not very precisely measured (both the unweighted and the weighted coefficients are insignificant at the 10 per cent level).

In sum, the results for the separate 1979 and 1989 tests show strong negative effects of recent immigrants on African-American earnings only for men. Comparing the findings for the beginning and end of the decade suggests that there may have been some increase in the negative impact of recent immigrants, but our evidence is only weakly supportive of this prediction – we see an increase in the negative effect of recent immigrants only in the unweighted tests.

Table 10.7 presents the results for our wage change tests for men (253 jobs) and women (240 jobs).[12] The first two rows show that for both NBB male and female workers, the mean level of NBB educational attainment in jobs in 1980 had no effect on subsequent earnings growth. Given the payoff to schooling shown in Tables 10.8a and 10.8b, this is rather surprising. Strikingly different are the results for the 1979 mean NBB income in the job, the inclusion of which dramatically improves the fit of the model: the adjusted R^2 increases from 0.193 to 0.275 for males, and from 0.098 to 0.255 for females. We have no satisfactory explanation for the magnitude of this impact.

Change in the relative demand for workers across jobs appears to play no role in changes in NBB earnings for either men or women. Jobs with an over representation of NBB workers in 1980 had slower earnings growth and this is particularly strong for men. But for our purposes, *the key result is that an increasing share of recent immigrant workers in jobs is strongly negatively associated with the earnings of both male and female African-Americans.* The new immigrant coefficient in the second column indicates that a ten percentage point increase in the recent immigrant share of employment is associated with about a 15 per cent lower increase in earnings over this decade. Interestingly, the change in the concentration of native-born blacks in jobs has a far smaller and less precise impact on NBB male and female earnings change than the increasing concentration of recent immigrants. Indeed, the change in recent immigrant share has a strong negative effect in all but the first female test (which is poorly fitted, with educational attainment instead of NBB earnings).

Conclusion

This chapter has employed jobs-level data for the New York metropolitan area, generated by aggregating individual-level Census data into detailed occupation–industry cells, to identify changes in the quality of jobs held by African-American and recent immigrant workers and to test for whether changes in the recent immigrant share of job employment have had a measurable effect on the mean job earnings of native-born black workers.

Changes in the structure of employment were examined by grouping jobs into six job contours defined by job quality (following Gittleman and Howell 1995). Limiting ourselves to those strongly attached to the labour market (working at least 20 weeks in the previous year) male and female African-American and female new immigrant workers show substantial improvements in their employment distribution, shifting from the two 'worst' (secondary) job contours toward the two 'best' (independent primary) contours. On the other hand, recent male immigrants *increased* their concentration in secondary jobs. While both male and female immigrants increased their share of employment in each of the six job contours, this growth was most pronounced in the secondary contours – particularly for men.

Native-born black workers are concentrated in specific job niches within each of these job contours. We identified 12 male and 12 female African-American job niches, defined by both overrepresentation and the absolute size of native-born black employment. As previous work has shown (Waldinger 1996), African-American job niches tend to have high shares of workers employed in the public sector. Foreign-born workers substantially increased their share of employment in every male and female African-American job niche. By 1990, foreign-born workers accounted for over 25 per cent of the workforce with over 20 weeks of work in all 12 African-American male niches, compared to just 4 per cent in 1980. Among female job niches, at least 20 per cent of employment was foreign-born in each of the 12 niches in 1990; ten years earlier there were only five niches with at least this foreign-born share. Particularly for female job niches, the increases corresponded to declining native-born black employment shares. But in most cases, it appears that much of the foreign-born gain was at the expense of white native-born workers who have migrated from the region.

Did the change in the ethnic mix of jobs, demonstrated both at the contour and the job niche levels, affect African-American earnings in the New York City labour market? Our results show strong negative effects for men in 1979 and 1989 and for both male and female workers in tests of earnings change over the decade. Although alternative variable specifications consistently produced statistically significant negative effects on the recent immigrant share of employment on mean African-American job earnings, we need to do much more work to confirm these findings and to develop a good explanation for them. For example, we need to know whether workers in other minority groups are equally disadvantaged by immigrant competition, by what means recent immigrants affect the wages of other workers in a given job (for example, lower wage increases or the replacement of higher wage workers), and whether the results for New York City hold for other major immigrant-receiving metropolitan areas.

Notes

1. Since the first draft of this chapter, several important studies have found more support for a negative effect on native-born, and particularly African-American, workers (see Hamermesh and Bean 1998).
2. For example, truck driving positions in light manufacturing industries, food service occupations in hospitals, or secretarial positions in the financial sector.
3. We use 'African-American' and 'native-born black' interchangeably in this chapter.
4. The rate for African-American men was 63.2 per cent in 1980, for foreign-born men it was 79.3 and for foreign-born black men it was 74.3.
5. Based on our calculations, using the 1980 and 1990 5 per cent Public Use Microdata Samples, the rate for African-American men in 1990 was 61.9 per cent, for foreign-born women, above 65 per cent.
6. African-American women increased their employment rate from 50 per cent to 58.7 per cent and their employment share from 15.7 per cent to 16.3 per cent.
7. We use as our definition of the New York City labour market the five boroughs that make up the city itself (Manhattan, Brooklyn, the Bronx, Queens and Staten Island), and Westchester county to the north and Nassau county to the east. For convenience, throughout the remainder of the chapter we will refer to this metropolitan area as 'New York City'.
8. Demographic characteristics like gender, race, age and marital status were not employed in the cluster analysis.

9. Throughout the remainder of the study we use the 5 per cent Public Use Microdata Sample from the Census of Population for 1980 and 1990. By including individuals ages 18–65 who worked at least 20 weeks in the year prior to the census, we limit ourselves to those with work experience who are strongly attached to the labour market. It should be noted that one of the effects of an increasing supply of low-skill foreign-born labour may be to push African-Americans out of the labour market altogether, a result that Ong and Valenzuela (1996) report for Los Angeles. We focus only on those who are more than intermittently employed in the above-ground labour market as reported in the Census.

10. This 150 per cent threshold follows Model (1993) and Waldinger (1996). But we add the constraint that the niche must account for a relatively large number of workers. In this study, a job qualifies as an African-American job niche if it meets the 150 per cent threshold and has at least 99 NBB male (female) workers with at least 20 weeks of work experience in 1979 in the 5 per cent PUMS sample for the seven counties. Since the PUMS is a 5 per cent sample, our 99 worker threshold means that there had to be at least 1980 native-born male (female) black workers employed in a job for it to qualify as an African-American 'niche' in 1980.

11. It might be argued that some of these niches could probably be merged together without losing too much information. We have preferred to go with the full detail available in the Gittleman–Howell classification, on the grounds that industry differences can have important effects on the wage and skill characteristics within the same occupation classification (Gittleman and Howell 1995). Even employment trends can vary sharply, as illustrated by the three general office clerk jobs (282, 283 and 333) which appear at the bottom of Table 10.5. While similar in their 1980 native- and foreign-born black employment shares, by 1990 native-born black office clerks had declined in their share of employment in the medical services and education industries, but experienced a huge increase in public administration, from 35 per cent to 49 per cent. Even more striking, the last column shows that the share of employment in the public sector varies dramatically across these three office clerk 'jobs', from 18 per cent in transportation, communications and public utilities, to 40 per cent in medical services and hospitals, to 100 per cent in public administration.

12. There are fewer jobs in these tests since the constraint of at least 100 native-born black and 100 recent immigrant workers in each job had to hold for *both* 1980 and 1990.

11

The Ethnic Division of Labour in Greater London: a Spatial Analysis of Workplace–Residence Relations

Alisdair Rogers

Introduction

Social exclusion arises from the articulation of various distinct processes, many of which possess spatial correlates and outcomes. Among these processes, the geographical relations between workplace and residence are relatively under-explored. There is a well-established literature on the urban residential distribution of ethnic groups, not least of all in the UK. Rather less attention has been paid to the work-related geography of such groups, that is where they work or the spatial relationships between work and residence. Furthermore, how this interaction of living and working spaces shapes the patterns of incorporation and exclusion of minority ethnic groups is largely unknown. This neglect may derive in part from the preference in urban social geography for analyses based on residence and housing markets rather than work and labour markets. But it may also be because of the limited availability of appropriate data at a national level. Robinson (1987), for example, has identified a lack of research on the accessibility to employment opportunities by minority ethnic groups in Britain. Elsewhere he has stated that:

> low rates of car ownership among sectors of the ethnic minority population and the decentralisation of manufacturing from urban cores...mean that *it would be essential to extend study to patterns of diurnal circulation as well as migration.*
>
> (Robinson 1992: 196, emphasis added)

The first and most general question which might be raised on this topic is simply the degree to which Britain's minority ethnic population works and lives in the same places. The settlement patterns of minority ethnic groups in Britain are relatively stable at the regional and metropolitan scales; they tend to reside in the same broad areas in which they initially settled. These areas are disproportionately located within the economically disadvantaged parts of Britain, mainly metropolitan areas, inner cities and industrial towns (Owen 1995; Robinson 1989). The implication of this is that, as Cross and Johnson (1988: 87) state, 'ethnic minorities are now totally dependent upon the fortunes of inner city economies'. But this claim is only valid in so far as minority ethnic groups are dependent on the areas in which they live for employment. Do they live and work within the same areas, and do they do so to a greater or lesser degree than the majority white ethnic population who live in those same areas? Given that there are often marked intra-metropolitan variations in labour demand and economic advantage, residence in inner cities need not imply employment in inner cities.

A specific hypothesis relating to workplace–residence relations and social exclusion is the spatial mismatch. As first proposed by Kain (1968), it addresses spatial causes of the economic disadvantage of some social groups, notably African-Americans in USA metropolitan areas. The general proposition is that, because of discrimination in the housing market, racial minorities are unable to adjust their residential location in accordance with their workplace location. An 'additional travel burden' is imposed upon disadvantaged groups, as well as higher levels of unemployment. The condition is exacerbated in metropolitan areas by a combination of structural circumstances. These include the residential concentration of minorities in central cities, the collapse of central city economies because of de-industrialization and the outwards movement of blue-collar employment to the metropolitan fringes. Trapped in the centre, USA racial minorities are either discouraged from finding work in the suburbs or, if they are not, are obliged to undertake lengthy commutes in order to get there. This process is central to some of the debate on the formation of a USA underclass.

The growing amount of research on spatial mismatch in the USA has failed to provide conclusive answers for or against the hypothesis. Holzer's (1991) thorough review of existing research suggests that, although there is some evidence for longer commutes, these are unlikely to contribute substantially to the observed levels of African-American unemployment. Jargowsky (1997: 125) claims that there is a growing body of evidence in support of Kain's original hypothesis, and that the effect seems to be growing. Much of the dispute centres on the different methodologies and variables employed, as Kain (1992) himself has recognized. It appears to be the case that research needs to be more sensitive to social differences such as age, ethnicity and, above all, gender. It should also pay more attention to changes over time and inter-metropolitan variation. Above all, there are many instances within USA cities of poor African-American neighbourhoods with chronic levels of joblessness juxtaposed with areas of high employment, not least of all in Chicago. Even if there is any substance to the spatial mismatch thesis, there are clearly other mechanisms of social exclusion at work other than physical distance.

An alternative thesis has been advanced by, among others, Cross (1992b) for London and Waldinger and Bozorgmehr (1996) for Los Angeles – the ethnic division of labour. British minority ethnic groups do not occupy common positions within the labour market and occupational structure. Different minorities will be affected by, and react to, economic restructuring in different ways. Some, notably Bangladeshis, Pakistanis and black Caribbeans, are disproportionately located within lower-status occupations, with a history of dependence on manufacturing (Peach 1996a). The Indian social class distribution is more bipolar, while Pakistanis now show signs of moving out of their former dependence on a relatively narrow range of manual occupations. Chinese and other Asians have above average representation in the professional and managerial classes. Furthermore, several groups demonstrate high levels of business ownership and self-employment. These often coincide with particular niches in the economy, specializations in terms of activity and occupation. An exceptionally high percentage of Bangladeshis work in the catering trade. Over forty per cent of British Chinese are also in catering. Among London's Irish, there is a substantial overrepresentation in the construction industry.

There are also good reasons to believe that the factors giving rise to a spatial mismatch in USA metropolitan areas are more muted in Britain. Levels of both racial residential segregation and metropolitan decentralization are lower in Britain for example. This is the case for Greater London (Peach 1996b). Moreover, the main focus group for USA studies – African-Americans – is not an immigrant community. About half the minority ethnic population of London is still first-generation immigrant, although proportions vary from group to group. Even if the conditions for a US-style spatial mismatch are largely missing, there are some suggestions that ethnic minorities are confined by discrimination and exclusion to inner city labour markets. Both Moore (1992) and Roberts, Connolly and Parsell (1992) report that Liverpool's black population is deterred from searching for jobs in some areas because of the threat of racism and violence. Over half of Roberts *et al.*'s sample of young black men reported some harassment in public places, while eight out of ten felt unsafe in the north of the city. Further, Wrench and Solomos (1993) surveyed job seekers in the West Midlands. They argue that employer preference for local labour in the suburbs not only militates against ethnic minorities, but is itself a racially mediated preference. Since inner city employers show no equivalent preference for local labour, minority ethnic residents are doubly disadvantaged. The existing research on spatial mismatch in British cities is therefore inconclusive, just as it is in the USA. But if any one metropolitan region would be suited to explore the hypothesis in Britain it would be Greater London.

Greater London as a global city

This study is taken from a much longer, more detailed analysis of journey-to-work patterns in all UK metropolitan areas.[1] Because Greater London contains the largest visible minority population of any British city, as well as large communities of the principal British ethnic groups, it is the most appropriate case for analysis.

There is no necessary connection between spatial mismatch and global cities; the processes may operate in any urban area. But it is plausible that the processes associated with globalization will accentuate any exclusion arising from the disjunctions between labour and housing markets. If nothing else, the greater size of the London metropolitan area and the longer distances involved in commuting must make a difference. (Greater London measures 1580 square km.) London also shows all the signs of a post-industrial metropolis, that is, decline in manufacturing, growth in service industries and a net decentralization of economic activity. Between 1981 and 1991, manufacturing lost over 250 000 jobs, reducing its share of London's workforce from 17 per cent to just 10 per cent (Howes 1997). Over the same period, banking and finance added 202 000 jobs and, together with other services, increased its share of employment from 43 per cent to 52 per cent. Outside London, in the rest of the south east, employment continued to grow. The regional upturn in employment from the late 1980s was sustained by a disproportionate growth in long-distance commuting, to the disadvantage of inner London residents. The overall decline of

250 000 jobs in London between 1981 and 1991 was particularly concentrated in the centre. Central London contains five of the ten most deprived wards in the country and by any standard of social disadvantage, compares poorly with almost every other UK metropolitan area (*Economist* 9 November 1996).

Greater London is the most cosmopolitan or multicultural of cities in the UK, and by European standards has a very high representation of immigrants and minority ethnic groups. With just 12.2 per cent of the total British population it contains 44.6 per cent of the minority ethnic population (Storkey and Lewis 1996). Just over a fifth of London's residents were enumerated as minority ethnic groups by the 1991 census – totalling 1.3 million. All ten of the ethnic groups recognized by the Census are overrepresented in the capital compared with the rest of the country. The largest single communities are Indians (347 000), black Caribbeans (291 000) and black Africans (163 000) (and the Irish-born account for over 250 000). However, a broad distinction can be drawn between Indians, Pakistanis and other Asians, who are disproportionately located in Outer London, and blacks and Bangladeshis who are more concentrated in the inner city. The analysis of spatial mismatch, therefore, focuses on these latter communities. Almost all the minority ethnic groups who live in London, also work in London, that is, their rates of out-commuting are negligible (Howes 1997).

Data and sources

The main data source on which the analysis below is based is the two per cent random sample of all individuals in the 1991 UK Census known as the Samples of Anonymised Records. For the first time in Britain it provides cross-tabulations of variables by individual. The most comprehensive Special Workplace Statistics do not include the ten category ethnic group classification. The SARs are, therefore, the first and only systematic and national data set which facilitate the analysis of journey-to-work and place of work patterns by ethnic group. There are, however, two main limitations to the data which inevitably render the analysis provisional. First, the sample produces relatively small sub-samples for minority ethnic groups – ranging from 17 025 for Indians to 3382 for Bangladeshis at the national scale. Second, in order to ensure the confidentiality of records, the data are only published at the scale of the local authority – 32 boroughs of London in this case.

From the SARs three relevant variables can be obtained: (a) distance to work in kilometres, expressed here in frequency distribution, mean and median distances; (b) place of work – whether at home, inside or outside the local authority of residence, expressed here as a ratio (I : O) between the numbers working inside the area of residence and the numbers working outside – ratios of above 0.5 indicate that a group works within the borough boundaries more than it commutes across them; (c) main mode of transport to work. Two 'missing' variables make the data less than ideal. Journey-to-work data do not include the unemployed, which might be a significant component of any spatial mismatch. Further, the SARs do not provide information about the destination of journey-to-work, only the distance travelled.

Analysis

By ethnic group[2]

The first question to answer is the extent to which, as suggested by Robinson, Owen and Cross above, employed minority ethnic workers are dependent on the areas in which they live for work.

Because London boroughs are relatively small in size, one would expect lower I : O ratios than for other British metropolitan areas. Although between a half and two-thirds of all groups commute outside their district of residence, the proportions are clearly lowest among Bangladeshis and Pakistanis (Tables 11.1 and 11.2). Almost two in five

Table 11.1 Ethnic group and workplace 1991, Greater London

Group	Numbers	Home	Inside SAR AUR	Outside SAR AUR	I : O ratio
White	46 531	12	30	58	0.53
Black Caribbean	2 142	7	30	63	0.48
Black African	782	8	25	67	0.38
Black Other	357	9	26	66	0.39
Indian	2 723	10	30	60	0.50
Pakistani	363	7	32	51	0.51
Bangladeshi	221	11	38	51	0.74
Chinese	421	11	22	67	0.33
Other Asian	902	8	26	66	0.39

Note: Home includes At Home and No Fixed Place: SAR AUR = SAR Area of Usual Residence.
Source: 2 per cent individual SAR for Great Britain (Crown copyright).

234

Table 11.2 Ethnic group and distance to work 1991: Greater London percentage travelling to work

Group	0–2 km	3–4 km	5–9 km	10–19 km	20–29 km	30–39 km	40+ km	med. km	mean km
White	24	16	27	24	5	1	2	6.45	8.02
Black Caribbean	24	18	32	23	2	0	1	6.00	7.06
Black African	21	18	34	22	3	0	1	6.25	7.39
Black Other	19	18	36	22	3	1	2	6.43	7.56
Indian	22	18	28	25	5	1	2	6.44	8.02
Pakistani	25	17	26	24	5	0	3	6.22	7.62
Bangladeshi	33	16	20	21	5	1	4	5.22	7.20
Chinese	14	15	31	33	4	1	1	7.68	9.23
Other Asian	22	13	27	31	4	1	2	7.16	8.52

Source: 2 per cent Individual SAR for Great Britain (Crown copyright).

of London's Bangladeshi workers live and work in the same local authority, compared with only 30 per cent of whites. At the other extreme, Chinese, other Asians, black others and black Africans are the least dependent on their districts of residence for work.

The longest mean journeys-to-work are found among Chinese (mean 9.23 km (5.8 miles)) and other Asians (mean 8.52 km (5.3 miles)). Two-thirds of Chinese and other Asians in London work outside their local authority district of residence. At the other extreme, black Caribbeans and Bangladeshis are the two most spatially confined working populations. A third of Bangladeshis work within 2 km, compared with 14 per cent of Chinese. Differences among the remaining groups are small. Although whites have the third longest mean journey to work, as many as 30 per cent live and work within the same district. This is probably because whites are disproportionately suburban and outer boroughs are larger than inner ones.

Are Inner London minority ethnic groups more dependent on the inner city for work than their white counterparts? The answer would seem to be that they are not. The proportion of each ethnic group who live in the inner boroughs and work within 9 km of their residence is more or less the same, in the range 76–80 per cent. The only exceptions are the black Caribbean and black other populations, of which 87 and 86 per cent respectively travel less than 9 km. These differences are not great, and certainly not large enough to suggest that minority ethnic groups are significantly more attached to the inner city labour market than whites living in the same area. For all ethnic groups, therefore, somewhere between a quarter and a fifth of Inner London residents commute over 9 km to work. Whether this is within the inner city or to the suburbs, the data cannot show.

The fact that inner city black Caribbeans (and others) are not travelling further to work than their suburban counterparts indicates that a strong spatial mismatch does not seem to be happening. That black Caribbeans in Inner London appear to journey no further than whites living in the same area also suggests that there is no additional travel burden. However, since these data include all social classes it may be premature to draw a conclusion (see below). As many as 45 per cent of Outer London Chinese commute between 10 and 19 km to work; two-thirds travel over 10 km, compared with only 35 per cent of Indians or 40 per cent of whites. This suggests that the lengthy commutes observed in London among Chinese and other Asians, are not simply a function of their disproportionate location in the suburbs. Inner London Chinese also have the longest mean and median commutes.

An alternative way of viewing these figures is to regard them as indications of the degree to which various ethnic groups are participating in the full range of metropolitan labour market opportunities. The assumption might be that, the longer the journeys to work and the less the dependence on area of residence for employment, the more a given group is taking advantage of the city's mix of industries and workplaces. Although there is very little commuting from London to the rest of the south east by minority groups (Howes 1997), within London there are significant differences suggestive of an ethnic division of labour. Bangladeshis stand at one extreme, the Chinese at the other.

By ethnic group and gender

Studies of journeys to work have consistently shown that men commute further than women. USA research has differentiated data sets by gender and found some evidence of greater mismatch among female workers (for example, McLafferty and Preston 1991, 1992). Among the UK minority ethnic groups, rates of female labour force participation vary. For example, while men slightly outnumber women in the workforce (as recorded in the SARs) among whites, Chinese, other Asians and Indians, among the three black groups, women outnumber men. Three-quarters or so of the working population of Pakistanis and Bangladeshis are male. There are also marked differences in occupational and employment profiles between men and women. Some of the observed differences in commuting among ethnic groups may be a function of differences in the ratios of male to female workers. All things being equal, groups with a higher proportion of female workers will have shorter distances to work.

As expected, male distances to work are consistently longer than female (see Table 11.3). Furthermore, the differentiation by gender does little to alter the relative rankings of ethnic groups. Overall, the data suggest that the varying gender ratios among ethnic groups have little impact on the observed differences. Perhaps the main noteworthy finding is that, although white males travel further than all black males, the reverse is true among females. Black African women have the second longest mean distance to work among women, for example. In Greater London alone, 49 per cent of white females work within 4 km of home, compared with 43 per cent of black African females but 54 per cent of Bangladeshi women.[3] Among males, the proportions working within 4 km fall into the range of 31 to 37 per cent for most groups, with Chinese and other Asians lower (28 and 23 per cent respectively) and Bangladeshis notably higher (48 per cent). In other words, male Bangladeshis 'behave' more like women than other men in so far as working close to home is concerned. Conversely, Chinese women 'behave' more like men, with less than one in three working within 4 km of place of residence.

Ethnic groups and social class

It will be recalled that one test of the spatial mismatch hypothesis could be assessing whether minority ethnic workers had to travel further to work than whites. Because higher status workers generally travel further than lower status workers, the comparison can only be meaningfully made by controlling for social class. In many of the USA studies, the mismatch is held to apply mainly to skilled manual or blue-collar workers, those most affected by geographical shifts in the location of manufacturing. Other studies suggest that the impact of reduced spatial access among minority workers is strongest on entry-level jobs, for example part skilled and unskilled employment. Furthermore, as the spatial mismatch is generally held to affect inner city workers, an examination based on an inner urban area alone would be appropriate. Sample sizes for social classes III–V (skilled manual and non-manual, partly skilled and unskilled) within Inner London are sufficient to afford testing the proposition for some minority ethnic groups.

Among black Caribbeans in Inner London, the mean distances to work of both skilled non-manual and skilled manual workers (6.63 km

Table 11.3 Distance to work by ethnic group and gender 1991, Greater London

Group	Male			Female		
	mean	median	% < 4 km	mean	median	% < 4 km
White	9.07	7.52	32	6.71	5.17	49
Black Caribbean	7.98	6.80	35	6.35	5.34	47
Black African	7.93	6.72	36	6.89	5.81	43
Black Other	8.91	7.36	31	6.74	5.95	41
Indian	9.07	7.41	33	6.67	5.23	49
Pakistani	8.41	7.14	37	5.86	4.58	55
Bangladeshi	7.48	5.48	48	–	–	54
Chinese	9.69	8.19	28	8.74	7.24	30
Other Asian	10.13	8.71	23	6.64	5.00	50

Source: 2 per cent Individual SAR for Great Britain (Crown copyright).

and 6.42 km) are longer than whites in the same classes (6.26 km and 5.71 km). Skilled non-manual Indians (6.80 km) and black Africans (6.05 km) also have longer mean journeys to work than their white counterparts. These differences are, however, minor. The absolute distances are also small; 6.63 km is just over 4 miles, which is a journey within Inner London rather than from the centre to the suburbs. About the same proportion of black Caribbean skilled manual workers as whites commutes over 10 km to work, around 18 per cent. There is no evidence that a higher proportion of inner city black Caribbean skilled manual workers is travelling from the centre to the suburbs than whites, which would be the case if there were a marked spatial mismatch of the specific kind discussed above.

If anything, the journey to work data suggest an inversion of the usual expectation of the spatial mismatch. Whereas 54 per cent of skilled manual whites find work within 4 km of home, only 46 per cent of skilled manual black Caribbeans do so. A similar gap exists among skilled non-manual workers, among whom 50 per cent of whites but only 40 per cent of black Caribbeans, find work within 4 km of home. The disparity lies not in the proportions travelling long distances, but in the relative numbers travelling shorter distances. Put another way, the median white skilled manual worker travels 500 m less than their black Caribbean counterpart, while the median white skilled non-manual worker journeys about 1 km less.

This additional travel burden compared with white workers is more apparent among the lowest status social classes (see Table 11.4). Sample

Table 11.4   Ethnic group and distance to work for social classes IV and V 1991, Inner London

Group	Numbers	Mean	Median	% within 4 km
White	2148	4.38	3.52	67
Black Caribbean	278	5.34	4.66	55
Black African	122	6.23	5.00	60
Indian	90	5.81	5.00	50

Source: 2 per cent Individual SAR for Great Britain (Crown copyright).

sizes permit the inclusion of Black Africans and Indians in the comparison. White part skilled and unskilled workers (classes IV and V) do not travel as far to work as their counterparts in other ethnic groups. Two-thirds of Inner London whites in these social classes go no further than 4 km, compared with between 55 and 50 per cent of black Caribbeans, black Africans and Indians. The median white worker in social classes IV and V has a daily commute of more than 1km less than these others. The difference is most striking between whites and black Africans, whose mean distance to work in 6.23 km, almost as far as white skilled workers. Even walking, an additional kilometre in a journey is not far, and the vast majority of all groups are probably working within Inner London rather than the suburbs.

Not only do minority ethnic workers in low status occupations have to travel further to work, but they are more likely to have to pay to do so. The cost of the additional travel burden may not simply be in terms of time alone. The SAR allow for a cross-tabulation of ethnic group and social class by mode of transport to work. For Inner London, among social classes III–V, only white males make use of cars to get to work more than public transport. In general, over 70 per cent of black workers in these four social classes use some form of public transport. Whites however, when they do not drive, tend to travel by foot or by bicycle. For example, 28 per cent of white female part skilled employees and 48 per cent of white female unskilled employees walk or cycle. These are more than double the rates among minority ethnic group females. Whereas over a third of white unskilled workers cycle or walk, only 15 per cent of black Caribbean unskilled workers do so. Rates of private car ownership among Inner London minority ethnic groups are generally low. Sixty per cent or more of black Africans, black others and Bangladeshis reside in households with no access to a private vehicle. By contrast, almost two-thirds of white skilled manual employees have the use of a car or van.

This presents a paradox. The groups with the highest levels of personal mobility in terms of access to private vehicles in fact travel the least distances to work. Blacks and Bangladeshis, though not Indians and Pakistanis, are very dependent on public transport, just as they are on public housing and public sector employment. Their additional travel burden is made worse by their reliance on the timing and routes of public transport systems, as well as the cost.

Residential segregation and distance to work compared

Analyses of segregation have been used as measures or surrogates for the social integration or assimilation of minority ethnic groups. By the same token, degrees of work-related concentration or dispersal might illuminate processes of social and economic inclusion. All things being equal, one might argue that the greater the level of work-related concentration the less a given group is incorporated into a society's labour markets and job opportunity structure. At least, low levels of dispersal among commuting patterns might be regarded as indicative of an inability to take advantage of the full range of metropolitan jobs. Moreover, ethnic residential communities are structured by labour markets as well as by housing markets. The argument might be that, the tighter the connections between living and working spaces, the greater the degree of community. To give one example, Moore (1992) argues that the Bangladeshi community in Spitalfields, East London, fought to maintain a residential base in the area in order to secure access to the clothing industry located there. The Indian community in west London's suburbs is partly shaped by its close connection with Heathrow airport's job opportunities (Baumann 1996). The extent to which residential and workplace geographies overlap or reinforce each other can be regarded as an indicator of the degree and nature of incorporation of social groups into the wider society.

Place of work

Structural location within both housing and labour markets and their geographies are, therefore, important conditions of ethnicity as a form of social organization. Furthermore, degrees of residential concentration and workplace concentration need not coincide. There may be a range of possible combinations. Two groups whose degrees of residential segregation are comparable differ in their degree of workplace concentration and vice versa. Or it may be that residential and workplace concentrations are closely related and reinforce one another.

Table 11.5 presents a series of measures for Greater London (the indices of segregation are taken from Peach 1996b). By and large the two types of measure confirm one another. The rankings at the extremes are the same for residential as work-related space. The Chinese and other Asians are the least segregated groups, they show the lowest mean distances to work and they are among the three groups who work least inside their districts of residence. Bangladeshis are the most residentially segregated and the most or second most constrained in the work-related dimension.

The Bangladeshi population is the most recently arrived of the main immigrant groups and the group with the lowest overall socio-economic status and the highest levels of residential segregation. They are also the most confined in terms of daily work patterns. Of all the British minority ethnic groups they most closely fit the description of a ghetto or a spatial enclave economy. About one-third of Bangladeshis active in the labour market are unemployed, while two-thirds of males are in some form of manual employment. But at the same time, levels of self-employment among males aged 30–44 are almost double the national rate. Bangladeshis can be characterized as a mostly working-class population but with high levels of entrepreneurship. Two-thirds of employed males are in distribution and catering alone. They are also physically concentrated, with almost one-quarter of the British population resident in just one London borough, Tower Hamlets. On average, their levels of residential segregation are ten or so points above the next most segregated group, Pakistanis (Peach 1996b). This is reinforced by levels of workplace concentration and personal mobility. Fifty-nine per cent of Bangladeshis live in households with no access to a private vehicle. Half work within 4 km of home, rising to 54 per cent in Inner London. In all metropolitan areas, one in five walks to work, the highest levels for this mode of transport. Much of this spatial concentration of daily work patterns may be due to their heavy concentration in Tower Hamlets, which supports not only the catering enclave but also affords access to the garment industry. This is not unusual among recently arrived immigrant groups. A further factor may be heavy dependence on public housing, which accounts for over two-fifths of Bangladeshi households. It has been argued that dependence on public housing introduces disincentives to residential mobility. This may affect their future social and spatial integration into metropolitan labour markets.

The workspace findings complete a picture of a strongly (by British standards) encapsulated community with a relatively enclosed residential

Table 11.5 Greater London 1991: comparison of residential segregation, distance to work and place of work

Group	Index of segregation	I:O ratio	Mean distance to work	% Inside SAR AUR
White	35	0.53	8.02	30
Black Caribbean	45	0.48	7.06	30
Black African	41	0.38	7.39	25
Black Other	36	0.39	7.56	26
Indian	49	0.50	8.02	30
Pakistani	49	0.51	7.62	32
Bangladeshi	63	0.74	7.20	38
Chinese	26	0.33	9.23	22
Other Asian	29	0.39	8.52	26

Source: 2 per cent Individual SAR for Great Britain (Crown copyright). Indices of segregation Peach (1996b).

and work-related geography. Many of the conditions associated with ghettoization are apparent, notwithstanding the evidence of a selective enclave economy.

Given the high levels of business ownership, particularly in catering, the Chinese community might be expected to conform most to the middleman minority type. But while this might account for a portion of the Chinese workforce, overall they appear more typical of an integrated, professional population. Although Chinese and other Asians appear consistently as the lengthiest commuters, there are important differences between them. Both are overrepresented in social classes I and II relative to whites (Cheng 1996), but other Asians have a below average level of self-employment. By contrast, 55 per cent of Chinese are in the catering and distribution industries. Given this concentration in the higher social classes, the lengthy commutes are not unexpected. But even within social classes I and II, they have the longest mean distances to work. There are signs of a bimodal distribution among the Chinese, but not other Asians. While for all metropolitan areas, 54 per cent work outside their district of residence, 14 per cent are recorded as working at home. This compares with only 10 per cent of whites. This bimodality does not appear as marked in Greater London as other metropolitan areas, where the at home proportion is less than that of whites.

Chinese and other Asians are the least segregated ethnic groups in Britain (Peach 1996b). Despite their concentration in Greater London, they are dispersed throughout the boroughs. Other Asians, like Indians, are found more in Outer than in Inner London. Storkey and Lewis (1996) suggest that this thin spread among the Chinese is 'partly because of the demands of the catering trade' (pp. 213–15). There may be some truth in this conjecture, but if catering was a significant factor in determining location then one might expect lower commutes. The evidence offers only partial support for this middleman type. Furthermore, Champion (1996) finds that for 1990–91, Chinese and other Asians have above average rates of inter-regional mobility but relatively low levels of short distance migration. Does this mean that long commutes are substituting for short distance residential mobility? Both men and women among the Chinese and men among the other Asians undertake long journeys to work. They do so with a level of access to private vehicles below that of whites and Indians. In London, they are the biggest users of the underground, about 30 per cent, and rely more on public transport than private vehicles. Is access to the underground an important factor in influencing location? A third or more of metropolitan Chinese and other Asians are commuting 10 km or more to work each day. A great proportion of these trips is to Central London, and Westminster in particular (Howes 1997). Other Asians tend to live more in the suburbs, while the Chinese are more central. Given the high rates of business ownership among the Chinese relative to other Asians, it may be that the two groups represent different paths to the same end, long distance commuting.

Summary and conclusion

The objective of this chapter was to describe and analyze data on daily work journeys for Greater London in order to shed a slightly different light on processes of social exclusion from the usual labour market or spatial concentration studies. The data were obtained from the 2 per cent individual Sample of Anonymised Records and, although they contain several limitations, they do provide a unique national quantitative survey hitherto not available.

A number of key questions were attempted. First, it has been observed by several authors that British minority ethnic groups are particularly dependent upon the fortunes of relatively disadvantaged local economies. This might be taken as an obstacle to social and spatial mobility. It was found that for the whole of London 60–70 per cent of most ethnic groups commute outside their borough of residence.

The exceptions are Pakistanis and Bangladeshis, among whom only half do so. Turning to figures for distance to work, only about 40 per cent of all workers travel less than 4 km. Again, Bangladeshis are the exception: one-third work within 2 km, compared with only 14 per cent of Chinese employees. In Inner London the vast majority of minority ethnic groups who live there also work there. But between one-fifth and one-quarter of those recorded in work commute outside these areas (that is over 9 km). But this dependency is generally shared with white residents of the inner city.

Furthermore, figures for commuting distances and ratios of people working inside and outside their local authority districts of residence demonstrate a wide variation in dependence upon the immediate area for work. The Chinese, other Asians and, to some degree, black Africans, travel longer distances than whites. Other groups, notably Bangladeshis and Pakistanis, are more generally spatially restricted. These broad patterns do not simply reflect relative location in inner and outer boroughs, social class distributions or variations in female labour force participation.[4] That is to say, there remains an 'ethnic' component. For example, even among the upper social classes, Chinese, other Asians and black Africans commute long distances. Furthermore, two of the most spatially contained groups, Bangladeshis and Pakistanis, have the lowest proportions of female workers.

There was little evidence of a US-style spatial mismatch, in which minority ethnic workers in inner areas are obliged to commute long distances to find work in the suburbs. There is some evidence that Inner London black Caribbean and black other workers are more likely to work within 9 km than whites, although the differences are not great. But there is no indication that black Caribbeans living in the centre commute further than those living in the suburbs, as would be the case if there were reverse commuting. Among unskilled and part skilled workers in Inner London, some minority groups had to travel further than whites. The additional travel burden is only of the order of 0.5–1km. If anything, the reverse is the case, that is, the disparity lies less in the proportion travelling long distances than in the relative numbers journeying short distances. For example, whereas 54 per cent of skilled manual whites in Inner London find work within 4 km of their homes, only 40 per cent of black Caribbeans do so. Furthermore, these workers were also more dependent on public transport than whites. Over 70 per cent of black workers in classes III–V use some form of public transport, while whites are more likely to make use of cars. Although the evidence for a spatial mismatch in terms of an 'additional travel burden' is small, there is a clear indication of a 'transport mismatch'. The groups with the highest rates of personal mobility among classes II–V are also those who are able to find work closest to home.

These negative findings for a spatial mismatch are, however, provisional. The data used exclude the unemployed, and many tests of the hypothesis argue that the effect is evident most in higher levels of minority unemployment. It might also be that a more fine-grained analysis based on age, skill and industry would reveal more. The spatial scale of analysis is too coarse to capture adequately the pockets of extreme social exclusion which undoubtedly exist in London. Last, the analysis raises questions of whether testing US-derived models in a European context is always appropriate. The study of migrants, race, ethnicity and space has been too often conducted in the shadow of USA cities. Despite the evident impact of globalization, there remain strong local differences. What is less certain is whether these local differences in any way constitute a common Western European model.

What the data do suggest is that there is a complex ethnic division of labour which includes different patterns of incorporation into the spatio-temporal matrix of the metropolis. The simple model of minority ethnic groups being concentrated in the inner and declining parts of metropolitan areas does not hold for Greater London. Comparisons of work-related spatial data and figures for residential concentration indicate that they operate together and not separately. Ethnic groups with high degrees of residential segregation have low levels of spatial incorporation into the metropolitan spatial labour market and vice versa. The example of three groups, Bangladeshis on the one hand and Chinese and other Asians on the other, illustrates these differences. The former are spatially encapsulated in their patterns of both living and working, while the latter are more dispersed residentially and undertake longer journeys to the workplace.

The data on journeys to work are, at best, only approximations of the experience of living, working and travelling in UK metropolitan areas. They reveal nothing of the times of day during which they are undertaken, the dependability or otherwise of public transport or the difficulties of combining work trips with other daily activities. Black Africans, particularly women, appear to undertake longer journeys to work than might be expected. Daley (1996) presents anecdotal evidence of the prominence of black African women among London's early morning commuters, presumably destined for office cleaning jobs around the capital. She also notes that there might be a high incidence of illegal work, part-time labour and multiple job-holding which together contribute to a diverse and complex position in the labour market.

Does this mean that there is a 'temporal mismatch' alongside a possible spatial one? Globalization involves a transformation in urban labour markets and working conditions, including new working practices among the salariat. These include both longer and more flexible working hours and, in some cases, a blurring of conventional distinctions between work and leisure or play, workplace and residence. But at the temporal margins of globalization, at the edges of the salariat's working day lie lower-wage, more part-time and less secure workers. They clean offices first thing in the morning or last thing at night, provide security, service restaurants, fast-food outlets and all-night stores. They probably include a high proportion of immigrant and minority ethnic workers. If there is any substance to Sassen's general thesis of a polarization or bifurcation of the labour force in global cities, then it presumably involves a restructuring of the working day at either end of the scale (Sassen 1996).

This opens up the possibility of what Doreen Massey (1993: 62) terms a 'politics of mobility and access', one which includes a temporal dimension. Castells writes of:

> the fundamental urban dualism of our time. It opposes the cosmopolitanism of the elite, living on a daily connection to the whole world (functionally, socially, culturally), to the tribalism of local communities.
>
> (1994: 30)

Although such disjunctures are commonly interpreted through both material and metaphorical spaces, it might be just as pertinent to inquire into the temporalities of such difference. Absence from socially significant times and the obstacles to reconciling personal, family and work times may be as strong modes of social exclusion as anything spatial. Residence in large cities necessitates the co-ordination of a range of individual and social activities within the time and space constraints of the city, its institutions and circulation patterns. The capacity of individuals to negotiate their daily paths through the city obviously differs from person to person. It may also differ systematically along lines of gender, class and, as discussed here, ethnicity. The SARs data used here isolate but one component of this geography, but they do suggest that social geographers' standing interest in residential patterns as a key to understanding social processes can be broadened to include other aspects of urban living. If there is any substance in concepts such as spatial marginalization or spatial exclusion, then it is probable that they will extend to the problems of co-ordinating and combining the demands of residence and workplace.

Acknowledgements

This work is based upon the Samples of Anonymised Records provided through the Census Microdata Unit of the University of Manchester with the support of the ESRC/JISC/DENI. All SAR data are reproduced with the permission of the controller of Her Majesty's Stationery Office and are subject to Crown copyright.

Notes

1. A copy of the full analysis – in the form of a first draft – is available from the author.
2. The strengths and limitations of the OPCS ethnic group classification have been discussed widely elsewhere (Ballard 1997; Peach 1996a) They are not perfect, containing as they do a number of portmanteau groups, such as Other Asian or Black Other. In the analysis, the Other group has been omitted as, by definition, it is a residual category including people who could not be placed elsewhere. Whites include Irish-born. The SARs do contain a place of birth variable, which would allow further classification.
3. The sample size for Bangladeshi women is too small to allow meaningful calculation of mean and median.
4. The full social class analysis is not presented here; a copy is available from the author.

References

Abramson, A. and M. Tobin (1995) 'The changing geography of metropolitan opportunity: the segregation of the poor in US metropolitan areas 1970–1990', *Housing Policy Debate* Vol. 6: 45–72.

Adams, T.K., G.J. Duncan and W.L. Rodgers (1988) 'Separate societies', in F.R. Harris and W.R. Wilkins (eds), *Quiet Riots: Race and Poverty in the United States*, New York: Pantheon.

Akbari, A.H. (1989) 'The benefits of immigrants to Canada: evidence on tax and public services', *Canadian Public Policy – Analyse de Politiques* Vol. 15 No. 4: 424–35.

Alba, R.D., J. Handl and W. Müller (1994) 'Etnische Ungleichheit im Deutschen Bildungssystem', *Kölner Zeitschrift für Soziologie und Sozialpsychologie* Vol. 46: 209–37.

Aldrich, H. and E. Auster (1984) 'Small business vulnerability, ethnic enclaves, and ethnic enterprises', in R. Ward and R. Jenkins (eds), *Ethnic Communities in Business*, Cambridge: Cambridge University Press: 39–54.

Allen, J.P. and E. Turner (1997) *The Ethnic Quilt: Population Diversity in Southern California*, Northridge CA: Center for Geographical Studies of California State University.

Altvater, E. and B. Mahnkopf (1996) *Grenzen der Globalisierung, Ökonomie, Ökologie und Politik in der Weltgesellschaf*, Münster: Westfälisches Dampfboot.

Amersfoort, van H. and C. Cortie (1996) 'Social polarisation in a welfare state? Immigrants in the Amsterdam region', *New Community* Vol. 22 No. 4: 671–87.

Anderson, E. (1990) *Streetwise*, Chicago: University of Chicago Press.

Arnold, F. (1984) 'West Indians and London's hierarchy of discrimination', *Ethnic Groups* Vol. 6: 47–64.

Arnold, F. (1996) 'Los Angeles West Indian immigrant women: "Claimin' De Not Black, De Jus' Tillin' De Bitter Harvest"', paper presented at the Annual Meeting of the American Sociological Association, New York.

Atkinson, A.B., L. Rainwater, and T.M. Smeeding (1995) *Income Distribution in OECD Countries: Evidence from the Luxembourg Income Study*, Paris: Organization for Economic Cooperation and Development.

Australian Bureau of Statistics (1982) *Labour Statistics – Australia*, Canberra: Commonwealth Government Printer.

Australian Bureau of Statistics (1984) *Census of Population and Housing, 1981: Persons Sample File, User's Guide for the Machine-Readable Data File*, Canberra: Australian National University Social Science Data Archives.

Australian Bureau of Statistics (1985) *Labour Force Status and Educational Attainment, Australia. Cat. No. 6235.0*, Canberra: Commonwealth Government Printer.

Australian Bureau of Statistics (1990) *Labour Force Status and Educational Attainment, Australia. Cat. No. 6235.0*, Canberra: Commonwealth Government Printer.

Baker, M. and D. Benjamin (1995) 'The receipt of transfer payments by immigrants to Canada', *Journal of Human Resources* Vol. 30 No. 4: 650–76.

Baker, M. and D. Benjamin (1997) 'The role of the family in immigrants' labor market activity: an evaluation of alternative explanations', *American Economic Review* Vol. 87: 705–27.

Baker, M., J. Sloan and F. Robertson (1994) *The Rationale for Australia's Skilled Immigration Program*, Canberra: Australian Government Publishing Service.

Ballard, R. (1997) 'The construction of a conceptual vision: "Ethnic Groups" and the 1991 UK Census', *Ethnic and Racial Studies* Vol. 20: 182–94.

Bamber, G.J. and R.D. Lansbury (1993) *International and Comparative Employment Relations – A Study of Industrialised Market Economics*, St. Leonards, NSW: Allen and Unwin.

Banfield, E.C. (1970) *The Unheavenly City: The Nature and Future of our Urban Crisis*, Boston: Little, Brown.

Bartel, A.P. (1989) 'Where do the new US immigrants live?', *Journal of Labour Economics* Vol. 7 No. 4: 371–91.

Baumann, G. (1996) *Contesting Culture: Discourses of Identity in Multi-Ethnic London*, Cambridge: Cambridge University Press.

Beggs, J.J. (1995) 'The institutional environment: implications for race and gender inequality in the US labour market', *American Sociological Review* Vol. 60: 612–33.

Bender, T. (1975) *Toward an Urban Vision: Ideas and Institutions in Nineteenth Century America*, Lexington: University of Kentucky Press.

Bericht der Sachverständigenkommission (1997) *Jahresgutachten des Sachverständigenrates zur Begutachtung der gesamtwirtschaftlichen Entwicklung 1996/97*, Bonn: Federal Department of Economics.

Berry, J.W., R. Kalin and D.M. Taylor (1977) *Multiculturalism and Ethnic Attitudes in Canada*, Ottawa: Minister of Supply and Services Canada.

Berthoud, R. (2000) 'Ethnic employment penalties in Britain', *Journal of Ethnic and Migration Studies* Vol. 26, No. 3: 389–416.

Bertone, S. and G. Griffen (1992) *Immigrant Workers and Trade Unions*, Canberra: Australian Government Publishing Service.

Bibby, R.W. (1995) *Social Trends Canadian Style*, Toronto: Stoddart Publishing.

Birrell, R. and T. Birrell (1987) *An Issue of People: Population and Australian Society*, 2nd edn., Melbourne: Longman Cheshire.

Blau, F.D. (1980) 'Immigration and labor earnings in early twentieth century America', *Research in Population Economics* Vol. 2.

Blau, F.D. and L.M. Kahn (1992) 'Race and gender pay differentials', National Bureau of Economic Research Working Paper No. 4120.

Blumer, H. (1958) 'Race prejudice as a sense of group position', *Pacific Sociological Review* Vol. 1: 3–7.

Blüthmann, H. (1996) 'Flüchtige Gewinne', *Die Zeit* 23 August, p.8.

Boli, J. and G.M. Thomas (1997) 'World culture in the world policy: a century of interorganizational non-governmental organization', *American Sociological Review* Vol. 62.

Bonacich, E. and J. Modell (1980) *The Economic Basis of Ethnic Solidarity*, Berkeley: University of California Press.

Borjas, G.J. (1985) 'Assimilation, changes in cohort quality, and the earnings of immigrants', *Journal of Labour Economics* Vol. 3 No. 4: 463–89.

Borjas, G.J. (1988) *International Differences in the Labour Market Performance of Immigrants*, Kalamazoo, Michigan: W.E. Upjohn Institute for Employment Research.

Borjas, G.J. (1989) 'Immigrant and emigrant earnings: a longitudinal study', *Economic Inquiry* Vol. 27.

Borjas, G.J. (1990) *Friends or Strangers*, New York: Basic Books.

Borjas, G.J. (1991) 'Immigration and self-selection', in J.M. Abowd and R.B. Freeman (eds), *Immigration, Trade, and the Labour Market*, Chicago: University of Chicago Press for the National Bureau of Economic Research, 29–76.

Borjas, G.J. (1993) 'Immigration policy, national origin, and immigrant skills: a comparison of Canada and the United States', in D. Card and R.B. Freeman (eds), *Small Differences that Matter: Labour Markets and Income Maintenance in Canada and the United States*, Chicago: University of Chicago Press, 21–43.

Borjas, G.J. (1994) 'The economics of immigration', *Journal of Economic Literature* Vol. 32, December: 1667–717.

Borjas, G.J. (1995) 'The economic benefits from immigration', *Journal of Economic Perspectives* Vol. 9: 3–22.

Borjas, G. (1996) 'The new economics of immigration', *The Atlantic* November, Vol. 278.

Borjas, G.J. and S.J. Trejo (1991) 'Immigrant participation in the welfare system', *Industrial and Labour Relations Review* Vol. 44 No. 2: 195–211.

Borjas, G.J., R.B. Freeman and L.F. Katz (1996) 'Searching for the effect of immigration on the labor market', National Bureau of Economic Research Working Paper No. 5454.

Bornschier, V. and H. Stamm (1990) 'Transnational corporations', in A. Martinelli and N.J. Smelser (eds), *Economy and Society*, Newbury Park: Sage, Chapter 8.

Bound, J. and R.B. Freeman (1992) 'What went wrong? The erosion of the relative earnings and employment of young black men in the 1980s', *Quarterly Journal of Economics* Vol. 107, February: 201–32.

Bourdieu, P. (1996) 'Champ politique, champ des sciences sociales, champ journalistique', *Cahiers de recherche du GRS*, Université Lumière-Lyon II: 5–42.

Bouvier, L. (1991) *Peaceful Invasions: Immigration and Changing America*, Maryland: Lanham Press.

Bovenkerk, F. (1992) *Testing Discrimination in Natural Experiments: A Manual for International Comparative Research on Discrimination on the Grounds of 'Race' and Ethnic Origin*, Geneva: International Labour Office.

Bradbury, B. (1993) 'Male wage inequality before and after tax: a six-country comparison', Kensington, NSW, Australia: Social Policy Research Centre, University of New South Wales, Discussion Paper No. 42.

Breton, R., W.W. Isajiw, W.E. Kalbach and J.G. Reitz (1990) *Ethnic Identity and Equality: Varieties of Experience in a Canadian City*, Toronto: University of Toronto Press.

Brown, C. and P. Gay (1994). 'Racial discrimination 17 years after the Act', in P. Burstein (ed.), *Equal Employment Opportunity* New York: Aldine de Gruyter, 315–27.

Buck, N. (1994) 'Social divisions and labour market change in London: global national and urban factors', unpublished paper for ESRC London Seminar, 28 October.

Bundesvereinigung der Deutschen Arbeitgeberverbände (1994) *Sozialstaat vor dem Umbau*, Köln: Bundesvereinigung.

Burgers, J. and G. Engbersen (1996) 'Globalisation, migration and undocumented immigrants', *New Community* Vol. 22 No. 4: 619–36.

Burridge, K., L. Foster and G. Turcotte (eds) (1997) *Canada–Australia: Towards a Second Century of Partnership*, Ottawa: International Council for Canadian Studies and Carleton University Press.

Butler, T. (1997) *Gentrification and the Middle Classes*, Aldershot: Ashgate.

Butler, T. and C. Hamnett (1994) 'Gentrification, class and gender: comments on Warde's "gentrification as consumption"', *Society and Space* Vol. 12: 477–93.

Cabinet Office (1996) Civil Service Data Summary 1996, Development and Equal Opportunities Division.

Canada, Statistics Canada (Dominion Bureau of Statistics) (1963) *1961 Census of Canada Population: Schooling by Age Groups*, Cat. No. 92–577, Ottawa: Queens Printer.

Canada, Statistics Canada (1974) *1971 Census of Canada Population: The Out-of-School Population*, Cat. No. 92–743, Ottawa: Information Canada.

Canada, Statistics Canada (1978) *1976 Census of Canada. Population: Level of Schooling, by Age Groups*, Cat. No. 92–827, Ottawa: Supply and Services Canada.

Canada, Statistics Canada (1984a) *1981 Census of Canada. Population: School Attendance and Level of Schooling*, Cat. No. 92–914, Ottawa: Minister of Supply and Services Canada.

Canada, Statistics Canada (1984b) *1981 Census of Canada Public Use Sample Tapes User Documentation: Individual File (2% Sample)*, 8–1200–69, Ottawa: Statistics Canada.

Canada, Statistics Canada (1989) *1986 Census of Canada: Schooling and Major Field of Study*, Cat. No. 93–110, Ottawa: Supply and Services Canada.

Canada, Statistics Canada (1993) *1991 Census of Canada: Educational Attainment and School Attendance*, Cat. No. 93–328, Ottawa: Supply and Services Canada.

Cardozo, L.A. (1993) 'Leveling the playing field', *Policy Options* Vol. 14, March: 27–30.

Castells, M. (1993) 'European Cities, the Informational Society, and the Global Economy', *Tijdschrift voor Economische en Sociale Geografie* Vol. 84: 247–57.

Castells, M. (1994) 'European cities, the informational society and the global economy', *New Left Review* Vol. 204: 18–32.

Chambliss, W.J. (1994) 'Policing the ghetto underclass: the politics of law and law enforcement', *Social Problems* Vol. 41 No. 2: 177–94.

Champion, T. (1996) 'Internal migration and ethnicity in Britain', in P. Ratcliffe (ed.), *Ethnicity in the 1991 Census, Volume Three: Social Geography and Ethnicity in Britain: Geographical Spread, Spatial Concentration and Internal Migration*, London: HMSO.

Charles, M. and D.B. Grusky (1995) 'Models for describing the underlying structure of sex segregation', *American Journal of Sociology* Vol. 100, January: 931–71.

Chase-Dunn, C. (1984) 'Urbanization in the world-system: new directions for research', in M.P. Smith (ed.), *Cities in Transformation. Class, Capital, and the State*, Urban Affairs Annual Reviews 26, Beverly Hills: Sage: 111–21.

Cheng, L. and P.W. Yang (1996) 'Asians: the model minority deconstructed', in R. Waldinger and M. Bozorgmehr (eds) *Ethnic Los Angeles*, New York: Russell Sage Foundation.

Cheng, Y. (1996) 'The Chinese: upwardly mobile', in C. Peach (ed.), *Ethnicity in the 1991 Census, Volume Two: The Ethnic Minority Populations of Great Britain*, London: HMSO: 161–80.

Chiswick, B. and P. Miller (1995) 'The endogeneity between language and earnings: international analyses', *Journal of Labour Economics* Vol. 13: 246–88.

Chiswick, B. and P. Miller (1996) 'The languages of the United States: What is spoken and what it means', *READ Perspectives* Vol. 3: 5–41.

Chiswick, B.R. (1986) 'Is the new immigration less skilled than the old?', *Journal of Labour Economics* Vol. 4 No. 2: 168–92.

Chiswick, B.R. (1988) 'Immigration policy, source countries, and immigrant skills: Australia, Canada, and the United States', in L. Baker and P. Miller (eds), *The Economics of Immigration*, Proceedings of a Conference at the ANU, 22–23 April 1987, 163–206.

Clark, K.B. (1965) *Dark Ghetto: Dilemmas of Social Power*, New York: Harper.

Clark, W.A.V. (1998) 'Mass migration and local outcomes: Is international migration to the United States creating a new urban underclass?', *Urban Studies* Vol. 35: 371–83.

Clark, W.A.V. and M. McNicholas (1996) 'Re-examining economic and social polarization in a multi-ethnic metropolitan area: the case of Los Angeles', *Area* Vol. 28 No. 1: 56–63.

Clark, W.A.V. and F. Schultz (1997a) 'Evaluating the local impacts of recent migration to California: realism versus racism', *Population Research and Policy Review* Vol. 16: 475–91.

Clark, W.A.V. and F. Schultz (1997b) 'The geographical impacts of welfare reform in the United States', *Environment and Planning* A Vol. 29: 757–61.

Coleman, J. (1988) 'Social capital in the creation of human capital', *American Journal of Sociology*, Supplement Vol. 94: 95–120.

Collins, R. (1979) *The Credential Society: An Historical Sociology of Education and Stratification*, New York: Academic Press.

Cornelius, W. (1997) 'The structural embeddedness of demand for immigrant labor: new evidence from San Diego and Japan', presentation to the Research Seminar of the Center for US–Mexican Studies, University of California, San Diego, 15 January.

Costrell, R.M. (1990) 'Methodology in the "Job Quality" debate', *Industrial Relations* Vol. 29 No. 1, Winter: 94–110.

Cross, M. (1989) 'Moving targets: the changing face of racism', *New Statesman and Society* Vol. 2, April 7: 35.

Cross, M. (1992a) *Racial Minorities and Industrial Change in Europe and North America*, Cambridge: Cambridge University Press.

Cross, M. (1992b) 'Race and ethnicity', in A. Thornley (ed.), *The Crisis of London*, London: Routledge, 103–18.

Cross, M. (1993) 'Migration, employment and social change in the new Europe', in R. King (ed) *The New Geography of European Migrations* London: Belhaven Press, 116–34.

Cross, M. (1994) '"Race", class formation and political interests: a comparison of Amsterdam and London' in A. Hargreaves and J. Learman (eds), *Racism, Ethnicity and Politics in Contemporary Europe*, Aldershot: Edward Elgar.

Cross, M. and M. Johnson (1988) 'Mobility denied: Afro-Caribbean labour and the British economy', in M. Cross and H. Entzinger (eds), *Lost Illusions: Caribbean Minorities in Britain and the Netherlands*, London: Routledge, 73–105.

Cross, M. and R. Waldinger (1992) 'Migrants, minorities and the ethnic division of labour', in S. Fainstein, I. Gordon and M. Harloe (eds), *Divided Cities: New York and London in the Contemporary World*, Oxford: Blackwell, 151–74.

Dale, A. and C. Bamford (1989) 'Social polarization in Britain 1973–82. Evidence from the General Household Survey: a comment on Pahl's hypothesis', *International Journal of Urban and Regional Research* Vol. 13: 481–500.

Daley, P. (1996) 'Black-Africans: students who stayed', in C. Peach (ed.), *Ethnicity in the 1991 Census, Volume Two: The Ethnic Minority Populations of Great Britain*, London: HMSO, 44–65.

Dangschat, J.S. (1994) 'Concentration of poverty in the landscapes of "boom-town" Hamburg: the creation of a new urban underclass?', *Urban Studies* Vol. 31 No. 7: 1133–47.

Dangschat, J.S. (1996) 'Lokale probleme globale herausforderungen in deutschen städten', in B. Schäfers and G. Wewer (eds), *Die Stadt in Deutschland*, Opladen: Leske and Budrich, 31–60.

Daniels, P.W. (1991) *Services and Metropolitan Development: International Perspectives*, London: Routledge.

Darden, J. (ed.) (1981) *The Ghetto: Readings with Interpretations*, Port Washington, New York: Kennikat Press.

Dawkins, The Hon. J.S. (1988) *Higher Education: A Policy Statement*, Canberra: Australian Government Publishing Service.

Defreitas, G. (1988) 'Hispanic immigration and market segmentation', *Industrial Relations* Vol. 27 No. 2: 195–214.

DeFreitas, G. (1996) 'Immigration, inequality, and policy alternatives', unpublished paper delivered at the conference 'Globalization and Progressive Economic Policy', Washington DC: Economic Policy Institute, 21 June.

Deutsche Bundesbank (1991) *Die Kapitalverflechtung der Unternehmen mit dem Ausland nach Ländern und Wirtschaftszweigen*, Frankfurt/M.: Deutsche Bundesbank.

Deutsche Bundesbank (1996) *Kapitalverflechtung mit dem Ausland*, Frankfurt/M: Deutsche Bundesbank.

Devine, J.A. and J.D. Wright (1993) *The Greatest of Evils: Urban Poverty and the American Underclass*, New York: Aldine.

Devoretz, D. (ed.) (1995) *Diminishing Returns: The Economics of Canada's Recent Immigration Policy*, Toronto: C.D. Howe Institute.

Dicken, P. (1992) *Global Shift. The Internationalization of Economic Activity*, 2nd edn, New York, London: Guilford Press.

Dieleman, F.M. (1994) 'Social rented housing: valuable asset or unsustainable burden?' *Urban Studies* Vol. 31: 447–63.

Dieleman, F.M. and C. Hamnett (1994) 'Globalisation, regulation and the urban system: Editor's introduction to the special issue', *Urban Studies* Vol. 31: 357–64.

Dieleman, F.M. and W.A.V. Clark (1996) *Households and Housing: Choice and Outcomes in the Housing Market*, New Jersey: Rutgers University Press.

Donohue, J.J. III and J. Heckman (1991) 'Continuous versus episodic change: the impact of civil rights policy on the economic status of blacks', *Journal of Economic Literature* Vol. 29, December: 1603–43.

Drake, St. C. and H.R. Cayton (1945) *Black Metropolis: A Study of Negro Life in a Northern City*, 2 vols, rev. and enlarged edition, (1962) New York: Harper and Row.

Duleep, H.O. and M.C. Regets (1992). 'Some evidence of the effects of admissions criteria on immigrant assimilation', in B.R. Chiswick (ed.), *Immigration, Language, and Ethnicity: Canada and the United States*, Washington: The AEI Press, 410–39.

Duncan, G.J., J. Brooks-Gunn and P. Klebanov (1994) 'Economic disparities and early childhood development', *Child Development* Vol. 65: 296–318.

Edmonston, B. and J. Passel (1994) (eds), *Immigration and Ethnicity, The Integration of America's Newest Arrivals*, Washington DC: The Urban Institute Press.

Edsall, T.B. and M.D. Edsall (1991) *Chain Reaction: The Impact of Race, Rights, and Taxes on American Politics*, New York: Norton.

Edwards, J. (1995) *When Race Counts: The Morality of Race Preference in Britain and America*, London: Routledge.

Erikson, R. and J. Goldthorpe (1992) *The Context Flux*, Oxford: Clarendon Press.

Esping-Andersen, G. (1990) *The Three Worlds of Welfare Capitalism*, Cambridge: Polity Press.

Esping-Andersen, G. (ed.) (1993) *Changing Classes; Stratification and Mobility in Postindustrial Societies*, London: Sage Publications.

Esser, H. and Friedrichs, J. (1990) *Generation und Identität*, Opladen: Westdeutscher Verlag.

Esteban, J.M. and D. Ray (1994) 'On the measurement of polarisation', *Econometrica* Vol. 62: 819–51.

Evans, M. (1986) 'Sources of immigrants' language proficiency: Australian research with comparisons to the Federal Republic of Germany and the United States of America', *European Journal of Sociology* Vol. 2: 226–36.

Evans, M.D.R. and J. Kelley (1986) 'Immigrants' work: equality and discrimination in the Australian labour market', *Australia and New Zealand Journal of Sociology* Vol. 22 No. 2: 187–207.

Evans, M.D.R. and J. Kelley (1991) 'Prejudice, discrimination, and the labour market: attainments of immigrants in Australia', *American Journal of Sociology* 97, 3: 721–59.

Fainstein, S., I. Gordon and M. Harloe (1992) *Divided Cities: New York and London in the Contemporary World*, Oxford: Basil Blackwell.

Faludi, A. (1994) 'Coalition building and planning for Dutch growth management: the role of the Randstad Concept', *Urban Studies* Vol. 31: 485–508.

Feagin, J.R. and M.P. Smith (1987) 'Cities and the new international division of labour: an overview' in J.R. Feagin and M.P. Smith (eds), *The Capitalist City*, Oxford: Blackwell, 1–34.

Fernandez-Kelly P.M. and A.M. Garcia (1989) 'Informalization at the core: Hispanic women, homework, and the advanced capitalist state', in A. Portes, M. Castells and L.A. Benton (eds), *The Informal Economy*, Baltimore: Johns Hopkins University, Chapter 13.

Fielding, A.J. (1994) 'Industrial change and regional development in Western Europe', *Urban Studies* Vol. 31: 679–704.

Fligstein, N. (1977) 'Is globalization the cause of the crises of welfare states?', paper presented at the Annual Meeting of the American Sociological Association, Toronto, August.

Florette, H. (1975) *Black Migration: Movement North, 1900–1920*, New York: Anchor.

Forman, R.E. (1971) *Black Ghettos, White Ghettos, and Slums*, Englewood Cliffs: Prentice Hall.

Fortin, N.M. and T. Lemieux (1997) 'Institutional changes and rising wage inequality: is there a linkage?', *The Journal of Economic Perspectives* Vol. 11 No. 2, Spring: 75–96.

Foster, L., A. Marshall and L.S. Williams (1991) *Discrimination Against Immigrant Workers in Australia*, Canberra: Australian Government Publishing Service.

Fraundorf, M.N. (1978) 'Relative earnings of native and foreign-born women', *Explorations in Economic History* Vol. 15.

Freeman, G.P. and J. Jupp (eds) (1992) *Nations of Immigrants: Australia, the United States, and International Migration*, New York: Oxford University Press.

Freeman, R.B. and K. Needels (1993) 'Skill differentials in Canada in an era of rising labour market inequality', in D. Card and R.B. Freeman (eds), *Small Differences that Matter: Labour Markets and Income Maintenance in Canada and the United States*, Chicago: University of Chicago Press, 45–67.

Frey, W. (1996–97) 'Immigration and the changing geography of poverty', *Focus* Vol. 18.

Frey, W. and E. Fielding (1995) 'Changing urban populations: regional restructuring, racial polarization and poverty concentration', *Cityscape* Vol. 1: 1–66.

Friedberg, R.M. and J. Hunt (1995) 'The impact of immigrants on host country wages, employment and growth', *Journal of Economic Perspectives* Vol. 9 No. 2: 23–44.

Friedman, J. (1986) 'The world city hypothesis', *Development and Change* Vol. 17: 69–84.

Friedmann, J. and G. Wolff (1982) 'World city formation: an agenda for research and action', *International Journal of Urban and Regional Research*: 309–43.

Friedrichs, J. (1985) 'Ökonomischer strukturwandel und disparitäten von qualifikationen der arbeitskräfte', in J. Friedrichs (ed.), *Die Städte in den 80er Jahren*, Opladen: Westdeutscher Verlag, 48–70.

Friedrichs, J. (1993) 'A theory of urban decline: economy, demography and political elites', *Urban Studies* Vol. 30: 907–17.

Friedrichs, J. (1996) 'Intra-regional polarization: cities in the Ruhr area' in J. O'Loughlin and J. Friedrichs (eds), *Social Polarization in Post-Industrial Metropolises*, Berlin, New York: de Gruyter.

Friedrichs, J. and H. Alpheis (1991) 'Housing segregation and immigrants in West Germany' in E. Huttman, W. Blauw and J. Saltman (eds), *Urban Housing Segregation of Minorities in Western Europe and the United States*, London: Duke University Press.

Frisbie, W. P. and L. Neidert (1977) 'Inequality and the relative size of minority populations: a comparative analysis', *American Journal of Sociology* Vol. 82, March: 1007–30.

Gans, H.J. (1992) 'Second-generation decline: scenarios for the economic and ethnic futures of the post-1965 American immigrants', *Ethnic and Racial Studies* Vol. 15 No. 2.

Ganzeboom, H., P. DeGraaf and D. Treiman (1992) 'A standard socio-economic index of occupational status', *Social Science Research* Vol. 21: 1–56.

Ganzeboom, H. and D. Treiman (1996) 'Internationally comparable measures of occupational status for the 1988 international standard of occupations', *Social Science Research* Vol. 25: 201–39.

Gaskell, J. (1991) 'Education as preparation for work in Canada: structure, policy and student response', in *Making Their Way: Education, Training and the Labour Market in Canada and Britain*, Toronto: University of Toronto Press, 61–84.

Gershuny, J. (1983) *Social Innovation and the Division of Labour*, Oxford: Oxford University Press.

Gildas, S. (1995) *Géodynamiqie des Migrations Internationales dans le Monde*, Paris: Presses Universitaires de France.

Gittleman, M. and D.R. Howell (1995) 'Changes in the structure and quality of jobs in the United States: effects by race and gender, 1973–1990', *Industrial and Labor Relations Review* Vol. 48 No. 3, April 420–40.

Glazer, N. and D.P. Moynihan (1963) *Beyond the Melting Pot: The Negroes, Puerto Ricans, Jews, Italians and Irish of New York City*, Cambridge, MA: MIT Press.

Goldfield, D.R. and J.B. Lane (eds) (1973) *The Enduring Ghetto*, Philadelphia: J.B. Lippincott Company.

Goldthorpe, J.H. (1987) *Social Mobility and Class Structure in Modern Britain*, 2nd edn, Oxford: Clarendon Press.

Goldthorpe, J.H. (1995) 'The service class revisited', in T. Butler and M. Savage (eds), *Social Change and the Middle Classes*, London: UCL Press, 61–84.

Gordon, D.M., R.C. Edwards and M. Reich (1982) *Segmented Work, Divided Workers: The Historical Transformation of Labour in the United States*, Cambridge: Cambridge University Press.

Gordon, M. (1964) *Assimilation in American Life*, New York: Oxford University Press.

Gottdiener, M. and N. Komninos (eds) (1989) 'Introduction', *Capitalist Development and Crisis Theory: Accumulation, Regulation and Spatial Restructuring*, New York: St Martin's Press.

Groh, G.W. (1972) *The Black Migration*, New York: Weybright and Talley.

Grossman, J. (1989) *Land of Hope: Chicago, Black Southerners, and the Great Migration*, Chicago: The University of Chicago Press.

Haeusermann, H. and T. Kraemer-Badoni (1989) 'The change of regional inequality in the Federal Republic of Germany', in M. Gottdiener and N. Komninos (eds), *Capitalist Development and Crisis Theory: Accumulation, Regulation and Spatial Restructuring*, New York: St Martin's Press.

Hall, P. (1977) *The World Cities*, 2nd edn, London: Weidenfeld and Nicolson.

Hamermesh, D.S. and F.D. Bean (eds) (1998) *Help or Hindrance? The Economic Implications of Immigration for African Americans*, New York: Russell Sage Foundation.

Hamnett, C. (1994a) 'Socio-economic change in London: professionalization not polarization', *Built Environment* Vol. 20: 192–203.

Hamnett, C. (1994b) 'Social polarization in global cities: theory and evidence', *Urban Studies* Vol. 31 No. 3: 401–24.

Hamnett, C. (1996) 'Social polarization, economic restructuring and welfare state regimes', *Urban Studies* Vol. 33 No. 8: 1407–30.

Hamnett, C. (1997) 'La polarisation sociale: deconstruction d'un concept chaotique', in A. Martens and M. Vervaeke (eds), *La Polarisation Sociale des Villes Europeennes*, Paris: Economica, 111–23.

Hamnett, C. and W. Randolph (1988) 'Ethnic minorities in the London labour market: a longitudinal analysis 1971–81', *New Community* Vol. 14: 333–46.

Hamnett, C. and D. Cross (1998) 'Social polarisation and inequality in London – the earnings evidence, 1979–1995', *Environment and Planning C: Government and Policy* Vol. 16: 659–80.

Handler, J.F. (1995) *The Poverty of Welfare Reform*, New Haven: Yale University Press.

Handlin, O. (1959) *The Newcomers: Negroes and Puerto-Ricans in a Changing Metropolis*, Cambridge, MA: Harvard University Press.

Hannerz, U. (1969) *Soulside: Inquiries into Ghetto Culture and Community*, New York: Columbia University Press.

Harding, A. (1994) 'Urban regimes and growth machines: towards a cross-national research agenda', *Urban Affairs Quarterly* Vol. 29: 356–82.

Harrington, M. (1962) *The Other America*, New York: Pantheon.

Harrison, A. (1991) *Black Exodus: the Great Migration from the American South*, Jackson: University Press of Mississippi.

Harrison, B. and B. Bluestone (1988) *The Great U-Turn, Corporate Restructuring and the Polarizing of America*, New York: Basic Books.

Hartwich, H.-H. (1997) 'Die entwicklung der deutschen staatsverschuldung seit der wiedervereinigung', *Gegenwartskunde* Vol. 2: 213–18.

Häussermann, H., W. Petrowsky and J. Pohlan (1995) 'Entwicklung der städte: stabile polarisierung', in T. Jäger and D. Hoffmann (eds), *Demokratie in der Krise? Zukunft der Demokratie*, Opladen: Leske and Budrich, 191–213.

Haveman R. and B. Wolfe (1995) 'The determinants of children's attainments: a review of methods and findings', *Journal of Economic Literature* Vol. 33: 1829–78.

Hawkins, F. (1989) *Critical Years in Immigration: Canada and Australia Compared*, Kensington, NSW: New South Wales University Press (published jointly with McGill – Queens University Press).

Heinz, W. and C. Scholz (1996) *Public Private Partnership im Städtebau: Erfahrungen aus der kommunalen Praxis*, Stuttgart: Kohlhammer.

Henri, G. (1975) *Black Migration: Movement North, 1900–1920*, New York: Anchor.

Henry, F. and E. Ginsberg (1984) *Who Gets the Work?: A Test of Racial Discrimination in Employment*, Toronto: The Urban Alliance on Race Relations and the Social Planning Council of Metropolitan Toronto.

Hill, P.J. (1978) 'Relative skill and income levels of native and foreign born workers in the United States', *Explorations in Economic History* Vol. 12.

Hirst, P. and G. Thompson (1992) 'The problem of globalisation: international economic relations, national economic management and the formation of Trading Blocs', *Economy and Society* Vol. 21: 358–96.

Hirst, P. and G. Thompson (1996) *Globalization in Question: The International Economy and the Possibilities of Governance*, Cambridge: Polity Press.

Hodge, R.W. (1973) 'Toward a theory of racial differences in employment', *Social Forces* Vol. 52, September: 16–31.

Hollifield, J.F. (1992) *Immigrants, Markets, and States; The Political Economy of Postwar Europe*, Cambridge, Mass: Harvard University Press.

Holzer, H. (1991) 'The spatial mismatch: what has the evidence shown?', *Urban Studies* Vol. 28: 105–22.

Holzer, H. (1996) *What Employers Want: Job Prospects for Less-Educated Workers*, New York: Russell Sage Foundation.

Howell, D. and E.N. Wolff (1991) 'Trends in the growth and distribution of skills in the US workplace, 1960–1985', *Industrial and Labor Relations Review* Vol. 44 No. 3.

Howes, E. (1997) *London's Workers*, London: London Research Centre.

Hughes, M.A. (1990) 'Formation of the impacted ghetto – evidence from large metropolitan-areas, 1970–1980', *Urban Geography* Vol. 11 No. 33: 265–84.

Huttman, E., J. Saltman and W. Blauw (1991) *Urban Housing Segregation of Immigrants in Western Europe and the United States*, Durham N. C.: Duke University Press.

Inglis, C., A. Birch and G. Sherington (1994) 'An overview of Australian and Canadian migration patterns and policies', in H. Adelman, A. Borowski,

M. Burstein and L. Foster (eds), *Immigration and Refugee Policy: Australia and Canada Compared*, Toronto: University of Toronto Press, 3–30.

Jaeger, D.A. (1995) 'Skill differences and the effect of immigrants on the wages of natives', unpublished paper, US Bureau of Labor Statistics, November.

Jargowsky, P. (1997) *Poverty and Place: Ghettos, Barrios and the American City*, New York: Russell Sage Foundation.

Jargowsky, P. and D. Ellwood (1990) 'Ghetto poverty: a theoretical and empirical framework', Working Paper H-90-7, October, Malcolm Wiener Center for Social Policy.

Jargowsky, P. and M.J. Bane (1991) 'Ghetto poverty in the United States, 1970–1980', in C. Jencks and P.E. Peterson (eds), *The Urban Underclass*, Washington DC: The Brookings Institution, 235–73.

Jaynes, G.D. and R.M. Williams, Jr. (eds) (1989) *A Common Destiny: Blacks and American Society*, Washington DC: National Academy Press.

Jencks, C. and P. Peterson (eds) (1991) *The Urban Underclass*, Washington DC: The Brookings Institution.

Jenkins, S.P. and F.A. Cowell (1994) 'Dwarfs and giants in the 1980s: trends in the UK income distribution', *Fiscal Studies* Vol. 15: 99–118.

Jensen, L. (1988) 'Patterns of immigration and public assistance utilization, 1970–1980', *International Migration Review* Vol. 22 No. 1: 51–83.

Johnson, C.S. (1943) *Patterns of Negro Segregation*, New York: Harper & Brothers.

Jowell, R., L. Brook, G. Prior and B. Taylor (1992) *British Social Attitudes: the 9th Report*, Aldershot: Dartmouth.

Kain, J. (1968) 'Housing segregation, Negro employment, and metropolitan decentralisation', *The Quarterly Journal of Economics* Vol. 82: 175–97.

Kain, J. (1992) 'The spatial mismatch hypothesis: three decades later', *Housing Policy Debate* Vol. 3: 371–460.

Kain, J. and J. Persky (1969) 'Alternatives to the Gilded Ghetto', *The Public Interest* Vol. 14 (Winter): 74–87.

Kalleberg, A.L. and T. Colbjørnsen (1990) 'Unions and the structure of earnings inequality: cross-national patterns', *Social Science Research* Vol. 19: 348–71.

Karrenberg, H. and E. Münstermann (1996) 'Gemeindefinanzbericht 1996. Städtische Finanzen '96 – in der Sackgasse', *Der Städtetag* Vol. 3: 115–93.

Kasarda, J.D. (1992) 'The severely distressed in economically transforming cities', in A.V. Harrell and G.E. Peterson (eds), *Drugs, Crime, and Social Isolation*, Washington: The Urban Institute Press.

Kasarda, J.D. (1993) 'Inner-City concentrated poverty and neighborhood distress: 1970–1990', *Housing Policy Debate* Vol. 4: 253–302.

Kasarda, J.D. and J. Friedrichs (1985) 'Comparative demographic–employment mismatches in the U.S. and West Germany', in R.L. and I.H. Simpson (eds), *Research in the Sociology of Work* Vol. 3, Greenwich, CT: JAI Press, 1–30.

Katz, M.B. (1989) *The Undeserving Poor*, New York: Pantheon.

Katz, M.B. (1995) *In the Shadow of the Poorhouse*, New York: Basic Books.

Katzman, D.M. (1973) *Before the Ghetto: Black Detroit in the Nineteenth Century*, Urbana: University of Illinois Press.

Kelley, J. (1990) 'The failure of a paradigm: log-linear models of social mobility', in J. Clark, C. Modgil and S. Modgil (eds), *John H. Goldthorpe: Consensus and Controversy*, London: Falmer Press, 319–46.

Kennedy, D. (1996) 'Can we still afford to be a nation of immigrants?', *Atlantic Monthly* Vol. 278: 52–68.

Kerchkoff, A.C. (1990) *Getting Started: Transition to Adulthood in Great Britain*, Boulder CO: Westview Press.

Kerner Commission [1968] (1989) *The Kernert Report. The 1968 Report of the National Advisory Commission on Civil Disorders*, New York: Pantheon.

Kirschenman, J. (1991) 'Gender within race in the labour market', paper presented at the conference on Urban Poverty and Family Life, University of Chicago.

Kloosterman, R.C. (1994) 'Three worlds of welfare capitalism? the welfare state and the postindustrial trajectory in the Netherlands after 1980', *West European Politics* Vol. 17 No. 4: 166–89.

Kloosterman, R.C. (1996a) 'Mixed experiences: post industrial transition and ethnic minorities on the Amsterdam labour market', *New Community* Vol. 22 No. 4: 637–54.

Kloosterman, R.C. (1996b) 'Double Dutch: polarization trends in Amsterdam and Rotterdam after 1980', *Regional Studies* Vol. 30.

Knight, R. (1989) 'The emergent global society', in R.V. Knight and G. Gappert (eds), *Cities in a Global Society*, Newbury Park: Sage.

Korff, R. (1987) 'The world city hypothesis: a critique', *Development and Change* Vol. 18: 483–95.

Kumar, P. (1993) *From Uniformity to Divergence: Industrial Relations in Canada and the United States*, Kingston, Ontario.: Queen's University, Industrial Relations Centre.

Kusmer, K.L. (1976) *A Ghetto Takes Shape: Black Cleveland, 1870–1930*, Urbana: University of Illinois Press.

Kusmer, K.L. (1995) 'The enduring ghetto: urbanization and the color line in American history', *Journal of Urban History* Vol. 21 No. 4: 458–504.

Kuttner, B. (1983) 'The declining middle', *Atlantic Monthly*, July: 60–72.

Lawrence, R.Z. (1984) 'Sectoral shifts and the size of the middle class', *The Brookings Review*, Fall: 3–11.

Leslie, D., S. Drinkwater and N. O'Leary (1997) 'Little white lies: ethnic variations in male and female earnings', unpublished manuscript, Department of Economics and Economic History, Manchester Metropolitan University.

Lever-Tracy, C. and M. Quinlan (1988) *Divided Working Class: Ethnic Segmentation and Industrial Conflict in Australia*, London: Routledge and Kegan Paul.

Levy, F. and R.J. Murnane (1992) 'US earnings levels and earnings inequality: a review of recent trends and proposed explanations', *Journal of Economic Literature* Vol. XXX, September: 1333–81.

Levy, P. (1987) 'The middle class: is it really vanishing?', *The Brookings Review*, Summer: 77–122.

Lieberson, S. (1980) *A Piece of the Pie*, Berkeley: University of California Press.

Light, I. (1988) 'Los Angeles', in *The Metropolis Era*, Vol. 2, *Mega-Cities*, Beverly Hills: Sage.

Light, I. (1996) 'Globalisation and migration networks', unpublished paper presented to a conference on 'Globalisation', Utrecht University, November.

Light, I. (1999) 'Globalization and migration networks', in J. Rath and R. Kloosterman (eds) *Immigrant Businesses: An Exploration of their Embeddedness in the Economic, Politico-Institutional, and Social Environment*, Basingstoke: Macmillan – now Palgrave.

Light, I., G. Sabagh, M. Bozorgmehr and C. Der-Martirosian (1994). 'Beyond the ethnic enclave economy', *Social Problems* Vol. 41: 65–80.

Light, I. and C. Rosenstein (1995) 'Expanding the interaction theory of entrepreneurship' in A. Portes (ed.), *The Economic Sociology of Immigration: Essays on Networks, Ethnicity and Entrepreneurship*, NewYork: Russell Sage Foundation, 166–212.

Light, I. and E. Roach (1996) 'Self-employment: mobility ladder or economic lifeboat?', in R. Waldinger and M. Bozorgmehr (eds), *Ethnic Los Angeles*, New York: Russell Sage.

Light, I., R. Bernard and R. Kim (1999) 'Immigrant incorporation in the garment industry of Los Angeles', *International Migration Review* Vol. 33: 5–2.

Lipset, S.M. (1989) *Continental Divide: The Values and Institutions of the United States and Canada*, Toronto: C.D. Howe Institute and Washington: National Planning Association.

Logan, J., R.D. Alba and T.L. McNulty (1994) 'Ethnic economies in Metropolitan regions: Miami and beyond', *Social Forces* Vol. 73, March: 691–724.

Logan, J. and T. Swanstrom (eds) (1990) 'Urban restructuring: a critical view', in *Beyond the City Limits*, Philadelphia: Temple University.

Lopez, D., E. Popkin and E. Telles (1996) 'Central Americans: at the bottom, struggling to get ahead', in R. Waldinger and M. Bozorgmehr (eds), *Ethnic Los Angeles*, New York: Russell Sage.

Lubove, R. (1962) *The Progressives and the Slums: Tenement House in New York City, 1890 to 1917*, Pittsburgh: University of Pittsburgh Press.

Lum, J.M. (1995) 'The Federal Employment Equity Act: goals vs. implementation', *Canadian Public Administration* Vol. 38, Spring: 45–76.

Lyon, M. and B. West (1995) 'London Patels: caste and commerce', *New Community* Vol. 31 No. 3: 399–419.

Marger, M.N. (1997) *Race and Ethnic Relations: American and Global Perspectives*, 4th edn, Belmont, CA: Wadsworth Publishing.

Markusen, A.R. (1985) *Profit Cycles, Oligopoly, and Regional Development*, Cambridge, MA, London: MIT Press.

Massey, D. (1990) 'American Apartheid: Segregation and the Making of the Underclass', *American Journal of Sociology* Vol. 96: 329–57.

Massey, D. (1993) 'Power-geometry and a progressive sense of place', in J. Bird, B. Curtis, T. Putnam and L. Tickner (eds), *Mapping the Futures: Local Cultures, Global Change*, London: Routledge.

Massey, D. and N. Denton (1989) 'Hypersegregation in US metropolitan areas: black and Hispanic segregation among five dimensions', *Demography* Vol. 26 No. 3: 373–91.

Massey, D. and N. Denton (1993) *American Apartheid: Segregation and the Making of the Underclass*, Cambridge, Mass.: Harvard University Press.

Massey, D.S. (1988) 'Economic development and international migration in comparative perspective', *Population and Development Review* Vol. 14 No. 3: 383–413.

Massey, D.S., J. Arango, G. Hugo, A.K.A. Pellegrino and J.E. Taylor (1993) 'Theories of international migration: a review and appraisal', *Population and Development Review* Vol. 19.

McKey, J.B. (1993) *Sociology and the Race Problem: The Failure of a Perspective*, Urbana: University of Illinois Press.

McLafferty, S. and V. Preston (1991) 'Gender, race and commuting among service sector workers', *Professional Geographer* Vol. 43: 1–15.

McLafferty, S. and V. Preston (1992) 'Spatial mismatch and labor market segmentation for African-American and Latina women', *Economic Geography* Vol. 68: 406–31.

McLean Petras, E. (1983) 'The global labor market in the modern world economy', in M.M. Kritz, C.B. Keely and S.M. Tomasi (eds), *Global Trends in Migration*, New York: Center for Migration Studies.

McMahon, D. (1997) 'Ethnic differences in the labour market: unemployment, self-employment and salaried employment', paper presented at the International Sociological Association's RC 28 Conference on Social Inequality in Multiethnic and Immigrant Societies, Tel Aviv.

Mead, L. (1992) *The New Politics of Poverty*, New York: Basic Books.

Miller, J. (1996) *Search and Destroy: African-American Males in the Criminal Justice System*, Cambridge: Cambridge University Press.

Miller, Z.L. (1992) 'Pluralism, Chicago School style: Louis Wirth, the ghetto, the city, and integration', *Journal of Urban History* Vol. 18 No. 3: 251–79.

Model, S. (1991) 'Caribbean immigrants: a black success story?', *International Migration Review* Vol. 25 No. 2: 248–76.

Model, S. (1993) 'The ethnic niche and the structure of opportunity: immigrants and minorities in New York City', in M.B. Katz (ed.), *The 'Underclass' Debate: Views from History*, Princeton, NJ: Princeton University Press.

Model, S. (1997) 'An occupational tale of two cities: minorities in London and New York', *Demography* Vol. 34, November: 539–50.

Model, S. (1999). 'A cross-national look at Chinese immigrant occupations', in A. Dale, C. Holdsworth, and E. Fieldhouse (eds), *The Analysis of Census Microdata*, London: Edward Arnold.

Model, S. and D. Ladipo (1996) 'Context and opportunity: minorities in London and New York', *Social Forces* Vol. 75, December: 485–510.

Model, S. and G. Fisher (1997) 'Black immigrants in three white societies', paper presented at the Annual Meetings of the American Sociological Association, Toronto.

Model, S., G. Fisher and R. Silberman (1999) 'Black Caribbeans in comparative perspective', *Journal of Ethnic and Racial Studies* Vol. 25 No. 2, April: 187–212.

Modood, T. (1992) *Not Easy Being British: Colour, Culture and Citizenship*, Stoke on Trent: Trentham Books.

Modood, T. (1996) 'The changing context of "race" in Britain: a symposium', *Patterns of Prejudice* Vol. 30, January: 3–42.

Modood, T. (1998) 'Anti-essentialism, multiculturalism and the recognition of religious groups', *Journal of Political Philosophy* Vol. 6 No. 4.

Modood, T., R. Berthoud, J. Lakey, J. Nazroo, P. Smith, S. Virdee, and S. Beishon (1997) *Ethnic Minorities in Britain: Diversity and Disadvantage*, London: Policy Studies Institute.

Mollenkopf, J.H. (1993) *Key Urban Nodes in the Global System*, New York: Social Science Research Council.

Mollenkopf, J.H. and M. Castells (eds) (1992) *Dual City. Restructuring New York*, New York: Russell Sage.

Moore, J. and R. Pinderhughes (eds) (1993) 'Introduction', *The Barrios: Latinos and the Underclass Debate*, New York: Russell Sage.

Moore, R. (1992) 'Labour and housing markets in inner city regeneration', *New Community* Vol. 18: 371–86.

Moss, P. and C. Tilly (1996) '"Soft" skills and race: an investigation of black men's employment problems', *Work and Occupations* Vol. 23, August: 252–76.

Mueller, E.J. and D.R. Howell (1996) 'Immigrants as workers in New York City: a review of current debates and evidence', Working Paper No. 3, The International Center for Migration, Ethnicity and Citizenship at The New School for Social Research.

Multhaupt, T. (1996) *Strukturelle Arbeitslosigkeit und Mismatch*, Münster: Universität, Institut für Siedlungs und Wohnungswesen.

Murray, C. (1990) *The Emerging British Underclass* Choice in Welfare Series No. 2, London: Institute of Economic Affairs.

Musterd, S. (1994) 'A rising European underclass', *Built Environment* Vol. 20: 1985–91.

Myrdal, G. and B. Sissela (1944) *An American Dilemma: The Negro Problem and Modern Democracy*, New York: Harper & Brothers.

Nanji, A. (1983) 'The Nizari Ismaili Muslim community in North America: background and development', in E. Waugh, B. Abu-Laban and R. Qureshi (eds), *The Muslim Community in North America*, Edmonton: The University of Alberta Press, 149–64.

Nederveen Pieterse, J. (1994) 'Globalization as hybridization', *International Sociology* Vol. 9.

OECD (1992) *Globalisation of Industrial Activities. Four Case Studies: Auto Parts, Chemicals, Construction and Semiconductors*, Paris: OECD.

Ogbu, J.U. (1987) 'Variability in minority school performance: a problem in search of an explanation', *Anthropology and Education Quarterly* Vol. 18: 312–34.

Olzak, S. (1992) *The Dynamics of Ethnic Competition and Conflict*, Stanford: Stanford University Press.

Ong, P. and E. Blumenberg (1996) 'Income and racial inequality in Los Angeles', in A.J. Scott and E.W. Soja (eds), *The City: Los Angeles and Urban Theory at the End of the Twentieth Century*, Los Angeles: University of California.

Ong, P. and A. Valenzuela, Jr. (1996) 'The labor market: immigrant effects and racial disparities', in R. Waldinger and M. Bozorgmehr (eds), *Ethnic Los Angeles*, New York: Russell Sage Foundation.

Orfield, G. (1983) *Public School Desegregation in the United States, 1968–1980*, Washington DC: Joint Center for Political Studies.

Orfield, G. (1987) 'The end of the integration dream', in M. Weir, A.S. Orloff and T. Skocpol (eds), *The Politics of Social Provision in the United States*, Princeton NJ: Princeton University Press.

Ortiz, V. (1996) 'The Mexican-origin population: permanent working class or emerging middle class?', in R. Waldinger and M. Bozorgmehr (eds), *Ethnic Los Angeles*, New York: Russell Sage Foundation, 247–78.

Osofsky, G. (1971) *Harlem: The Making of a Ghetto – Negro New York, 1890–1930*, 2nd edn, New York: Harper & Row.

Owen, D. (1995) 'The spatial and socio-economic patterns of minority ethnic groups in Great Britain', *Scottish Geographical Magazine* Vol. 111: 27–35.

Pahl, R. (1988) 'Some remarks on informal work, social polarization and the social structure', *International Journal of Urban and Regional Research* Vol. 12 No. 2.

Park, R.E., E.W. Burgess and R.D. McKenzie (1925) *The City*, Chicago: The University of Chicago Press.

Parkin, F. (1979) *Class Analysis: a Bourgeois Critique*, London, Tavistock.

Peach, C. (ed.) (1996a) *Ethnicity in the 1991 Census, Volume Two: The Ethnic Minority Populations of Great Britain*, London: HMSO.

Peach, C. (1996b) 'Does Britain have ghettos?', *Transactions*, Institute of British Geographers Vol. 21: 216–35.

Penn, R. and H. Scattergood (1992) 'Ethnicity and career aspirations in contemporary Britain', *New Community* Vol. 19 No. 1: 75–98.

Persson, T. and G. Tabellini (1994) 'Is inequality harmful to growth?', *American Economic Review* Vol. 84 No. 3: 600–21.

Peterson, P.E. (1981) *City Limits*, Chicago: University of Chicago.

Philpott, T.L. (1978) *The Slum and the Ghetto: Neighborhood Deterioration and Middle-Class Reform, Chicago 1880–1930*, New York: Oxford University Press.

Phizacklea, A. and M. Ram (1996) 'Being your own boss: ethnic minority entrepreneurs in comparative perspective', *Work, Employment and Society* Vol. 10 (June): 319–39.

Pinch, S. (1993) 'Social polarization: a comparison of evidence from Britain and the United States', *Environment and Planning* A Vol. 25: 779–95.

Pineo, P. (1977) 'The social standing of ethnic and racial groupings', *Canadian Review of Sociology and Anthropology* Vol. 14: 147–57.

Piore, M.J. (1979) *Birds of Passage: Migrant Labour and Industrial Societies*, Cambridge: Cambridge University Press.

Porter, J. (1965) *The Vertical Mosaic: An Analysis of Social Class and Power in Canada*, Toronto: University of Toronto Press.

Portes, A. (1981) 'Modes of structural incorporation and present theories of labour immigration', in M.M. Kritz, C.B. Keely and S.M. Tomasi (eds), *Global Trends in Migration: Theory and Research on International Population Movements*, New York: Center for Migration Studies, 279–97.

Portes, A. (1995) 'Transnational communities: their emergence and significance in the contemporary world system', Working Papers Series No. 16, Department of Sociology, The Johns Hopkins University.

Portes, A. and J. Sensenbrenner (1993) 'Embeddedness and immigration: notes on the determinants of economic action', *American Journal of Sociology* Vol. 98, May: 1320–50.

Portes, A. and M. Zhou (1993) 'The new second generation: segmented assimilation and its variants', *The Annals of the American Academy of Political and Social Science* Vol. 530: 74–96.

Portes, A. and MacLeod, D. (1999) 'Educating the second generation: determinants of academic achievement among children of immigrants in the United States', *Journal of Ethnic and Racial Studies* Vol. 25 No. 3: 373–96.

Priemus, H. and F.M. Dieleman (1997), 'Social rented housing: recent changes in Western Europe', Introduction to Special Issue, *Housing Studies* Vol. 12 No. 4: 421–25.

Reid, L. and N. Smith (1993) 'John Wayne meets Donald Trump: the Lower East Side as Wild Wild West', in G. Kearns and C. Philo (eds), *Selling Places: The City as Cultural Capital. Past and Present*, Oxford: Pergamon, 193–209.

Reimers, D.M. and H. Troper (1992) 'Canadian and American immigration policy since 1945', in B.R Chiswick (ed.), *Immigration, Language, and Ethnicity: Canada and the United States*, Washington DC: The AEI Press, 15–43.

Reitz, J.G. (1998) *Warmth of the Welcome: The Social Causes of Economic Success for Immigrants in Different Nations and Cities*, Boulder, CO: Westview Press.

Reitz, J.G. and R. Breton (1994) *The Illusion of Difference: Realities of Ethnicity in Canada and the United States*, Toronto: C.D. Howe Institute.

Rex, J. (1970) *Race Relations in Sociological Theory*, London: Weidenfeld & Nicolson.

Reyneri, E. (1997) 'The informalization of migrant labour: oversupply of illegal migrants or pull-effect by the underground receiving economy? The Italian case', paper presented at the University of Warwick International Conference on 'Globalization, Migration, and Social Exclusion', 31 May.

Rhein, C. (1996) 'Social segmentation and spatial polarization in greater Paris', in J. O'Laughlin and J. Friedrichs (eds), *Social Polarization in Post Industrial Metropolises*, Berlin: Walter de Gruyter.

Riach, P.A. and J. Rich (1991) 'Testing for racial discrimination in the labour market', *Cambridge Journal of Economics* Vol. 15.

Riach, P.A. and J. Rich (1992) 'Measuring discrimination by direct experimental methods', *Journal of Post Keynesian Economics* Vol. 14 No. 2.

Richard, K. (1989) 'The emergent global society', in R.V. Knight and G. Gappert (eds), *Cities in a Global Society*, Newbury Park: Sage.

H.W. Richardson (1978) *Urban Economica*, Hinsdale, IL: Dryden Press.

Roberts, K., M. Connolly and G. Parsell (1992) 'Black youth in the Liverpool labour market', *New Community* Vol. 18: 209–28.

Robinson, V. (1987) 'Race, space and place', *New Community* Vol. 14: 186–97.

Robinson, V. (1989) 'Economic restructuring, the urban crisis and Britain's Black population', in D.T. Herbert and D.M. Smith (eds), *Social Problems and the City: New Perspectives*, Oxford: Oxford University Press, 257–70.

Robinson, V. (1990) 'Changing stereotypes of Indians in Britain', *Indo-British Review* Vol. 16: 79–95.

Robinson, V. (1992) 'The internal migration of Britain's ethnic population', in T. Champion and T. Fielding (eds), *Migration Processes and Patterns volume 1: Research Progress and Problems*, London: Belhaven.

Robinson, V. (1993) 'Marching into the middle classes? The long-term resettlement of East African Asians in the UK', *Journal of Refugee Studies* Vol. 6: 230–47.

Robinson, V. (1995) 'The migration of East African Asians to the UK', in R. Cohen (ed.), *The Cambridge Survey of World Migration*, Cambridge: Cambridge University Press, 331–6.

Rodwin, L. and H. Sazanami (eds) (1991) *Industrial Change and Regional Economic Transformation: The Experience of Western Europe*, London: HarperCollins Academic.

Rosenfeld, R.A. and A.L. Kalleberg (1990) 'A cross-national comparison of the gender gap in income', *American Journal of Sociology* Vol. 96 July: 69–106.

Runnymede Trust (1997) 'Islamophobia: Its Features and Dangers: A Consultation Paper', London: Runnymede Commission on British Muslims and Islamophobia.

Sabagh, G. and M. Bozorgmehr (1996) 'Population change: immigration and ethnic transformation', in R. Waldinger and M. Bozorgmehr (eds), *Ethnic Los Angeles*, New York: Russell Sage Foundation.

Sánchez-Jankowski, M. (1996) 'Change and persistence in low-income communities', unpublished paper, Department of Sociology, University of California, Berkeley.

Sandefur, G. (1988) 'The persistence of urban poverty', in F. Harris and R. Wilkins (eds), *Quiet Riots: Race and Poverty in the United States*, New York: Pantheon.

Sassen, S. (1988) *The Mobility of Labor and Capital: A Study in International Investment and Labor Flow*, Cambridge: Cambridge University Press.

Sassen, S. (1990) 'Beyond the city limits: a commentary', in J. Logan and T. Swanstrom (eds), *Beyond the City Limits*, Philadelphia: Temple University.

Sassen, S. (1991) *The Global City: New York, London, Tokyo*, Princeton, NJ: Princeton University Press.

Sassen, D. (1993) 'Economic internationalization: the new migration in Japan and the United States', *International Migration* Vol. 31 No. 1: 73–102.

Sassen, S. (1994) *Cities in a World Economy*, Thousand Oaks, Cal.: Pine Forge Press.

Sassen, S. (1996) 'New employment regimes in cities: the impact on immigrant workers', *New Community* Vol. 22 No. 4: 579–95.

Sassen, S. (1996) 'Rebuilding the global city: economy, ethnicity and space', in A.D. King (ed.), *Re-presenting the City: Ethnicity, Capital and Culture in the 21st-century Metropolis*, Basingstoke: Macmillan, 23–42.

Sassen, S. (1999) *Guests and Aliens*, New York: The New Press.

Sassen-Koob, S. (1984) 'The new labour demand in global cities', in M.P. Smith (ed.), *Cities in Transformation. Class, Capital, and the State*, Urban Affairs Annual Reviews 26, Beverly Hills: Sage, 139–71.

Sassen-Koob, S. (1985) 'Capital mobility and labor migration: their expression in core cities', in M. Timberlake (ed.), *Urbanization in the World Economy*, Orlando: Academic Press.

Sassen-Koob, S. (1986) 'New York City: economic restructuring and immigration', *Development and Change* Vol. 17: 85–119.

Sassen-Koob, S. (1989) 'New York City's informal economy', in A. Portes, M. Castells and L.A. Benton (eds), *The Informal Economy*, Baltimore: The Johns Hopkins University.

Saunders, P. (1994) *Welfare and Inequality: National and International Perspectives on the Australian Welfare State*, Melbourne: Cambridge University Press.

Savitch, H.V. (1990) 'Post-industrialism with a difference: global capitalism in world-class cities', in J. Logan and T. Swanstrom (eds), *Beyond the City Limits*, Philadelphia: Temple University.

Saxenian, A. (1994) *Regional Advantage: Culture and Competition in Silicon Valley and Route 128*, Cambridge, Mass.: Harvard University Press.

Schaefer, R. (1995) *Racial and Ethnic Groups*, Boston: Little, Brown.

Schimek, P. (1989) 'Earnings polarization and the proliferation of low-wage work', in *The Widening Divide: Income Inequality and Poverty in Los Angeles*, Los Angeles: Graduate School of Architecture and Urban Planning of the University of California.

Schmitter-Heisler, B. (1994) 'Housing policy and the underclass: the United Kingdom, Germany and the Netherlands', *Journal of Urban Affairs* Vol. 16 No. 3: 203–20.

Schoeni, R.F., K.F. McCarthy and G. Vernez (1996) *The Mixed Economic Progress of Immigrants*, Santa Monica: Rand Corporation.

Schram, S. (1995) *Words of Welfare*, Minneapolis: University of Minnesota Press.

Scott, A.J. (1988) *Metropolis*, Berkeley: University of California.

Scott, A.J. (1993) *Technopolis: High Technology Industry and Regional Development in Southern California*, Berkeley: University of California Press.

Scott, A.J. and M. Storper (eds) (1993) 'Industrialization and regional development', in *Pathways to Industrialization and Regional Development*, London: Routledge.

Shachar, A. (1994) 'Randstad Holland: a "world city"?' *Urban Studies* Vol. 31: 381–400.

Shergold, P.R. (1976) 'Relative skill and income levels of native and foreign born workers: a re-examination', *Explorations in Economic History* Vol. 13: 451–61.

Simon, G. (1995) 'Par une sorte de logique en boucle, la migration engendre la migration', *Géodynamique des Migration Internationales dans le Monde*, Paris: Presses Universitaires de France.

Simon, J. (1989) *The Economic Consequences of Immigration*, Cambridge: Basil Blackwell.

Simon, P. (1997) 'La statistique des origines: l'ethnicité et la "race" dans les recensements aux États-Unis, Canada et Grande Bretagne', *Sociétés Contemporaines*, No. 26, April.

Small, C. (1995). 'Social theory: an historical analysis of Canadian socio-cultural policies, "race" and the "other": a case study of social and spatial segregation in Montreal', unpublished D.Phil. thesis: University of Oxford.

Smith, M. (1988) *City, State and Market*, New York: Basil Blackwell.

Smith, T.W. (1990) *GSS Topical Reports No. 19*, Chicago: National Opinion Research Center, University of Chicago.

Smith, T.W. (1991) *What Do Americans Think About Jews?*, New York: American Jewish Committee.

Soja, E. (1987) 'Economic restructuring and the internationalization of the Los Angeles region', in M.P. Smith and J.R. Feagin (eds), *The Capitalist City*, London: Basil Blackwell.

Soja, E. (1989) *Postmodern Geographies*, London: Verso.

Soja, E., R. Morales and G. Wolff (1983) 'Urban restructuring: an analysis of social and spatial change in Los Angeles', *Economic Geography* Vol. 59.

Sorensen, E., F.D. Bean, L. Ku and W. Zimmerman (1992) *Immigrant Categories and the U.S. Job Market: Do They Make a Difference?*, Washington DC: The Urban Institute Press.

Spear, A.H. (1967) *Black Chicago: The Making of a Negro Ghetto, 1890–1920*, Chicago: The University of Chicago Press.

Srinivasan, S. (1992) 'The class position of the Asian petit-bourgeoisie', *New Community* Vol. 19 No. 1: 61–74.

Stadt München (1991) *Münchner Armutsbericht '90*, München: Sozialreferat der Stadt München.

Statistics Canada (1994) *User Documentation for Public Use Microdata File on Individuals*, Ottawa: Statistics Canada, 1991, Census of Canada.

Statistics Canada (1995) *Occupation According to the 1991 Standard Occupational Classification, 1991. Census Technical Reports, Reference Products Series*, Ottawa Minister of Industry, Science and Technology.

Steinberg, S. (1995) *Turning Back: The Retreat from Racial Justice in American Thought and Policy*, Boston: Beacon Press.

Storkey, M. and R. Lewis (1996) 'London: a true cosmopolis', in P. Ratcliffe (ed.), *Ethnicity in the 1991 Census, Volume Three: Social Geography and Ethnicity in Britain: Geographical Spread, Spatial Concentration and Internal Migration*, London: HMSO, 201–25.

Teaford, J.C. (1993) *Cities of the Midwest*, Baltimore: The Johns Hopkins University Press.

Thrift, N. (1987) 'The fixers: the urban geography of international commercial capital' in J. Henderson and M. Castells (eds), *Global Restructuring and Territorial Development*, Newbury Park: Sage.

Thrift, N. (1994) 'Globalisation, regulation, urbanisation: the case of the Netherlands', *Urban Studies* Vol. 31 No. 3: 365–80.

Thurow, L.C. (1975) *Generating Inequality: Mechanisms of Distribution in the US Economy*, New York: Basic Books.

Tonry, M. (1995) *Malign Neglect: Race, Class, and Punishment in America*, New York: Oxford University Press.

Trotter, J.W. (1995) 'African Americans in the city: the industrial era, 1900–1950', *Journal of Urban History* Vol. 21 No. 4: 438–57.

Trotter, J.W. and E. Lewis (1996) *African Americans in the Industrial Age*, Boston: Northeastern University.

Troyna, B. (1988) 'Ghetto', in E. Ellis Cashmore (ed.) *Dictionary of Race and Ethnic Relations*, 2nd edn, London: Routledge.

Turner, M.A., M. Fix and R.J. Struyk (1991) *Opportunities Denied, Opportunities Diminished: Discrimination in Hiring*, Washington DC: The Urban Institute.

UNESCO (1975) *Statistical Yearbook, 1975*, Paris: UNESCO.

UNESCO (1985) *Statistical Yearbook, 1985*, Paris: UNESCO.

UNESCO (1993) *Statistical Yearbook, 1993*, Paris: UNESCO.

United States Bureau of the Census (1983) *Census of Population and Housing, 1980: Public-Use Microdata Samples Technical Documentation*, Ann Arbor, Michigan: Inter-university Consortium for Political and Social Research.

United States Bureau of the Census (1988) *Statistical Abstract of the United States: 1988*, Washington DC: US Government Printing Office.

United States Bureau of the Census (1993) *Statistical Abstract of the United States: 1993*, Washington DC: US Government Printing Office.

Vernez, G. (1993) 'Mexican labor in California's economy', in A.F. Lowenthal and K. Burgess (eds), *The California-Mexico Connection*, Stanford: Stanford University.

Vernez, G. and A. Abrahamse (1996) *How Immigrants Fare in US Education*, Santa Monica, CA: Rand.

Wacquant, L. (1996) 'De l'état charitable à l'état pénal: notes sur le traitement politique de la misère en Amérique', *Regards sociologiques* Vol. 11: 30–8.

Wacquant, L. (1997) 'Les pauvres en pâture: la nouvelle politique de la misère en Amérique', *Hérodote* Vol. 85, Spring: 21–33.

Wacquant, L. (1998) '"A black city within the white": revisiting America's dark ghetto', *Black Renaissance/Renaissance Noire* Vol. 2 No. 1: 141–51.

Wade, R.C. (1990) 'The enduring ghetto: urbanization and the color line in American history', *Journal of Urban History* Vol. 17 No. 1: 4–13.

Waldinger, R. (1986–87) 'Changing ladders and musical chairs: ethnicity and opportunity in post-industrial New York', *Politics and Society* Vol. 15: 369–401.

Waldinger, R. (1996) *Still the Promised City: African-Americans and New Immigrants in Postindustrial New York*, Cambridge: Harvard University Press.

Waldinger, R., H. Aldrich and R. Ward (1990) *Ethnic Entreprenurs: Immigrant Business in Industrial Societies* Newbury Park, Ca.: Sage.

Waldinger, R. and M. Bozorgmehr (1993). 'From Ellis Island to LAX: immigration and urban change in gateway cities', paper presented at the annual meeting of the American Sociological Association, Miami.

Waldinger, R. and M. Bozorgmehr (eds) (1996) *Ethnic Los Angeles*, New York: Russell Sage Foundation.

Walton, S.F. Jr. (1994) *A Geonomical Solution to the Problem of Haphazard Black Migration*, San Ramon: San Ramon Valley Counseling, Consultation, and Education Services.

Ward, D. (1989) *Poverty, Ethnicity, and the American City, 1840–1925*, Cambridge: Cambridge University Press.

Warner, S.B. Jr. and C.B. Burke (1969) 'Cultural change and the ghetto', *Journal of Contemporary History* Vol. 4, October: 173–88.

Waters, M.C. (1993) 'West Indian immigrants, African Americans and Whites in the workplace: different perspectives on American race relations', unpublished manuscript, Harvard University.

Waters, M.C. (1996) 'The intersection of gender, race, and ethnicity in identity development of Caribbean American teens', in B.J. Ross Leadbeater and N. Way (eds), *Urban Girls: Resisting Stereotypes, Creating Identities*, New York: New York University Press, 65–81.

Weaver, R. (1948) *The Negro Ghetto*, New York: Russell and Russell.

White, S.B. and W.F. McMahon (1995) 'Why have earnings per worker stagnated?', *Journal of Urban Affairs* Vol. 17.

Whiteford, P. (1992) 'Are immigrants over-represented in the Australian social security system?', Kensington, NSW: Social Policy Research Centre, University of New South Wales, Discussion Paper No. 31.

Williams, C.C. and J. Windebank (1995) 'Social polarization of households in contemporary Britain', *Regional Studies* Vol. 29 No. 8: 723–8.

Willis, P. (1977) *Learning to Labour*, New York: Columbia University Press.

Wilson, W.J. (1979) *The Declining Significance of Race*, Chicago: Chicago University Press.

Wilson, W.J. (1987) *The Truly Disadvantaged: The Inner City, the Underclass and Public Policy*, Chicago: The University of Chicago Press.

Wilson, W.J. (1991a) 'Studying inner-city social dislocation: the challenge of public agenda research', *American Sociological Review* Vol. 56 No. 1: 1–14.

Wilson, W.J. (1991b) 'Public policy research and the truly disadvantaged' in C. Jencks and P. Peterson (eds), *The Urban Underclass*, Washington DC: Brookings Institution, 460–81.

Wilson, W.J. (1994) 'New urban poverty and the problem of race', *Michigan Quarterly Review* Vol. 33 No. 2: 247–64.

Wilson, W.J. (1996) *When Work Disappears: the World of the New Urban Poor*, New York, Alfred A. Knopf.

Wirth, L. (1928) *The Ghetto*, Chicago: The University of Chicago Press.

Woodward, R. (1995) 'Approaches towards the study of social polarization in the UK', *Progress in Human Geography* Vol. 19 No. 1: 75–89.

Wrench, J. and J. Solomos (eds) (1993) 'The politics and processes of racial discrimination in Britain', in *Racism and Migration in Western Europe*, Oxford: Berg, 157–76.

Wright, E.O. (1994) 'Inequality', in E.O. Wright (ed.) *Interrogating Inequality: Essays on Class Analysis, Socialism and Marxism*, London: Verso.

Wright, E.O. (1997) *Class Counts: Comparative Studies in Class Analysis*, Cambridge: Cambridge University Press.

Wrigley, J. (1997) 'Immigrant women as childcare providers' in I. Light and R. Isralowitz (eds), *Immigration and Immigrant Absorption in Israel and the USA*, Aldershot: Ashgate, Chapter 9.

Zipp, J.F. (1994) 'Government employment and black-white earnings inequality, 1980–1990', *Social Problems* Vol. 41, August: 363–82 .

Zolberg, A.R. (1991) 'Bounded states in a global market: the uses of international labor migrations', in P. Bourdieu and J.S. Coleman (eds), *Social Theory for a Changing Society*, Boulder CO: Westview.

Index